I was lucky enough to be one of Sarah's organ scholars at Selwyn (2011-14), and I learned so much from this remarkable musician. Her infectious passion for what she does, and her seemingly endless resources of energy and creativity, have been hugely influential to me and countless church musicians across the world.

Timothy Parsons
Director of Music, St Edmundsbury Cathedral

It has been an absolute pleasure to work as producer and engineer with Sarah MacDonald and her choirs at Selwyn College and Ely Cathedral over the last fourteen or so years in over twenty-five recordings for the Regent label. Many of these have been first recordings of new sacred choral music, and Sarah's boundless energy and enthusiasm for exploring the work of both young and more established composers has been an inspiration to us all!

I'm delighted that her perceptive and entertaining essays on the state of choral music scene in the UK have been collected together for this new publication.

Gary Cole, MA (Cantab), GRSM, FRCO, ARCM,
HonRSCM, (Producer, Regent Records Ltd, UK)

Cathedrals, Chapels, Organs, Choirs

CATHEDRALS, CHAPELS, ORGANS, CHOIRS

a personal view by

SARAH MACDONALD

This material was published in its original form in The American Organist magazine and is reprinted by permission of the American Guild of Organists.

Published in 2022 by August Press, LLC.
PO Box 486
Burns, Tennessee USA 37029

ISBN 979-8-218-04214-1

Library of Congress Cataloging-in-Publication Data is on file at the Library of Congress, Washington, DC

www.cathedralschapelsorganschoirs.com

This book is dedicated to my parents, Bob and Diana,
with gratitude for their wisdom, imagination,
love, discipline, and musicianship.
Their commitment to each other, to my three younger brothers,
Jeremy, Simon, and James, and to me, has shaped everything that I am.

FOREWORD

BY JOHN RUTTER

The clearest view of a society and its institutions is often provided by an outsider, and so it is with this lively and multi-faceted collection of essays on the theme of cathedral and collegiate choirs in England. Our intrepid author arrives from her home in Western Canada and is plunged headlong into the role of Director of Music at Selwyn College, part of the ancient university of Cambridge where May Week is in June, the Easter Term begins after Easter is over, and an exhibition is a type of scholarship formally awarded to students rather than a public showing of art. In search of further adventure, she takes on the additional job of directing the first-ever girls' choir at nearby Ely Cathedral, where for a thousand years only men and boys sang.

With an insider's knowledge but an outsider's perspective she lifts the lid on a choral tradition which is admired worldwide but mysterious in its inner workings to most of those not involved in it. How do you train a liturgical choir—whether its members are children or young adults—to the highest possible standard? How do you choose the right music for them to sing? How do you get to be a member of one of these choirs? How do you organise a choir tour or a recording? These and many other questions are addressed, and the daily trials and tribulations of a busy choir director—who is also a fine and active organist—are entertainingly chronicled. There are informative essays on (for example) the too-often overlooked body of sacred music by women composers . . . where to place final consonants in English church music . . . and how to design and equip a perfect choir vestry. A miscellany? More than that: a cornucopia.

In the course of reading through this book, the baffling structure of our two oldest universities, Oxford and Cambridge, will be revealed. But in case you are as confused by it as is most of the rest of the world, and would be glad of a clue before you start, I'll attempt an explanation.

Oxford and Cambridge Universities were founded over 800 years ago, part of a Europe-wide movement to establish new seats of learning. The students were young men (younger than today's students) who were mostly destined to serve either the Church, or the Crown and the nobility. They needed somewhere to live while they studied, as did the older men who taught them, so colleges were established as halls of residence—in effect, dorms. Some of these were founded by kings and queens, some (like my *alma mater* Clare College) by the nobility, some, in more recent times, by wealthy private individuals. Our author's *alma mater* Robinson College was set up by a kindly philanthropist who made his money from television rentals. The older colleges were modelled on the pattern of monasteries, built around central quadrangles, with dining halls and chapels. The chapels range from my own college's modest eighteenth-century 100-seater to the vaulted splendour of our next-door neighbour along the River Cam, King's. Cambridge has thirty-one colleges, which in modern times function as almost self-contained communities within the university. If you wish to study at Cambridge University, you apply to one of those colleges, not to the university or to the faculty (i.e., specialist department) in your chosen subject. (In most British universities, undergraduates focus on just one subject, though many aspects of it are covered during their three-year or, in a few subjects, four-year course.) You may well receive some of your tuition within your own college, because the senior membership will probably include one or more who teach in your subject faculty. These days most of the senior members no longer live in college, they just have 'rooms' there. Much of the tuition you receive will also come from your faculty, where there will be lecture and seminar rooms. Faculty buildings in Cambridge are mostly modern, some designed by renowned architects, located away from the historic city centre.

The university, unlike some in the USA, is not a confederation of colleges. A Cambridge college cannot confer a degree: that is the prerogative of the university. As you wander around Cambridge, a few of the buildings you see are university buildings, like the elegant eighteenth-century Senate House, where degree ceremonies are held. A few are (mostly now re-purposed) faculty buildings, such as the Divinity Faculty in Trinity Street. The majority are college buildings. These are where you will find all those chapels with their resident choirs, and although they are private chapels anyone is welcome to attend their choral evensongs and other worship services. The choirs are maintained by their colleges, not by the university—so King's College Choir is not a university choir but a college choir.

If you are now more confused than ever, start your journey through this valuable and enlightening book and all will become clear.

JOHN RUTTER
May 2020

INTRODUCTION AND ACKNOWLEDGEMENTS
SPRING 2020

As with many of you, the COVID-19 pandemic of 2020 provided me with an unexpected and unprecedented amount of free time. Having agreed to compile this book some time in the halcyon days of 2019, I then proceeded (uncharacteristically, I hasten to add) to miss a number of proposed copy deadlines with my ever-patient publisher, Wes Ramsay. Of course, neither of us would have wished for a global health emergency to be the catalyst for completing the project. Nevertheless, having cancelled two international choir tours, several concerts, a CD recording, two residential courses, four workshops, cathedral services for Holy Week and Easter, as well as the entirety of the Easter Term at Cambridge, I sat at my kitchen table, #WorkingFromHome, along with so many in the world, finally having the time required. I read through old columns, reminiscing and cringing in equal measure, and hoping that people would enjoy reading this collection of essays at some point in a healthier future.

The columns are organised into chapters according to topic, and they appear chronologically within those chapters. Sometimes you will find the same words as were published in The American Organist magazine (TAO); some columns have been edited slightly since, particularly where they were uncomfortably anachronistic; some are in a pre-TAO unedited state, or a post-TAO extended version. As part of the introduction, I will start with the very first column (very good place to start), which was published in 2009, before I had composed anything beyond undergraduate harmony and counterpoint exercises, before I was permanent director of the girl choristers at Ely Cathedral, and before I had completed my first decade as Director of Music at Selwyn College, Cambridge, let alone begun my third. Much has changed since I began writing this column, in my life, and in the world around us. And yet, reading them through again, I can see that the things which influenced and shaped me from a very early age remain constant: music, rigour, high (often unattainable) standards, liturgy, the Anglican (Episcopal) church, community, teaching, a fascination with England coupled with a longing for home (Canada), and, I hope, a good dose of humour.

I would like to express my thanks to successive editors of The American Organist magazine, who have been most helpful and accommodating over the years. For permission to reprint my columns in this format, I am particularly grateful to Todd Sisley and James Thomashower. I am indebted to Wes Ramsay and Carol McClure for their support and encouragement over many years of friendship, to August Press for being willing to sponsor and promote this venture, and to Chase Neely for brokering the arrangement with the American Guild of Organists. I am also thankful to John Rutter for writing such a generous and engaging foreword and for going well beyond the call of duty by proof-reading the manuscript. The discovery of his 1988 'Faire is the heaven' recording with the Cambridge Singers (Collegium COLCD107) was the single-most important influence in my change from being a first-study keyboard player to being a choral conductor, so his support for this project is particularly appreciated. My colleagues in the UK and on the Continent have kindly provided respite by writing guest issues, a few of which are published here with their authors' permission, widening the column's horizons, and also giving readers a break from the sound of my voice. I owe much to Marcus, without whose editing and proof-reading, especially during the first few years, these columns would have been significantly more verbally clumsy and considerably less concise and communicative. Finally, I am grateful to you, the many readers who have written to me over the years. I have been touched by every one of your "fan letters", and I have enjoyed meeting many of you, in person on both sides of the Atlantic, and electronically over social media. I hope that this collection delivers edification and entertainment, and also provides an historical snapshot of the preoccupations of a Canadian church musician in England during the early decades of the twenty-first century.

GLOSSARY OF COMMONLY USED ACRONYMS

ABRSM	Associated Board of the Royal Schools of Music
ABCD	Association of British Choral Directors
ACDA	Association of Choral Directors of America
AGO	American Guild of Organists
BBC	British Broadcasting Corporation
RCO	Royal College of Organists
RCCO	Royal Canadian College of Organists
RSCM	Royal School of Church Music
TAO	The American Organist magazine
CRCO/CAGO/ CRCCO	Colleague diploma (of the relevant organisation)
ARCO/AAGO/ ARCCO	Associateship diploma (of the relevant organisation)
FRCO/FAGO/ FRCCO	Fellowship diploma (of the relevant organisation)

A Note about Terminology and Spelling

Throughout this book, North American musical vocabulary is used (i.e., quarter notes, 8th-notes, 16th-notes, etc.) since the columns were originally aimed at an American readership, and because as a Canadian, that terminology constitutes my musical mother tongue. For British readers, a handy table can be found below. Conversely, I have begged permission from my editor for British spelling to be used throughout (e.g., 'colour', 'modernise'), since that is the correct Canadian spelling. It is typical that Canada sits compromisingly between Britain and the States, using aspects of both cultures as convenient.

NORTH AMERICAN		BRITISH
Double whole note		Breve
Whole note		Semibreve
Half note		Minim
Quarter note		Crotchet
Eighth note		Quaver
16th note		Semiquaver
32nd note		Demisemiquaver
64th note		Hemidemisemiquaver

A VIEW FROM THE OTHER SIDE
AUGUST 2009

In 1834 Edward Hodges, a musician who had studied at Cambridge, reflected upon English music and concluded that "if the English, as a nation, excel in any department of the art, it is in that of *church* music".[1] Rather more recently, Mickey Butts, an American music critic, began a concert review with the sentence "England has always been an artistic, even choral, superpower. You don't have to be an Anglophile to appreciate that England has produced one of the world's richest choral traditions." [2]

As a Canadian organist living in the UK (and, if truth be told, just a bit of an Anglophile), I should be well-placed to offer some objective reflections on the organ and choral tradition here, and how it compares with that on the other side of the Atlantic. At a recent meeting of the RCO, of which I am a trustee and examiner, we were discussing the ways in which we could ensure that other organists in the world knew what was going on over here. "So I got to thinking" that it might be of interest to AGO and RCCO members to have a view from the other side as a regular column in TAO, a magazine to which I have subscribed for about 25 years, and which I always enjoy reading, possibly even more now, since it keeps me connected with the organ world in North America. The Editor of TAO also thought this might be a popular idea, and thus, the purpose

1. *An Apology for Church Music and Music Festivals*, London, 1834, p. 66
2. San Francisco 'Classical Voice', 25 February 2006

of this first column is to introduce myself, and to give an idea of what I propose to do in this space over the next few months.

To introduce myself then: I grew up in various cities in Canada, starting in Ottawa, and then working my way west to Victoria, which I now consider home. I began my post-secondary studies at the Royal Conservatory of Music in Toronto, and then continued them in the UK as Organ Scholar of Robinson College, Cambridge. My present post is that of Director of Music in Chapel at Selwyn College, Cambridge, where I have been for 10 years, and where I was the first woman to hold this sort of post in either Cambridge or Oxford Universities (the combination is known as "Oxbridge"—contrary to what I believed as a child, this is not a separate institution). I spent the calendar year 2008 running the Girls' Choir at Ely Cathedral as well, where I was covering for maternity leave. In my spare time, I teach for the University Music Faculty, play recitals, do a lot of recording (conducting, playing, producing), and run the university Organ Scholarships competition; I am also a strict vegetarian, a mediocre tennis player, and an avid 'Doctor Who' fan.

As indicated in the quotation above, there is a significant North American fascination with the so-called English Choral Tradition—indeed, my own version of that fascination is exactly what brought me here in the first place. For me, it was watching 'The Boast of Kings'[3] as a child, and deciding then that I had to get over here somehow (I doubt my father's bank manager has yet forgiven me completely). In forthcoming manifestations of this column, I propose to address various issues and questions which have been raised by American and Canadian visitors over the years. For example, there is a belief that choral sight-reading is better on this side of the Atlantic—is this actually the case, and if so, what is the reason for it? Have any English choral conductors ever actually had any conducting lessons? As one of only a handful of women in this line of work, (not to mention being a foreigner), am I hampered by prejudice? What is it like studying in the UK as compared to North America? What are some of the linguistic and practical differences between the two traditions?

---

3. 'The story of King's College Choir: The Boast of Kings', 1981 television documentary, now available on DVD (Regis RDVD101)

I hope that this sounds as if it might be of interest. I would welcome questions, and suggestions for future topics from TAO readers as well: please do write to me at Selwyn College, Cambridge UK, CB3 9DQ, or email me on seam100@cam.ac.uk. In particular, I need a name for the column. Although it is catchy, my working title perhaps doesn't quite fit the bill: 'Sesquialtera and the City'.

TABLE OF CONTENTS

Chapter 1

Terminology and Tradition

This chapter brings together columns about linguistic difference, ceremony, and tradition. In addition, I attempt to debunk a number of commonly-held but erroneous assumptions about the musical world in the UK. Topics range from the use of vibrato to meeting the Queen, and from hemidemisemiquavers to ancient universities.

Divided by a Common Language

September is a busy time in Cambridge University. We have just endured two weeks of organ and choral scholarship auditions. This involved listening to 25 young organists and nearly 200 teenaged singers from Britain and elsewhere, including both Canada and the United States. Sight-reading and aural tests were administered; there were additional transposition and harmonisation exercises for the organists, while the vocal range and technique of the singers was probed. These were long and tiring days: the auditions began every morning at 9am, and decision meetings commenced at 9pm. As a final punishment, the University's Michaelmas Term started only two days after this process had ended. In the midst of all this busy-ness, I wondered what topic I should choose for this column, and it seemed appropriate to focus on a subject that had first confronted me when I myself auditioned for an organ scholarship at Cambridge, one busy September many years ago.

The Irish playwright George Bernard Shaw allegedly observed that England and America are "divided by a common language"[4], and this separation frequently provokes amusement and confusion in equal measure: a UK tourist in the States who asks someone to lend him a rubber

---

4. widely attributed, e.g. *Reader's Digest* (November 1942). Not found in his published works.

(a pencil eraser) may not receive quite what he is expecting. Since these sorts of intricacies bedevil the English language in general, it is no surprise to find that they complicate musical terminology as well. As a student in Toronto, I spent a semester learning musical vocabulary in French, but it would have been just as useful to learn the main words and phrases used by English musicians. During my aforementioned audition for an organ scholarship, I was asked to produce a written analysis of a score as part of the admissions process. I was vaguely aware that I could not use my usual nomenclature, and I had to resort to asking one of the other applicants what a '32nd-note' was called. It was disconcerting to find myself applying to study for a degree in Music at one of the most prestigious universities in the world only to discover that my knowledge of even the most basic vocabulary was alarmingly inadequate.

To spare you a similar fate, I offer the following guidance. The UK uses various rather quaint and archaic words to describe the rhythmic values of notes. Double-whole-notes, whole-notes, and half-notes retain their historical names from mensural notation: they are called breves, semibreves, and minims respectively. A quarter-note is called a crotchet (from the Old French diminutive of 'croc', meaning 'little hook', because the note was hooked in mensural notation). To add to the general confusion, in many Cambridge first-year undergraduate essays, this kind of note is not infrequently referred to as a 'crochet', but it is important to note (as it were) that this is not a musical term at all, but rather a mildly esoteric form of knitting. Unhelpfully, in French, the eighth-note is called a 'croche', since in modern notation it is the hooked note. For UK musicians, an eighth-note is called a quaver, a word that comes from the Middle English verb 'quaveren' meaning 'to tremble or quiver'—a state familiar to terminologically naive conductors from across the pond who are rehearsing a British choir for the first time. The subdivisions of the quaver produce the arithmetical relationships with which North Americans are familiar: the 16th-note is a semiquaver, the 32nd-note a demisemiquaver, the 64th-note a hemidemisemiquaver, the 128th-note a semihemidemisemiquaver. Try saying that after a wee (post-Evensong) dram!

But note values are not the only troublemakers. A 'measure' is a 'bar', and this no doubt reveals an etymological connection with the name of the place where singers generally gather after a rehearsal. The two small-est diatonic intervals are called tones and semitones; the words 'step' and 'half-step' are not understood here, though Britons and North Americans generally agree on 'major second' and 'minor second'. The evocatively named 'deceptive cadence' is here labelled (rather dully) an 'interrupted cadence'. An orchestra's 'concertmaster' is merely the 'leader' in the UK; concerts have intervals (though not of the 'minor third' variety), rather than intermissions; and a small choir is never called a chorus.

I hope that this guide for the perplexed will be of some use. Don't forget, though, that, in the end, these differences are trivial and cosmetic: we are all striving for the same perfection, whether we have cookies or biscuits at coffee hour, and whether we wear braces on our trousers, our pants—or even on our teeth.

February 2013

Please Check Your Vibrato at the Door

In the hectic run-up to what is fondly known as "Bridgemas" (Cambridge's liturgically-muddled conglomeration of Advent and Christmas, which is marked by an incalculable number of concerts and services in the space of about four days at the end of November) I was grateful to a friend for rescuing me from an uncharacteristic case of writer's block by suggesting that I tackle the potentially amusing subject of "The most commonly-held erroneous assumptions that Americans make about the English Choral Tradition". Accordingly, this month's column deals with one of my favourites: UK choirs never sing with vibrato.

Two key issues need to be considered in refuting this manifestly incorrect assumption: first, the technical definition of vibrato, and second, the passage of time and musical fashions, and the associated advancement of musicological scholarship. My only caveat is that it is important for readers to remember that the best known UK choirs (i.e., those which are exported most frequently by means of broadcasts and recordings) constitute an exceedingly small minority of the choirs in the country, and that the sound of a "typical English choir" is impossible to codify.

'Vibrato' is defined as a regular, pulsating variation in pitch, above and below the fundamental frequency, used to add expression to vocal and instrumental music.[5] Both the range and the speed of fluctuation can be measured and adjusted. In most academic references to vibrato in singing (as opposed to vibrato in string playing), a clear distinction is drawn between 'vibrato', a natural by-product of a healthy, free singing technique, and 'warble' (or 'wobble'), when the pitch oscillation is too wide and/or the speed of fluctuation too slow, which is normally symptomatic of poor technique and/or ageing (and occasionally of abused or over-used vocal folds), and which adversely affects both pitch and sound quality.[6] Technically speaking, the misconception here is perhaps more accurately expressed by saying that the best UK choirs do not sing with 'wobble', rather than that they do not sing with 'vibrato'.

It probably goes without saying that the humorous sign "Choir Room: Please Check your Vibrato at the Door" is most commonly directed at sopranos. Since both age and technique are known to play a crucial role in the distinction between a natural vibrato and an undesirable warble, it is necessary to consider the normal make-up of an English choir's soprano section to ascertain why the latter is not perceived in the sound. In the majority of England's best-known choirs, the soprano sections consist of young, individually-trained singers: boys or girls in Cathedral choirs; those in their late teens/early twenties in mixed Oxbridge choirs; young professionals in the best-known specialist choirs. Conductors in all of these places are at liberty to encourage healthy vibrato, even in sopranos, since the combination of youth and technical training safeguards against warble, whereas healthy vibrato enriches choral colour, improves tuning, and facilitates a sound which is free, relaxed, and vibrant—and I have chosen this word advisedly. However, unsurprisingly, across this country there are many thousands *more* choral singers who are ageing and/or whose technique is unreliable, and consequently, warble is equally as present here as it is in choirs in North America. The question to be asked is whether comparing an average village parish choir with a professional London ensemble is necessarily appropriate or fair.

---

5. https://en.wikipedia.org/wiki/Vibrato
6. A well-explained generalisation can be found here: http://www.sci.brooklyn.cuny.edu/~jones/Shirlee/vibrato.html

Historically, the early music revival, which gathered momentum in the 1960s, has of course influenced both fashion and taste. Vibrato has always been considered an essential expressive device, and its use by singers and players alike is well documented in 16th- and 17th-century theoretical treatises.[7] So, although Baroque string players do not use vibrato continuously with equally wide pitch fluctuation on every note as they might when playing Romantic repertoire on a modern instrument, removing it entirely is an unsuitably extreme and unstylistic interpretation of the sources. By extension, the same is true for singers.

Nevertheless, it is true to say that when the early music revival began, there was an unhealthy fashion for some choral conductors to ask grown women to sing like pre-pubescent boys. This now-dated practice resulted in a vocal production which was artificially straight, constrained, thin, and often sharp (not to mention that it was both psychologically and vocally traumatic for a whole generation of sopranos). Unfortunately this sound was recorded for posterity and widely distributed, since this trend coincided with the invention of CD recordings in the 1980s. Thankfully now, most UK choir directors have outgrown this hazardous practice, and at any rate, there have always been plenty of pre-pubescent boys, particularly in Europe, who have sung with vibrato, so it was a flawed constraint from the outset.

Notwithstanding the above refutations of the original misconception, there must be a particular quality that Americans have perceived in English choral singing (and not just on 1980s recordings), since this characteristic misapprehension continues to be surprisingly widespread. It probably is true to say that the best-known UK choirs' sounds are characterised by unity of purpose and by what is usually called 'good blend'. Personally, I dislike the word 'blend' in a choral context, since it appears to deny choir members the opportunity to make an individual contribution to the corporate sound, and I know that most of my director-of-music colleagues agree with me. Instead, I try to achieve a *unified* choral sound

---

7. A commonly cited source is Ludovico Zacconi, *Prattica di Musica*, Venice, 1592, Libro I, f. 55r: "Il tremolo nella musica non è necessario; ma facendolo oltra che dimostra sincerità, e ardire; abbellisce le cantilena." ["The tremolo in music is not necessary; but in doing so, it shows sincerity and daring; embellishes the songs."]

in my own choirs by encouraging vocal independence and courage. The singers do, of course, have to listen to each other and co-operate musically, and ensemble of diction, expression, and intent are obviously crucial in order to turn 30 individuals into one musical force, but true vibrato does not—indeed, *should* not—be checked at the door in order to achieve this end. In my experience, this philosophy creates a fresh, colourful, free, in tune, and most importantly *healthy* choral sound, to which every singer contributes individually and naturally.

I hope I've managed to refute this particular misconception successfully. And if, even after reading this, you still believe that UK choirs never sing with vibrato, do a Google search for videos of one of the UK's finest professional choirs, the BBC Singers. In future columns I might look at the mistaken belief that all English choirs can sight-read, that all UK clergy are musically literate and supportive, that university organ and choral scholarships are in any way similar to rugby and basketball scholarships, and most bizarrely of all, that the main reason that English choirs are so good is because they sing with English accents.

When You Sing,
You Begin with Do-Re-Mi

Following on from last month's column which started to explore commonly-held erroneous assumptions about the English Choral Tradition, my second favourite misconception is that all UK choirs can sight-read. In reality, there are just as many ordinary choirs in ordinary towns here, who take just as long to learn new music as the ordinary choirs in ordinary towns everywhere else in the world. Once again, this misconception stems from the fact that the cathedral, Oxbridge, and professional choirs which are most frequently exported from the UK, are the ones which determine the expectations of non-Brits. Most foreign conductors and singing teachers who visit the UK arrange to observe rehearsals in cathedrals and college chapels, and not in the Parish Church of Saint-Alphege-the-Bald in the suburban outskirts of a city somewhere in the West Midlands.

Whilst it probably *is* true to say that the majority of members of cathedral, Oxbridge, and professional choirs read music better than a typical singer in a village choral society, this does not constitute a like-for-like comparison. Cathedral choristers receive daily training, usually involving lessons in sight-singing and the study of at least two instruments. Although they may not sight-sing fluently when they join the choir as seven-year-olds, after five years, they are usually pretty adept. Oxbridge choirs consist (apparently) of exceptionally intelligent students, many of whom go on to run the country or win Nobel Prizes. Even if they cannot sight-read when they arrive as first year undergraduates (and in the less-accomplished Oxbridge choirs, most of them cannot) they are so accustomed to the swift processing of information, regardless of the specific technical skills involved, that they figure out how to learn music quickly enough to convince visiting Americans that they *can* sight-read—I've seen it with my own eyes (or rather heard it with my own ears). The UK's professional choirs are, of course, made up of the best of the former cathedral and Oxbridge singers, who have learned to read through either or both of the above-mentioned experiences.

I believe that teaching singers to read is a crucial responsibility of any choral conductor, particularly for those who direct young singers who sing liturgically. Teaching all children to read their mother tongue is a matter of course in primary school; teaching even only modestly musical children to sight-sing is hardly more complicated. If a child can carry a tune (and the overwhelming majority of them can), then some basic theory and some basic aural training can give them educated access to music for the rest of their lives. Obviously there will be the few who are exceptionally gifted, and who will learn to read anything fluently; on the other hand, there will be the large masses of those for whom sight-reading may never come as naturally as reading texts, but for whom learning the basics will provide them with both musical independence and leadership skills.

There are, of course, as many methods for teaching sight-singing as there are teachers and students. I have developed my own techniques over the years, which combine a number of the practices that influenced me. Most importantly, I encourage my singers to maintain a sense of a tonal framework in their heads, so that they relate everything to the tonic, or *doh*. Inspired by a combination of the Kodály method, Julie Andrews in 'The Sound of Music', and 'Sesame Street' (!), each daily sight-singing exercise can be "brought to you by" a particular key. After singing the scale up and down, to the letter names of the notes (ironically, I consciously avoid tonic *solfege*, thus removing the need for translation when faced with notes on a stave), I call out letter names (in my speaking voice), and the choir sings the notes back. I also play notes on the piano, and the choir identifies them by singing their letter names. I start simply, keeping intervals small, and within one octave. I maintain strict diatonic tonality, only introducing accidentals once the choir is fully confident in every key. This not only solidifies the singers' tonal frame of reference, but it is also good for diction: try singing an F# major scale quickly, to the letter names of the notes.

In addition, other tricks can be useful: as a pianist, I found as a child that I could mime the playing of a passage on the desk in front of me, and I would usually sing the right notes instinctively (though I do not have perfect pitch). I have used this image successfully with university students who are accomplished instrumentalists, but less experienced choral musicians. I remember auditioning an alto at Selwyn who now sings professionally: she had her ABRSM diploma on the flute, but was struggling to sing a line of Palestrina at sight. I asked her to sing along with herself as if she were playing the flute, and the passage was completely accurate. All she then needed to do was to continue to use this trick without raising her arms into flute-playing position, since that looked a little silly in the choir stalls.

I also ensure that singers remember repeated pitches from previous bars, learn to read the spacing of the rhythms within the bar as well as their arithmetic values, and I give them a few seconds in advance to work out tricky passages in their heads. I never play the top part when rehearsing girl or boy trebles; I rarely use the piano for full rehearsals except in particularly dissonant contemporary repertoire; I always provide a harmonic context when rehearsing a section on its own, and I often don't give notes again after verbal instructions. Most crucially, I assiduously avoid use the "this is how it goes, sing it back to me" method. It also has to be said that having to sing three or four, and in many cases six or seven, services per week, contributes a good deal to a singer's ability to read—but it must be remembered that this sort of training is available to just a tiny minority of the choral population in the UK.

I hope that I have persuaded you that the ability to sight-sing is not bestowed upon the English at birth, but that it can be acquired without too much pain. In a very small proportion of high-profile cases, intense childhood and university training has produced an elite group of singers with fluent reading skills, but I have heard just as impressive reading from professional choral singers in Boston, New Haven, and New York (to name just three places) as I have heard in London, Oxford, and Cambridge. Members of The Upper and Lower Gigglesborough Combined Village Choral Societies, on the other hand, are absolutely no different from their counterparts anywhere else in the world.

Some Choirs are More Equal than Others

This column, the third in my series on the most commonly held misconceptions about the English Choral Tradition, is inspired by a comment made to me a few years ago by a disappointed North American audience member, after hearing a performance by a rather humble volunteer student choir from one of the smaller Cambridge colleges. "I had assumed that because it was an English choir, and from Cambridge University, that it would be absolutely amazing." The moral of this story (and the topic of this column) is that not all English choirs are by definition "amazing" and neither is every Oxbridge choir necessarily brilliant just by virtue of its connection with one of the ancient universities.

As demonstrated by the disillusioned reaction to a less-than-King's-like performance by a less-than-famous collegiate choir, it should be clear that even across these two great choral universities there is much divergence of musical standards. In a number of Cambridge colleges, and in the majority of Oxford colleges, the chapel choir consists of groups of volunteer (often unauditioned) singers, many of whom have no serious musical or vocal training, who are directed and accompanied by two undergraduate organ scholars. These types of choirs are often devoid of a convincing tenor section (*plus ça change . . .*), and the senior organ scholar (the student responsible for the conducting) is often learning on the job with little or no professional advice or tuition. In addition, he or she will normally run the choir for a maximum of two years, after which another undergraduate will take up the post, in order to learn the same lessons from scratch all over again. As you can imagine, this lack of continuity frequently produces choral singing that is enthusiastic if rather rough around the edges, and that will inevitably startle North American audiences who are disappointed to find that they do not hear professional quality consort singing every time an Oxbridge undergraduate opens his or her mouth.

A little history might elucidate this further. Whereas the colleges which still maintain men-and-boys choirs with chorister choir schools (King's and St John's in Cambridge, and Christ Church, New College, and Magdalen in Oxford), have had directors of music for well over a century, the employment of professional conductors to take responsibility for mixed undergraduate choirs is a relatively recent phenomenon. When previously all-male colleges began to admit women in the 1970s, a small number of pioneering colleges appointed professional directors of music to run their newly-formed mixed choirs. In Cambridge, Clare, Selwyn, and Gonville & Caius Colleges were the first to do this (in the mid-70s), followed closely by Trinity, and then by The Queen's College, Oxford, in the early-80s. Since then, a handful of other colleges have followed suit, and one or two of these choirs have gradually built international reputations for themselves.

However, given that a further 30 or so Oxbridge Colleges continued for many years with undergraduate-run choirs (with all of the potential musical inconsistencies that result from such an arrangement), it should not be surprising to find on occasion that one hears singing from a mixed Oxbridge choir which does not quite live up to the adjective "amazing". Interestingly, over the second decade of the 21st century, in order to counteract this variability, nearly all of the Cambridge colleges appointed part-time directors of music to oversee the organ scholars' progress, and this professional guidance has much improved the general standard of mixed choral singing across the smaller Cambridge colleges. In Oxford, however, it is still the case that the majority of college choirs are run by talented but often unguided 18-year-olds, and therefore, the standard of singing from some of these choirs is inevitably unpredictable.

I hope that this little history lesson has explained the reality behind the myth. The question remains as to why the myth evolved in the first place, and why it is still prevalent. The five afore-mentioned men and boys choirs at the two university have long and distinguished histories, and all have had professional leadership throughout. However, as discussed above, the mixed-choir tradition is much more recent and the standards more variable. In the 1980s and 1990s, when the finest of the Oxbridge mixed choir really came into their own, the best singers (men and women) were concentrated in just a few colleges, so the benchmark was high to begin with. Colleges' academic entrance requirements were less rigorous, and the possession of a good singing voice was a positive feature on an undergraduate application form. While this is most certainly not the case any more, the tradition was established, and the mixed choirs' reputations secured. International tours, recordings, and broadcasts proclaimed to the outside world that the standard of Oxbridge mixed choirs was as good as that of the men and boys, and the development of successful professional mixed chamber choirs in London, with the likes of the Monteverdi Choir, the Tallis Scholars, the Sixteen, etc., has given the finest of these singers something to aspire to upon leaving university.

Meanwhile, the humbler Oxbridge choirs continue to thrive in their own less prestigious way, and many talented undergraduate organ scholars still learn conducting technique and musicianship by experimenting on unsuspecting volunteer singers. Indeed, a surprising number of distinguished cathedral organists were organ scholars at colleges that most people haven't heard of. Although these choirs do tour and record, their destinations tend on the whole to be more local (Britain and mainland Europe, rather than the New World), and recordings are not likely to be international commercial releases, but are primarily produced for college alumni and choir parents.

Perhaps this lack of transatlantic exposure, combined with the arguable *over*-exposure of a small number of college choirs, propagates the myth that all mixed Oxbridge choirs are outstanding, when in reality, although some are certainly "amazing", most are simply very ordinary groups of undergraduates who just happen to enjoy singing as a hobby—which is a commendable thing. Notwithstanding the myth, however, when a particularly gifted organ scholar has started to blossom, one might well hear unexpectedly lovely singing from a humble volunteer student choir, and the potential, the dedication, and the improvement can and should be described as "amazing".

July 2014

Meeting the Queen

Well, after over 20 years living the UK, this colonial's English life has now reached its apogee. Lat month, I experienced the kind of significant encounter that even the most lackadaisical anglophiles sometimes dream about: I was presented to Her Majesty, Queen Elizabeth II. The occasion was an organ recital in St George's Chapel, Windsor, to celebrate the 150th anniversary of the RCO, of which the Queen is Patron. Since I am aware that a number of my readers are organ-loving anglophiles (even if they ceased being colonials themselves in the 1770s), I thought it might be worthwhile to say something about this event.

Invitations to attend this significant anniversary recital itself were very limited, so I was surprised and delighted to receive one. The College had set aside a small number of tickets for those who were closely involved with its working (trustees, vice-presidents, staff, and the like), and I was invited as a recently retired trustee who continues to be involved in RCO examining and academic work. The remainder of the tickets were then allocated to the membership by public ballot, and not surprisingly, the event was heavily oversubscribed. Then, just a week before the recital, I received an email from the College asking me whether I would be willing to be presented to the Queen and Prince Philip. Amusingly, the invitation arrived on 1st April, so when I forwarded it to my family in Canada, their immediate reaction was that it was an elaborate April Fool! Needless to say, I indicated that I was indeed willing (I presumed that the question in the email was rhetorical), even though it meant that my "Plus 1" would have to sit separately. I don't normally subject my partner to organ recitals except when I am playing and he is turning pages, but this was a special occasion, after all.

In my preparations for the day, I had some advice from colleagues at Selwyn College, who were determined to tease me into a worried frenzy. On the subject of what to wear, apparently it makes a difference whether the presentation takes place inside or outside, but none of them could remember whether hats and gloves are necessary in the former or latter circumstance. I was comfortable with the need for conservative long sleeves and high collars, but was it really the case that I couldn't wear trousers? As an organist, my formal attire has not included a dress or skirt for years (though one of my colleagues helpfully suggested that my cassock might suffice as an alternative). Fortunately, the RCO assured me that no such directives had been set by the Palace. I also learned various other necessary lessons in etiquette, such as how to address the Queen: "Your Majesty" the first time, and then "Ma'am" (to rhyme with "jam") thereafter. Prince Philip, on the other hand, is firstly "Your Royal Highness" and subsequently "Sir". I practised my curtsy, which belied my churchmanship and came out looking rather more like an awkward genuflection (ironic, given that the Queen is the Head of the Church of England); so, in the end; I decided it was safer to opt for a slight dignified bow.

The day arrived, and fortunately the weather was fine. The English *adore* standing in queues, so an orderly line soon formed outside the gates of Windsor Castle, and we were amused to observe tourists taking our photographs. Presumably, they were conflating our immaculate attire and impeccable behaviour with importance. We were led into St George's Chapel, where security was tight: I daresay that will be the only time I have to show my passport in order to attend an organ recital. The audience was seated early, with about half an hour to wait for the afternoon's most important guests. Eventually, the organ broke into a fanfare, the audience arose, an entourage of be-cassocked vergers processed in, leading the Dean of Windsor with various other dignitaries; finally the Queen and the Duke of Edinburgh appeared, smiling and waving at the assembled throng. They took their special seats in the front row, and the recital began. Thomas Trotter gave a dazzling performance of music by Bach, Widor, William Harris, and Peter Hurford (the latter two both former presidents of the RCO).

After the recital, those of us to be presented were ushered into ordered lines at the front, while the rest of the audience remained in their seats. I was in the first group, which consisted of about ten vice-presidents and trustees. The royal couple was first introduced to Thomas Trotter, who explained that as all organs were very different, several hours of practice are required at a new instrument before a recital, regardless of how experienced the player is. He reassured them that although pedalboards are often different shapes, the notes are all in the same order, which made both of them laugh. I was standing beside Sarah Baldock, currently director of music at Chichester Cathedral, and one of only two women in top posts in cathedral music here. The Queen was gracious, delightful, and put us both at our ease immediately. Fortunately, she did not seem especially shocked that I was wearing trousers and was *not* wearing gloves. Both she and Prince Philip were intrigued to know how few women there are in top cathedral positions, and after a few minutes of discussion on this topic, the highlight of the day came for me, when Prince Philip looked me in the eye and said (as only Prince Philip can), "Now . . . you don't sound particularly native!" We then continued out conversation on the topic of Victoria, British Columbia, my hometown, which he and the Queen have visited a number of times. About 30 RCO members were presented that day, including a number of students who had recently been successful in diploma examinations.

The Queen was then presented with the College's highest honour, the RCO Medal, in a special issue to mark her patronage, and the Duke of Edinburgh was presented with a facsimile edition of a ceremonial organ work composed by Sir Walter Parratt (1841–1924), sometime organist of St George's Chapel, Windsor. They both then waved and smiled as graciously as can be, and departed, leaving the assembled organists to continue chatting. Needless to say, the RCO was honoured indeed to receive this kind of recognition in this our 150th year. It was truly a delightful day, and although the official photographer didn't have the best angle, there was one clear photo of me being presented to Her Majesty, which set a Facebook record for me in terms of the number of "likes"!

July 2015

The Ultimate Rivalry

As the child of two professional Anglican choral singers in the Commonwealth, I knew from a young age, not surprisingly, of the ancient English universities, and their significant choral traditions. Until I was about twelve, I assumed that there were actually three universities: Oxford, Cambridge, and Oxbridge. In reality, the latter term is a nickname referring to the combination of the former two, to distinguish these, the oldest and arguably most prestigious institutions, from the rest of the UK's universities.

The rivalry between Oxford and Cambridge is a long and well-documented phenomenon (it even has its own Wikipedia page).[8] My own loyalty was fixed long before I came to England—indeed, before I had finished elementary school—thanks in no small part to the 1981 documentary 'The Boast of Kings'[9] about the choir at King's College, Cambridge. Eventually, I came to Cambridge as an undergraduate, and have never left (as many of you know). Imagine my horror, then, when earlier this year, within the space of one month, both the journal of the RCCO (*Organ Canada*) and this august publication itself (i.e., TAO), attached titles to my columns which used the name of The Other Place! Both editors

---

8. https://en.wikipedia.org/wiki/Oxford%E2%80%93Cambridge_rivalry
9. 'The story of King's College Choir: The Boast of Kings', 1981 television documentary, now available on DVD (Regis RDVD101)

offered to print a correction, but I suggested that instead I devote an entire column to explaining the differences between the two universities, thus ensuring that the mix-up never be repeated.

Some historical and geographical background might be helpful. Oxford, a city of about 160,000, is located 60 miles west of London. Although there is no specific date for the University's foundation, there is evidence of teaching as far back as 1096 AD, making it the oldest university in the English-speaking world. In 1209, a group of scholars fled Oxford, following disputes with townsfolk. They settled in East Anglia, in the small market town of Cambridge, 60 miles north of London, which now has a population of about 120,000. The two universities have grown and thrived over the ensuing eight centuries, between them producing many great scientists (e.g., Isaac Newton, Charles Darwin), academics (Roger Penrose, F. R. Leavis), actors (Hugh Laurie, Emma Thompson), and musicians (Roger Norrington, David Willcocks), as well as numerous Prime Ministers (Margaret Thatcher, Tony Blair). Both are city universities, with colleges and departments scattered throughout the residential streets, rather than with traditional campuses. Both are collegiate universities: the colleges are independent, self-governing institutions, responsible for admitting their own students (undergraduate and postgraduate), who live and work in the college, but who attend university departments for lectures and examinations. Academics are employed by the university and/or by the colleges, depending on their positions, and all are independent scholars living and working together in small interdisciplinary communities. At lunch, you might find yourself chatting to a biochemist, a mediæval historian, and a linguist about the achievements of a brilliant undergraduate cricketer who is reading (the word we use for studying) Music.

As well as these various historical and institutional similarities, there are also many differences. Oxford is bigger, with 38 colleges compared to Cambridge's 31. Spelling denotes territory: at Cambridge we have Magdalene, Queens', and St Catharine's Colleges; at Oxford they have Magdalen, Queen's, and St Catherine's. The beautifully manicured lawns and their surrounding buildings which are many colleges' centrepieces are "courts" in Cambridge, but "quads" in Oxford. Academics are "Fellows" in Cambridge, and "Dons" in Oxford. Small-group teaching (whereby one leading academic instructs groups of just two or three undergraduates) is fundamental to the educational infrastructure at both Oxford and Cambridge, but they are called tutorials in the former, and supervisions in the latter. Most crucially, punters in the two universities stand on opposite ends of the boat.

The Oxbridge academical year is divided into three terms: the first term runs from early October to early December; the second from mid-January to mid-March; the third from mid-April to mid-June. In both universities, the first term is the Michaelmas Term, beginning just after 29 September. In Cambridge this is followed by Lent Term and Easter Term; in Oxford the second term is Hilary Term (his Feast Day is 13 January), and the third is Trinity Term. In Cambridge we count teaching weeks in cardinal numbers, whereas Oxford uses ordinals. Thus, we have Week 1, Week 2, Week 3, etc., but Oxford has First Week, Second Week, and Third Week, etc.. (This reminds me of the difference between many readers' early education and mine: in Canada, I went to Grade 4, Grade 5, and Grade 6, etc., but in the USA, you went to Fourth Grade, Fifth Grade, and Sixth Grade.)

Arguably the universities' most celebrated rivalry is that of the annual Boat Race on the River Thames in London, which (although it pains me to say it) Oxford is currently in the habit of winning. In other sports, although there are plenty of inter-university football (i.e., soccer), tennis, and rugby games across UK universities, it is only when Oxford plays against Cambridge that it is a Varsity Match. More light-heartedly, there is also the annual Goat Race, in which two Pygmy Goats, one wearing Cambridge's light blue, the other in Oxford's dark blue, battle for an "edible vegetable trophy" over a 200-metre farmyard course.

The academic rivalry is particularly significant, though, and I am delighted to say that we normally win that. Cambridge academics are the recipients of 120 Nobel Prizes in all disciplines since 1904, whereas Oxford have only 71.[10] It is telling that Cambridge is regularly ranked

---

10. Numbers updated in May 2020. See https://en.wikipedia.org/wiki/List_of_Nobel _laureates_by_university_affiliation

ahead of Oxford in university league tables, both nationally and interna-
tionally (we've topped the most recent national tables in the Times, the
Telegraph, and the Guardian newspapers). And, quite frankly, we have
King's College Chapel, and they do not.

June 2022

Dignissime Domine

On 1st April, I was invited by the Master of Selwyn College to act as Praelector in our graduation ceremony the next day. Having confirmed that this was not an April Fool, with some trepidation I agreed to take on this historic ceremonial role. Unexpected Covid-isolation meant that no-one who had done it before was available, and as a performer with some familiarity with Latin, I was supposedly the obvious substitute. Graduations are a quirky public Cambridge ritual, much photographed by bemused tourists, and I thought readers might enjoy hearing about this one.

Cambridge is a collegiate university, with 31 administratively-independent and academically-interdisciplinary colleges responsible for admitting their own students. During the degree, teaching is provided by a combination of university departments, faculties, and colleges, but examinations and formal academic assessment are administered by the university. Degrees are also conferred centrally, so whilst a student may have been a member of Selwyn College, s/he is a graduate of the University of Cambridge.

A Praelector is the senior academic in a college who is charged with presenting students to the university to receive their degrees. As well as having to vouch for their morals and learning, the Praelector is also vicariously responsible for students' actions and attire, and can be punished if students misbehave or are incorrectly dressed. Fortunately that punishment is not usually severe—traditionally it takes the form of being fined a bottle of Port.

In Cambridge, all undergraduates receive a BA (Bachelor of Arts) after their three-year degree, regardless of the subject they study. As long as the graduate stays out of jail for ten terms after taking their BA, the university upgrades it to an MA (Master of Arts). The Cambridge MA is a measure of rank, rather than an academic qualification *per se*. Holders of the degree may vote in university elections and policy decisions, and it also confers seniority at the college level, granting High Table dining rights, and even "grass rights" (i.e., MAs can walk across the lawn—Cambridge hierarchy at its most eccentric).

I made my Praelectorial debut at the admission to MA status of the students who "came up"[11] in 2015 (i.e., who graduated as BAs in 2018).[12] In addition, some were receiving the MB (Bachelor of Medicine), a six-year degree which includes postgraduate clinical placement. We began in Selwyn, with the 80 graduands being called individually for inspection. The Praelector is responsible for ensuring that all graduands are correctly dressed in the university's highly prescriptive ceremonial attire: dark suits, white shirts, black shoes, white bow tie and preaching bands, BA-status black academic gown, and hood of the highest Cambridge degree they hold (BA in most cases, though some had stayed on to complete MPhil, MSci, or other postgraduate qualifications). The Praelector must also wear a "square", the tasselled cap sometimes (though never in Cambridge) called a mortarboard, the doffing of which by way of greeting can never be done too often, nor too theatrically (apparently).

We then walked in a long black-and-white line procession through the college gardens and the town centre. The Master and I were at the

---

11. Undergraduates "come up" to or "go down" from Cambridge (regardless of where their home is) at the start and end of their degree, and also for the annual Christmas, Easter, and Long Vacations.

12. Unlike American universities, students' year groups are measured from when they arrive (matriculate) rather than when they leave (graduate). We don't use the phrase "class of [insert year]" but if you see "SE 2015" beside a name, this means that they began their degree at Selwyn College in 2015.

front of the procession, while the Head and Deputy Head Porters stopped traffic where necessary. Everyone smiled and waved at the many tourists who videoed us on our way. Our destination was the Senate House, a beautiful university building dating from the 1720s, where the graduands are presented by the Praelector to the Master of their college with the following Latin formula, which I was encouraged to recite dramatically (fortunately I had special dispensation not to have to do it from memory):

Dignissima domine,	*Most worthy*
Domine Procancellarie	*Lord Vice-Chancellor*
et tota Academia	*and the whole University,*
praesento vobis hunc virum (hanc mulierem)	*I present to you this man (this woman)*
quem (quam) scio	*whom I know*
tam moribus quam doctrina	*as much by character as by learning*
esse idoneum (idoneam)	*to be suitable*
ad gradum assequendum	*to proceed to the degree of*
Magister in Artibus (Baccalaurei in Medecina);	*Master of Arts (Bachelor of Medicine);*
idque tibi fide mea praesto	*for which I pledge my faith*
totique Academiae.	*to you and to the whole University.*

In non-pandemic times, the students, in groups of four, hold one finger of the Praelector's right hand, and are led to the dais where they kneel one-at-a-time in front of the Master's chair. He holds their hands in his and confers the degree (in Latin), while the Praelector ensures that they do not catch the bottom of their gown on their shoes. I was grateful that Covid restrictions meant that the ceremony was entirely non-contact, so all I had to do was worry about my Latin pronunciation.

Although I have never spoken Latin in public before, my training as a musician stood me in good stead: performance, ritual, and ceremony are very familiar. Indeed, I much enjoyed the day, and have even told the Master that I'd be willing to do it again if necessary!

Organist to the University of ____?

In the weeks leading up to the end of the academical year, there was a plethora of social media updates from my (numerous) organist friends alerting followers to the "busy season", as graduation ceremonies in their academic institutions approached. The role of University Organist in most places is ceremonial: the post-holder provides organ music for graduations every year. As these graduation posts appeared, I recalled having lessons many years ago with John Tuttle, then University Organist in Toronto, in Convocation Hall. For John, one of the rewards for accompanying lengthy graduation ceremonies every spring was the free teaching access to the otherwise underused instrument during the rest of the year. And so, with these various reminiscences running through my mind, I thought readers might be interested to know what the equivalent role is like in the ancient university city of Cambridge

The position of Cambridge University Organist (or, more properly, "Organist to the University of Cambridge") dates back to 1670, with the inaugural appointment of Dr Thomas Tudway (1650-c1726), Organist of King's College. It appears from the archives that this was a post traditionally held until retirement (historically equivalent to demise). For the first few hundred years of the post's existence, the average time of employment was about 35 years (the longest tenure was 56 years, a record shared by Tudway himself and another King's organist, the unfortunately-named

John Pratt (1772-1855). Until 2022, the position at Cambridge had been held by just 13 men: eight were organist of King's College, three of St John's, and two of Trinity. The most common name over the centuries was John (three in a row between 1777 and 1872); William, Robert, and Thomas also featured. During more recent centuries, the familiar names of Arthur Mann, George Guest, David Willcocks, Stephen Cleobury, and Andrew Nethsingha (King's, St John's, King's, King's, and St John's, respectively) held the position.

The post-holder in Cambridge is required to provide music for all university ceremonies and occasions. Ironically, this does not include graduations, since there is no organ in the building in which "General Admission to Degrees" takes place (the Senate House, which dates from the 1720s). Having said that, there is a University Organ, the west end instrument in Great St Mary's (GSM), the University Church, which is situated on the Market Square, opposite the Senate House. The University Organ was purchased in 1698, and continues this day to be maintained by the University, rather than by GSM (another organ, a 1991 III/33 instrument at the east end by the Irish builder Kenneth Jones, is the responsibility of the parish). The University Organ is a III/35 Thomas Hill/Father Smith instrument which includes what is thought to be the most significant collection of original Father Smith pipework of any playable instrument in the country. It was restored in the 1960s by Hill, Norman, and Beard, and then again in 1995 by Mander Organ Builders. The instrument is historic in every sense, including having no playing aids and a ratchet-swell-pedal. Legend has it that Tchaikovsky played the University Organ when he was in Cambridge to receive his honorary doctorate in 1893. It is much sought-after by visiting organists, and it is the responsibility of the University Organist to facilitate these visits.

Special services in GSM called University Sermons take place on Sunday mornings twice each term (six times per year), when a clerical alumnus is invited back to preach to the gathered academical community. The choir from the college which the preacher attended is invited to sing for these services, and the University Organist makes all musical arrangements for such occasions. The Director of Music of the preacher's college normally directs the choir from the gallery at the west end (so as to be close to the organ) and unsuspecting organ scholars from across the university recount tales of their first experience accompanying Howells or Britten on an instrument designed to play nothing more modern than Handel. Ironically, once the arrangements are in place with the relevant college and organ scholar, the University Organist can take the day off.

The Organist to the University is also required to provide music for ceremonies in the Senate House, and in particular for the annual Honorary Degree Day (see my UK Report of November 2012, which can be found on page 242, for further details on this peculiar ritual). Here, two college choirs (normally representing two of the honorands) sing unaccompanied music, the Cambridge University Brass Ensemble (CUBE) plays fanfares and processionals, and a student instrumentalist provides a solo performance. No organ music is required (nor even possible, due to the lack of an instrument) and only when his own college choir is involved is the University Organist actually required to be present.

The role in Cambridge is historic and important, but even more ceremonial (i.e., less practical) than in most other universities (including Oxford). In April 2022, I was delighted to make my own debut as Organist to the University of Cambridge by conducting the choir in the University's official memorial service for His Royal Highness, the Prince Philip, Duke of Edinburgh. I am honoured to be adding a new College—and a new gender—to the list of holders of this important office.

Chapter 2

Education and Examinations

Since I have spent the majority of my career working in educational institutions, it is no surprise that a number of columns over the years have dealt with the training of young singers and organists. In this chapter, you will find discussion of methods of teaching and assessment methods, curricula, syllabi, and other such edifying topics.

September 2009

Children's Instrumental Lessons

I n 1991, on my first visit to England, I participated in an Eton Choral Course,[13] a week for teenagers run at the famous 'public' school (the UK now uses the word 'independent' for fee-paying or private schools, as differentiated from 'state-maintained', which is what North Americans would call public schools). The courses were set up in 1980 to prepare high-school-aged singers for university choral scholarships. When they began, there was one course per year; now there is such a demand for places that there are six courses each summer, including one which focuses on young organists. When I arrived on my first course, despite jet-lag and culture-shock, I was astonished to find so many people my age who loved church music.

Like many young singers, my church choral experience at home had been mainly with adults—some superb professional singers in Toronto, to be sure, but few of my generation. Obviously I had had some interaction with younger singers: I sang in my city and provincial youth choirs as a student, and I knew several members of the National Youth Choir of Canada. Although I loved these experiences, the music was primarily secular, and usually too full of (dare I say it) patronising obligatory

---

13. These were renamed and rebranded under the auspices of the Rodolfus Foundation in 2019, and are now called Rodolfus Choral Courses.

'Canadian Content'.[14] During my first Eton Choral Course, I sang Howells, Byrd, Gibbons, Brahms, and Mendelssohn, and was surrounded by
like-minded young people who not only understood this repertoire, but
actually loved it, and wanted to sing it in its proper liturgical context.

This made me question what it is about UK schooling which produces so many more young liturgical singers. Obviously, cathedral choir
schools have a significant influence: there are 44 such schools in the UK,
compared with only two or three in North America. However, there are
also tens of thousands of schools in the UK where government cut-backs
are marginalising music as much as at home, and only a few of the largest
parish churches retain any significant youth involvement in their choirs.
However, it is still usually the case that in primary school (at least), children are encouraged to play an instrument or two, and take ABRSM
exams each year, even if only to grade 4/5.

I was surprised last summer at how few of the 50 girls on the St
Thomas Fifth Avenue Girl Chorister Course had actually had any instrumental lessons—only a handful, and of them, only one had taken graded
exams. In Canada and the UK, "what grade are you on the piano" is a
common childhood question thanks to Toronto's Royal Conservatory of
Music (RCM) and the ABRSM. Although there were some terrific young
singers at St Thomas, I was worried for their choir directors at home: as
far as I could tell, every aspect of their musical training, including simply
learning the names of the notes, was in the hands of overworked organists and choral conductors who might see them for only an hour a week.
If they all were having basic instrumental lessons, their reading and their
broader musical knowledge would be improving so much more quickly.
Eton Choral Courses regularly have a 'course orchestra', and though on
occasion one might be inclined to spell the first word 'coarse', at least 90%
of those teenagers can actually join in on a borrowed instrument of some
description for an ad hoc performance of Elgar's *Land of Hope and Glory*.

So, in my experience, one of the major differences over here is that
far more children have some basic musical literacy (despite funding cut-
backs), allowing a higher proportion of them to sing in choirs at a more

---

14. https://en.wikipedia.org/wiki/Canadian_content

advanced level. Those who are involved in liturgical singing are indeed often from cathedral schools, or independent schools which still maintain their chapels, though I have noticed that even those who come from secular singing experiences, like the UK's National Youth Choirs (note the plural), have such an understanding of music and choral singing, that they want to be challenged by serious great repertoire, and they quickly learn to appreciate it in the liturgical context for which it was written. It seems obvious to me that parents and music directors in North America should encourage their charges to take instrumental lessons alongside their choral singing, and to prepare for both practical and theory examinations such as those run by the Toronto's RCM or the ABRSM, as well as AGO certification for young organists. Perhaps then, fewer North American teenagers will have to cross the Atlantic in order to find choral courses that inspire and motivate them musically.

Oundle for Organists

I have just returned from a week in The Other Place (a.k.a. Oxford) where I was one of eight tutors for the annual "Oundle for Organists" Prospective Organ Scholars course, which is run in partnership with the RCO. 42 teenagers gathered for the six-day residential course which is based in Cambridge and Oxford in alternate years.

The course consisted of daily masterclasses on repertoire and keyboard skills (including, of course, the universally dreaded transposition exercises), recitals played by tutors and students, question-and-answer sessions on university organ scholarships, and lively social activities, including a very enjoyable punting trip. The students also participated in five public choral services in five different chapels, including two services of Compline, and three of Choral Evensong. Every piece of music in the services was conducted and accompanied by a different students, so by the end of the week, 23 conductors and organists (not to mention 14 Compline cantors) had helped to lead the services. The choir consisted of the remainder of the students, with a slight imbalance towards baritones with recently-changed voices.

This course provides an excellent illustration of how young organists are "trained" in the UK: they are simply told to stand in front of the choir, or to sit at an organ console, and get on with it. Of the students who directed, none had extensive (or indeed any, in some cases) conducting experience. We had sessions during the week on beat patterns, clarity of gesture, and preparation of scores, as well as reminders about singing and rehearsal technique, administration, recruitment, and numerous other essentials. But even before all of those basics had been covered, the students were pulled out of the choir stalls (usually, but not always, willingly) for masterclasses in directing singers, knowing that they would be part of a public service in a prestigious Oxford chapel only a few hours later.

The same is true with the accompanists: the "volunteers" were sent to an organ that they did not know, sometimes in the far distance at the other end of the chapel, and asked to accompany major repertoire (Howells, Gibbons, Mathias, as well as psalms and hymns) with no rehearsal, apart from the time that they had spent at home, learning the notes in advance. We did allow for a tutor in the organ loft, helping with registration and relaying the beat when the camera didn't work, but in general, the students were on their own, learning on the job about accompanying, playing ahead of the beat, registering, responding to verbal directions from the (often barely audible) conductor, giving notes/chords, etc., and then accompanying in the service later in the day. Once the day's rehearsal was over, the tutors took their places in the congregation, and all the musical leadership in the service was left to the students themselves. There is no question that there were many places in those five services that were (to put it kindly) musically unpolished, however, there were also moments of great beauty and enthusiasm, partly because the singers, the conductors, and the organists were all supporting, encouraging, and learning from each other.

As a North American, it is probably not surprising to hear that I would not advocate this type of training exclusively—standing in front of a mirror and honing stick technique is a crucial part of all students' preparation, as are the hours of solitary organ practice, watching the imaginary conductor on the blank TV screen or the empty mirror. However, it is certainly the case that the "learning on the job" method eliminates the fear of *doing* the job at a very young age: there were students last week who were very apprehensive at first, but once in front of the choir, conducting a successful performance in the service, they quickly gained in confidence and authority.

It is the norm for Oxbridge organ scholarships to place this sort of responsibility on undergraduate shoulders, especially in colleges where there is no professional director of music, and although it may have its drawbacks as an educational method, it also gives those who have the courage to rise to it incredible opportunities to develop quickly as leaders, despite an apparent lack of theoretical training. Anyone thinking of a university organ scholarship in the UK (and there will be more of this in next month's column) should certainly consider attending a "Prospective Organ Scholars" course. The courses are open to all, without audition, and really extremely enjoyable, as well as being educational.

Studying in the UK
as an Organ Scholar

Firstly, many thanks for your feedback: I am grateful to those who have suggested ideas for future articles, or who have written to say that they are enjoying the column. Several people have requested a discussion of the opportunities here for foreign organists to study or work as university or cathedral organ scholars. While there are logistical and legal hurdles to overcome, the musical rewards are certainly great.

I came to the UK specifically to spend three years as an organ scholar at Cambridge, while studying for an undergraduate degree in Music, so I have personal experience of being a student in the UK. There are organ scholarships available at a number of universities, though Oxford and Cambridge are the most popular, partly because they each offer about fifteen awards per year to students of the university. There is considerable diversity: you can work with a world-class choir in a high-profile venue, or you can run the show on your own, with little guidance but great freedom. Since Oxford and Cambridge are two of the greatest educational institutions in the world, students work with leading academics, and organ scholars can study a wide range of subjects, not just Music (present organ scholars are studying Classics, Law, Medicine, and Engineering, for example). Study at Oxbridge is intense, and the work is difficult: organ scholars need to be exceptionally able academically as well as musically.

Information about applying is available on the university websites. In brief, the deadline every year is September 1st, and the auditions ("Trials") take place at the end of September, with a view to beginning studies the following year. The majority of applicants who are competitive on paper are invited to audition (though travel costs are not covered). If you are offered a place, you need to obtain a student visa, and, most importantly, you need to show that you are able to afford tuition fees and living expenses for the duration of your course (usually three years for an undergraduate degree). Crucially, the "scholarship" is *not* worth a great deal of money: the only financial perks are a modest annual stipend (about £450 GBP) and free organ lessons. The overall cost amounts to about as much as undergraduate study at an American university—though Canadian readers might be rather more concerned! It is, however, a wonderful way to spend three years, and is certainly worth every penny.

It is also possible to come to the UK for a master's degree or doctorate, though Oxbridge organ scholarships are generally directed towards undergraduates, and the timing of the trials is not coordinated with the application process for postgraduate study. Candidates who wish to pursue this route should contact individual directors of music.

For those interested in spending a short time working in the UK, most cathedrals have a one-year organ scholarship, normally for students on a "gap" year, between school and university, or for those who have recently completed a university scholarship. The classified section of the UK's weekly newspaper, the *Church Times,* is available online, and all cathedral positions are advertised there. The RSCM also maintains a site listing scholarships in the UK and elsewhere. Cathedral organ scholars have a range of duties, some of which include attending chorister rehearsals, giving piano lessons, being choir librarian, and assisting at daily services. In all cases, the financial rewards are small (church musicians are simply not paid very well over here), but most cathedrals provide free (single) accommodation, and many also offer free school meals, so the organ scholar's stipend is ample for basic survival and pub visits.

The main legal hurdle is that of obtaining a work permit. Some cathedrals are on an approved list of educational establishments, and organ scholars qualify for a student visa; other cathedrals act as a sponsor for a full work permit; some organ scholars have applied under the Temporary Religious Worker category (though the last person I knew who did this had to apply—and pay—twice for this privilege).[15] The lack of consistency is partly due to the fact that the UK is presently changing its immigration policy. It is also the case that since 2001, movement between countries has been harder. However, a year immersed in the choral tradition here easily makes up for the administrative hassle.

In conclusion, read the websites if you are interested in a university organ scholarship, or keep your eye on the Church Times if you would like to apply to a cathedral. And of course, organists on holiday or sabbatical are always welcome: I, for one, am always willing to have lunch and chat with visitors, allow them to observe rehearsals, or play the Selwyn organ, so please do just get in touch.

---

15. After 2012, cathedral organ scholarships no longer qualified for international work visas, as none of them pays above the compulsory salary threshold. Some posts are considered educational positions, and can be applied for as such by non-UK citizens.

Cathedral Choir Schools

The Choir School is one of the most cherished features of England's choral tradition. Although children are involved in liturgical singing throughout the world, there is a unique and valuable intensity about the daily training that a choir school affords. As is well known, in a conventional cathedral choir, choristers (historically boys, more recently girls, and, very occasionally now, boys and girls together) sing the soprano or treble parts, while professional adult singers (lay clerks) provide the alto, tenor, and bass parts. The children range in age from seven to 17, and sing services every day of the week in most cathedrals, many of which originally followed a monastic pattern of regular and frequent daily liturgy which dictated the rhythm of the community. The standard that is expected from these choristers is high, and although expectations alone do not produce results, it is true to say that most cathedral trebles sing with impressive maturity and linguistic understanding, well beyond the typical capabilities of the average ten-year-old.

A few readers have asked me to write about this topic—indeed, two in particular enquired as to whether cathedral choristers are actually "normal" children (!). I suppose they may appear to be atypically angelic, disciplined, confident, and gifted when seen only at work in the cathedral. On the sports field or in the local Starbucks however, less exalted adjectives might be more apt. Of course, most of the children who audition will have an instinctive natural singing voice and a quick ear, but many of the youngest ones have had no formal musical training when they arrive, and very few indeed are child prodigies. As I have recently taken over as director of Ely Cathedral Girls' Choir (an appointment which I combine with my position as Director of Music at Selwyn College, Cambridge), and am now working regularly in a cathedral choir school, I am pretty well placed to offer an insider's view of life as a chorister—and some reassurances that they are indeed "normal" children.

The Ely choristers attend the King's School, Ely, a large, co-educational, independent (i.e., private) school, situated beside the cathedral. It was founded in 970AD and has about 1000 day and boarding pupils ranging in age from two to 17. The 18 girl choristers are members of the senior school (equivalent to the North American 'junior high' and 'high school'), beginning in the choir at the age of 13, and usually continuing as choristers for five years. The 22 boy choristers are pupils in the junior (elementary) school; they begin their choristership at age eight, and sing either until they move on to the senior school, or else until nature determines otherwise—whichever occurs first. All of the choristers are boarding students, in specially designated choir boarding houses, one for the boys and one for the girls, and they all receive a scholarship to help with their school fees. Each house has a live-in housemistress or housemaster who is responsible for the children's pastoral well-being, as well as a matron for practical issues like first-aid and laundry, a house tutor with academic responsibilities, a conductor, and an organist.

A chorister's day begins at about 6:30am, when those who are studying a musical instrument get up to practise before breakfast. Every morning I take the train from Cambridge to Ely, and then ride my bicycle up the hill to the Cathedral, as the wafting strains of scales on the flute and basic piano exercises mingle with the cathedral bell for Morning Prayer. Breakfast for all of the choristers and many of the choir-house staff takes place in the main school dining hall at 7:25am, and this is followed by a rehearsal five mornings a week at 8:00am. The boys rehearse in the cathedral song school, the girls in a (rather warmer) specially designed rehearsal room in their boarding house. The first ten minutes is spent warming up the voices and doing ear-training and sight-reading exercises

The remainder of the time is dedicated to rehearsing for the services to be sung that week.

After the rehearsal, the choristers head off to lessons (the UK word for 'classes'), along with the rest of the school. At this point, they do indeed become ordinary school children, indistinguishable from their peers, with lessons in Biology, French, Mathematics, and the like, as well as field hockey and soccer training, debating clubs, art classes, and drama practices. Lunchtime and other school breaks find the girls' boarding house buzzing with activity: the making of toast and tea, chatting with Matron in the office, running upstairs to perform crucial tasks such as the re-straightening of hair, texting each other on their mobiles, thoughtlessly stomping mud from the playing field into the hallway carpet, etc.—so far, very normal teenaged girls. What marks them out as choristers, though, is the concurrent musical activity: a quick run through a Gibbons solo, a theory lesson over lunch, a detailed discussion about the circle of fifths or Stanford in B flat with the organist, an impromptu rendering of the soprano suspensions in Noble in B minor, mingled with laughter, as two of the girls put their coats on before dashing outside.

After school on cathedral service days, the girls scurry back to the house, stop briefly for juice and cookies prepared by Matron, before donning royal red cassocks and flat black shoes, putting their music in order, and processing over to the cathedral for a short rehearsal (20 minutes). This is all followed by the singing of Evensong, after which a cursory hug of visiting parents precedes a return to the house, where cassocks are hung up again (not always as carefully as Matron would like), music is piled up for filing by the long-suffering choir librarian, and the school dining room provides some well-earned supper. The evening is spent doing "prep" (homework), more instrumental practice, and possibly the watching of some TV in the common room once everything is finished. Bedtime requires all lights to be turned off by 10:30pm at the latest, and, when the cathedral bell sounds the following morning, the whole routine begins again.

Watching the choristers go about their work in the candlelit stillness of a breathtaking mediæval cathedral, singing the daily psalmody, the ancient plainsong office hymns, and the great liturgical music written over the past 500 years, I suppose one can be forgiven for thinking that they are not "normal". However, although they are just ordinary children, they have certainly been given an extraordinary musical and educational opportunity, as well as the particular privilege of participating in the centuries-old rhythm of the Christian liturgy.

Easter Term Examinations

As I write, here in Cambridge, the Easter Term has ended, and, after a final week of celebration, the undergraduates have gone home for a much-needed summer break. As might be expected of such a prestigious university, the academic pressure placed on students is intense, with the spring subsumed in examinations worth 100% (grades do not accumulate over the year). During the Easter Term (a.k.a. Exam Term), the university becomes focussed: colleges are closed to the public; sports teams and choirs are depleted; libraries and laboratories are full; college bars are empty. Given this commendable focus on academic performance, it is ironic to remember that many of the things for which the university is known around the world are, in effect, extra-curricular: inspiring architecture, curious Brideshead-esque (Hogwarts-esque?) traditions, outstanding museums and galleries, celebrated acting and comedy, world-class rowing, and, of course, the choral tradition. Since the spring brings many tourists to Cambridge, I thought readers might like to know why visiting Cambridge in the Easter Term might not provide a particularly well-rounded view of student life.

Throughout the examination period, balancing the drive to succeed academically, with the need to preserve the sorts of pursuits mentioned above (let alone our sanity), requires careful management, especially for those who, like myself, are employed to direct undergraduates in an extra-curricular activity (namely, singing in a college choir). The university may be best known for the annual Oxford-Cambridge boat race and King's College carol services, but, when examinations loom, activities such as these are sidelined, and tourists hoping to experience charming Edwardian customs in practice, or see the next Monty Python or Fry & Laurie in performance, will be disappointed, as they encounter closed doors, locked gates, and enforced college Quiet Periods. This academic single-mindedness is also reflected in our admissions policy, where applicants are assessed solely on their academic record and their perceived intellectual potential. Admissions Tutors are rarely interested in extra-curricular activities—indeed, many are overtly suspicious of them. The number of musical instruments played, mountains climbed, rainforests planted, hospitals volunteered for, school prefectures held, and sports accolades obtained are of minimal concern, and those applying to study here must bear this in mind.

Indeed, applicants who are offered a place here, soon realise that there is little time for extensive extra-curricular commitments. To supplement the usual pattern of lectures and laboratories, Cambridge undergraduates also receive weekly small-group teaching sessions ("supervisions"), involving a leading scholar ("supervisor") teaching two or three students ("supervisees"). This "supervision system"—regular scrutiny of an undergraduate's written work by a leading academic—is a hallmark of a Cambridge education. For each supervision, undergraduates prepare essays or complete technical exercises. A typical "supervision essay" is between 1500 and 2000 words, and students might prepare two or three essays per week on a variety of topics. So, for example, in a given week, for three specialist supervisors, a Music student might write one supervision essay discussing Beethoven's influence on the development of the symphony, another providing an analysis of a movement from Bach's *B minor Mass*, and, in addition, would complete a piece of three-part Palestrina-style counterpoint. When time for preparation, reading, listening, writing, and composing is added to that spent in lectures and supervisions, a Humanities student can expect to devote about 50 to 60 hours a week to academic work. With additional laboratory time, a Science student may study for 60 to 70 hours a week. The three terms are short (just eight weeks) and intense. Falling behind is not a viable option. Very quickly, one begins to see that Admissions Tutors' suspicion of extra-curricular activities is well-founded. For an organised undergraduate, a choral scholar's commitment of 12 hours a week to a chapel choir, or a boatie's two hours a day on the river, is probably manageable. More than that would be impossible.

As mentioned above, one reason why the examination period is so pressurised, is that virtually no supervision work is officially assessed, but instead constitutes long-term preparation for exams in the Easter Term. Occasionally one wonders why students bother to prepare the work every week even though it "doesn't count". Of course, one would like to think that self-motivation and intellectual curiosity alone were sufficient explanation, though no doubt the prospect that the world's leading Beethoven scholar will read that symphony essay is also a contributing factor. More practically, that very topic might appear at the end of the year, on a three-essays-in-three-hours music history exam, so preparing well for a supervision on this topic is sensible.

With this sort of academic pressure, perhaps it is a wonder that any life at all occurs in Cambridge during the Easter Term. Although rowing, singing, acting, and the like do continue to an extent, the academic work becomes the primary focus. Consequently, those of us who run extra-curricular activities must allow flexibility: Evensong might be sung by 16 students instead of the usual 24; plays and stand-up comedy appear on weekends only; the university orchestra gives just one concert instead of six; sports teams train only twice a week instead of every day. Once examinations are over, however, visitors to Cambridge will find the most ridiculous outpouring of extra-curricular overindulgences imaginable. On offer is a multifarious selection of inter-collegiate rowing races and cricket matches, ground-breaking new drama, Shakespeare performances in college gardens, stand-up comedy, musicals, operas, orchestral concerts, organ recitals, choral performances, and even (for those who are that way inclined) the University Croquet Tournament finals. Astonishingly, undergraduates still find time to attend garden parties all day and "May Balls" all night. And this period of merry-making lasts just one week.

This extravagant week is called "May Week" (though, as befits our charming traditions, May Week actually occurs in the middle of June), and it is good to see that the artistic and sporting activities for which Cambridge is well known continue to thrive. Visitors to Cambridge need to be aware that for seven of the eight weeks of the Easter Term, observing that alluring Brideshead-esque vision is not really possible, but if you time your visit to coincide with May Week, you will not be disappointed.

February 2012

TJYP: A New Arrival

Every three or four years in most Cambridge colleges, a particularly important new "fresher" (first year) arrives to begin an undergraduate degree: a new organ scholar. At Selwyn, this past term, I have been "breaking in" our new Junior Organ Scholar, and have spent a good deal of time reflecting upon the training that every organ scholar undergoes.

My new arrival at Selwyn—let us call him Johann-Sebastian for convenience—followed a relatively conventional route to Cambridge. He was a chorister at a major English cathedral, where he was immersed in the English choral tradition, its discipline, its standards, and its repertoire. After five years at a senior school with an excellent music department, where he learned the organ and excelled academically, he spent his "gap" year (i.e., the year between school and university) as the organ scholar at another major English cathedral. He arrived at Selwyn at the beginning of this academical year, with this very solid background upon which to build.

Not surprisingly, one of the first things Johann-Sebastian needed to do was to accustom himself to the organs, our wonderfully substantial Létourneau (III/30) and our delightful little Tickell (I/3), as well as to the acoustic of the chapel itself. Obviously, both instrument and building contribute significantly to the way in which an organist plays. At Selwyn, the Létourneau's sensitive mechanical action, combined with a relatively dry acoustic, forces all of my organ scholars to adapt and exaggerate their legato technique rather more than they originally expected, particularly when playing 19th- and 20th-century repertoire (Stanford, Howells, et al).

Experienced accompanists are well aware of the importance of adjusting to a conductor's quirks in rehearsal, both physical and verbal. My previous two seasoned organ scholars, who had been here for three and four years respectively, were completely familiar with my rehearsal technique: they knew which bar I was starting from before I announced it to the choir; they understood instinctively when I wanted them to play along with a struggling part, and when I wanted them to leave the singers to work things out for themselves; they could follow my idiosyncrasies and they knew my foibles. Johann-Sebastian has been working all of these things out for the first time, and it has made me realise afresh that I am perhaps not always as clear as I would like to be.

One of the things that most organ scholars have to come to terms with is the difference between sight-reading, quick-study, and proper preparation. In an audition, we test the first and the third of these important skills, but it is less easy to test the second. In reality, though, it is the second skill that is most important in a Cambridge College chapel. Although I demand good sight-reading skills, I certainly do not expect an organ scholar to sight-read an accompaniment during Evensong. However, in reality, in the busy-ness of Full Term, there is rarely time for really detailed long-term preparation of music, so it is the quick-study skills which are most often called upon.

Most young organists spend much of the early years of their training learning solo repertoire, and this is a laudable pursuit. Gap-year organ scholars in a cathedral will play a fair number of complete services, but the majority of their contributions will be voluntaries, while the professional assistant organist does most of the accompanying. When Johann-Sebastian arrived in Cambridge, he was a little surprised to have to prioritise accompaniments instead of solo repertoire. Over the eight weeks of this past term, he has played (with aplomb, I might add) the not-insubstantial accompaniments of the Duruflé *Requiem*, Kodály's *Missa brevis*, Grayston Ives *Edington Service*, Stanford *Mag & Nunc in G,*

Howells *Worcester Service*, Bairstow's *Blessed city*, and Wood *Mag & Nunc in E flat No. 2*—to name but a few. In addition, there have been numerous psalms and hymns, as well as other more straightforward accompaniments on the Tickell chamber organ. Needless to say, learning extensive new voluntaries was not feasible on top of this load.

As well as dealing with these technical and methodological adjustments, learning new repertoire, accompanying a new choir, settling into a new environment, working with a new conductor, and a new organ teacher, Johann-Sebastian is also, of course, studying towards a degree. He is learning to juggle his academic commitments with his chapel duties, the latter of which are entirely extra-curricular. As some of you may remember from my recent column about the academic versus non-academic life in Cambridge,[16] a Cambridge Music student can expect to spend about 50 to 60 hours per week on academic work. All chapel and organ-playing duties (about 12 hours per week *before* organ practice time) are secondary.

Financially the position of organ scholar is a humble one—across the university, the stipend paid is just £450 GBP per year (about $700 USD). In addition, organ scholars also receive free organ lessons and a piano in their rooms. Although this may sound like a lot of work for little recompense, these responsibilities are recognised in terms of status (this is Cambridge, after all). In all Colleges, "Scholar" is a technical term, referring to those students who are part of the legal governing foundation of a College (the "Master, Fellows, and Scholars"). The Master is the Head, the Fellows are the Academics (called "Dons" in Oxford), and the Scholars are those students, undergraduates and post-graduates, who have achieved First Class university examination results, and have been admitted to the foundation of their College, normally by signing a large, dusty vellum book with an ageing fountain pen, after an elaborate ceremony in Latin. By definition, a first year, who has not yet taken university examinations, cannot be a Scholar—indeed, so-called Choral Scholars are actually technically merely Choral Exhibitioners, or Choral Award-holders. The only exception to this is the Organ Scholar.

---

16. See October 2011 on page 46.

The responsibilities of Johann-Sebastian's position are significant: over the past century, the Organ Scholarship at Selwyn has been held by the likes of Dr Percy Young, Sir David Lumsden, Dr Richard Marlow, Andrew Lawrence-King, Dr Gerald Hendrie, and Professor John Harper. Fortunately for me, our newest addition to this illustrious list is already living up to his predecessors. He is playing with accuracy, confidence, and flair, and I know that you will hear about him one day—though perhaps under a different name.

May 2012

WDPR: My Publisher's Son

As would be expected of a world-leading university, there is a high proportion of overseas students at Cambridge, particularly at the post-graduate level. However, only very infrequently does one find a foreign student at the organ console in a college chapel. Since the 1980s, only a handful of international students have held organ scholarships here, despite the fact that, with about forty organ scholars in residence at any one time, well over 100 organ scholars pass through the university every decade. Of the limited number of foreign organ scholars, all but one have been from Commonwealth countries such as Canada, Australia, and Hong Kong. None have been from continental Europe, and only one organ scholar in living memory has been American. As it happens, I had coffee with that particular American just a few days ago, and we discussed this very issue.

Most of you will know that the present Junior Organ Scholar of King's College, Cambridge is American. Parker Ramsay, originally from Tennessee, is currently in his second year of an undergraduate degree in History. Having been home-schooled until he was 16, Parker studied the organ in his early teens with Wilma Jensen. He came to the UK to complete his high school education in the Sixth Form at the King's School Ely (where the Ely Cathedral girl and boy choristers are educated). This gave him a taste of life in the UK, and he went on successfully to apply for what is arguably the most prestigious organ scholarship in the world. In addition to being academically exceptional, a talented organist, and a gifted composer, Parker is also an accomplished harpist, and is my accompanist-of-choice for Ely Cathedral Girls' Choir's annual performance of Benjamin Britten's *Ceremony of Carols*.

Over coffee the other day, Parker and I mused upon the reasons why the two of us were so unusual in having come to Cambridge from North America as undergraduate organ scholars. Since the opportunities available here to ambitious young musicians are so outstanding, it is surely unfortunate that relatively few foreigners have applied for these posts, especially as there are barely enough appropriately-qualified English students to fill all of the vacancies. We identified a number of hurdles, none of which is insurmountable, but many of which might dissuade academically able potential organ (and indeed choral) scholars from applying to Cambridge. I thought I would use this month's column to accomplish two things: firstly to give you an insight into life as an organ scholar, as seen through the eyes of Parker Ramsay, and secondly, to encourage academically and musically gifted North American organists and singers to consider applying for a place at Cambridge.

An Oxbridge undergraduate education is very different from that offered by universities in most other countries (to be fair, it is also very different from that offered by most other universities in the UK). Undergraduate courses are specialised and focussed on one academic discipline from the beginning; we expect undergraduates to think and work independently throughout the year, despite the fact that the vast majority of the assessment takes place in summer exams; we teach the writing of discursive essays in examination conditions (most Humanities exams require the writing of three essays in three hours); we demand original research using primary sources, especially towards the end of the course. Parker, as a student of History, spends approximately six or seven hours every day reading, writing, and attending lectures and supervisions. On average, he writes about 6000 words per week, in supervision essays, and in preparation for this year's submitted Long Essay on the topic of "The Politics of Space and the use of Church Music in Colonial Peru". This sort of specialised academic concentration at the undergraduate level is unusual in other universities, but for the right kind of motivated and focussed young academic, it can be intellectually liberating.

Musically, the skills demanded of an organ scholar are unlike those required of an organ major at a music conservatoire or in a university with a performance-based music degree. An organ scholar's daily playing is entirely liturgically focussed, and as much time is spent learning accompaniments, hymns, and psalms, as is dedicated to polishing solo repertoire. An organ scholar is primarily an ensemble musician, and, unlike a recitalist, is always working with other musicians, as an accompanist and a conductor. Parker is unusual in having to prepare for seven choral services every week during term (most college chapels only have two or three). He usually aims to spend about three hours a day at the organ (though depending on the time of day, his registration choices may be severely limited in order not to disturb the tourists). The skill of the 'quick study' is key: "it is not sight-reading, but it is definitely not polished either" says Parker of his daily service playing. Organ lessons are taught purely on a consultation basis, three times per term, and teachers are willing to work on accompaniments with their students as well as solo repertoire.

Perhaps surprisingly, another consideration must be financial. The delightful sentence "A football scholarship to an American university can cover some, and at times, all, of the costs associated with earning a university degree" (see www.firstpointusa.com) is sadly misleading if you replace "football" with "organ or choral" and "American university" with "Oxbridge". My father had to re-mortgage the family home to send me here—though I think he doesn't regret it. For more information on the advantages of status over financial reward, please see my UK Report from February 2012.[17]

Finally, does an organ scholar have a social life? On top of his daily six to seven hours of academic work, and three hours of organ practice, Parker also has a boys' rehearsal (an hour every morning) and rehearsal and Evensong (another two hours each afternoon). By my reckoning, that adds up to about a 12-hour day, so there is definitely a little bit of time for socialising. Meal times in college provide a chance to see friends, and the

---

17. This can be found on page 50 of this book.

interdisciplinary nature of Oxbridge college life, whereby one's immediate neighbours in residence might be a physicist, a musician, a classicist, and a veterinary medic, helps to keep a broader perspective. Given his hectic schedule, I was grateful that Parker managed to find time to sit down with me for a leisurely coffee between a boys' rehearsal and a lecture.

This sort of experience as a student and an organ scholar opens up many career possibilities. Former Oxbridge organ scholars are conductors of major international orchestras and opera companies, cathedral directors of music throughout the world, solo recitalists, collaborative pianists, professional singers, investment bankers, university academics, bishops, comedians. There has even been an English Prime Minister (Edward Heath). So, if you are a high-school-aged, over-achieving, academically-able organist, and you would like to know more about being a Cambridge organ scholar, then I suggest that you pop along to the AGO National Convention in Nashville this summer, and have a word with Parker, who will be a featured artist there. Failing that, you can find out more on the Cambridge website.

If you apply and are successful, then it is highly likely that I will arrange to meet you for coffee at some point shortly into your degree!

Meaningful Gestures:
Teaching Conducting

In 2009, the University of Cambridge developed a specialised Master's degree in Choral Studies, the MMus. Since the its beginnings, it has been modified and tweaked, taking into account suggestions from both students and lecturers. One of this year's additions to the established timetable of lectures, seminars, and masterclasses, is the provision of individual conducting lessons, to complement the group sessions which have been featured thus far. I am one of two directors of music to have taken on this teaching.

Until recently, the teaching of choral conducting as a technical practice has been rare in the UK. Historically, conductors have acquired their skills on the job as apprentices, rather than in a classroom. In college chapels, we thrust students in front of the choir, and expect them to prepare Evensong with little input from senior musicians. Remarkably, despite this ad-hoc approach, the English Choral Tradition is revered the world over, though it is not without its limitations. Many conductors here have technical flaws and failings which could have been addressed with more methodical teaching.

The recent establishment of postgraduate choral conducting courses at UK conservatoires and universities is a long-overdue and welcome development. The RCO also offers an examined diploma that is the choral conducting equivalent of an FRCO. As a rule, at the undergraduate level, university organ scholars still follow the traditional apprenticeship method, but many go on to further specialist conservatoire study to hone conducting skills. In addition, most of the younger generation of college directors of music have had some conducting training, so are they able to coach undergraduate organ scholars both musically and gesturally, as they learn on the job.

Over the years, I have done a great deal of conducting coaching, for my own organ scholars, in masterclasses and residential courses, and for the MMus. However this is the first time that I have given individual conducting lessons in the quiet privacy of my own college room. It has been educational for the students (I hope) but also for me: I have had to think about what I do, and why I do it, in an uncharacteristically analytical way, since, without the presence of a choir in the room, every movement is entirely theoretical. Unusually for a UK undergraduate, I had had two years of orchestral conducting lessons in Toronto before I came to Cambridge, so although I was also trained in the apprentice organ scholar method here, it was not wholly without technical grounding. This background has definitely helped me in my own career, and it is also helping me to teach this year's MMus students more effectively.

In our sessions, we have worked on score preparation, rehearsal technique, programme planning, and (most conspicuously) gesture, in any number of contexts. We have practised changing time signatures, indicating dynamic contrast, showing awkward upbeats, subdividing rallentandos, conducting Anglican chant and plainsong, communicating musical moods through facial expression and movement, and other such issues. This focussed concentration on physical gesture is important, of course: it is essential to be clear and precise. The video camera and mirror are used frequently, so that, as for an élite athlete or dancer, the conductors can see whether they are actually doing what they think they are doing.

However, it is crucial to remember that beauty of physical gesture must never be the ultimate goal for a conductor. If he/she is not listening and responding to the ensemble in front of him/her, but is simply waving about in an aural vacuum (or worse, while remembering a favourite recording), then perfect gesture is pointless. Likewise, if the movement does not spring fundamentally from an expression of the music itself, then "beautiful hands" are meaningless. For a group coaching session last term with a choir present, one of the conductors had prepared Peter Warlock's *Bethlehem Down*. We worked on simplifying the gesture, and making it smaller, more intense, and more intimate, because that created the profound and still atmosphere that the Warlock demands. When, six weeks later, I saw this particular student for our first individual session, the instruction about the Warlock had been taken out of its musical context, and was being applied everywhere—even in an ebullient forte passage from a Poulenc motet. Whilst efficiency of movement is to be lauded, the Poulenc requires generosity and freedom of gesture in order for the true musical intention to be expressed.

Earlier this term, my choir at Selwyn College had the great privilege of singing evensong for one of the UK's choral legends, Christopher Robinson. He has had a long and illustrious career, and is one of the most respected and revered musicians in the country. The choir particularly enjoyed his anecdotes about his time spent with that evening's composers, Howells, Sumsion, and Joubert. Christopher's conducting technique is idiosyncratic, to say the least. There is rarely a discernible beat pattern, he shows entries or cut-offs only sporadically, he points rather wildly in the direction of whichever section has a good phrase or colourful dissonance, he creates intensity by miming vibrato on a violin. He would undoubtedly be the bane of a professional conducting teacher, and yet there was more musical profundity in his gesticulations than in the textbook-perfect technique of any graduate of a choral conducting master's programme. How you look may be important, but what you express is far more so. This is the case in conducting, as it is in life.

October 2018

Organ Scholars: The Next Generation

Every summer, the RCO runs a five-day-long residential course for prospective organ scholars. The course is based each year at either Cambridge or Oxford, and is called "The Organ Scholar Experience", or TOSE for short. When I'm asked about the Jimi-Hendrix-esque name of the course, I generally reply that, although the attendees may not learn how to kiss the sky, they do often experience playing Bach using toes only for the first time, rather than the out-dated heel-toe technique which teachers of older generations are prone to advise.

This summer we were based in Cambridge, with 27 young hopefuls ranging in age from 15 to 18. Encouragingly, nine of these were girls—the highest proportion of young women since the courses began over three decades ago. A team of staff and tutors took care of everything from solo repertoire, hymn playing, keyboard skills, accompanying, conducting, to (of course) pastoral care. In addition, there were talks on the admissions processes for UK and EU universities and conservatoires, as well as plenty of social time (including a trip to the bowling alley—the "go-to activity" for groups who are too young for the pub!)

The musical focus of the course was the preparation of two services of Choral Evensong, as well as one public recital given by the most advanced players. I was the tutor responsible for choral services, and to that end had selected repertoire which ranged in difficulty to provide a challenge to the more advanced students without discouraging the less able ones. I also tracked down the appointed biblical readings, pointed psalms, chose hymns, and booked singing clerical friends to officiate.

In one service we sang William Byrd's *Second Service,* and his verse anthem *Teach me, O Lord.* To provide stylistic contrast, our other service featured Edwardian classics, with C. V. Stanford's *Mag and Nunc in B flat* and his hymn-anthem *O for a closer walk with God,* along with S. S. Wesley's *Thou wilt keep him in perfect peace.* Richard Ayleward's *Preces and Responses* completed the liturgical repertoire. This is not an especially adventurous list, though it has two particular merits: it is all in the public domain (and therefore free to photocopy), and little of it requires split soprano. Since the pupils form the choir themselves, thinking about *divisi* in advance is important. The many teen boys and several of the girls sang varying combinations of alto, tenor, and bass, leaving only three sopranos, who were bolstered by a staff member and two Selwyn graduate students who were bribed with post-evensong refreshment.

The aim of these services is to involve as few staff members as possible. The pupils themselves are responsible for all choral and solo singing, accompanying, conducting, and voluntaries. We changed musical leadership at every opportunity, so there was a different combination of organist and conductor for the Preces, the Responses, each psalm, hymn, canticle, and anthem, as well as voluntaries before and after the service. In our Byrd-fest, the music was led by nine organists, seven conductors (none of whom also played the organ), and five different solo singers for the verse sections of canticles and anthem. In addition, two others read the lessons.

It can be frustrating trying to cajole the shyer teenagers to volunteer to play or conduct, especially with some of the more reticent girls, of which there was more than one. As much as I could, given the 60/30 proportion of male and female participants, I tried to achieve gender parity in the services, by arranging for a boy organist to be directed by a girl conductor, and vice versa. I was quite surprised—and secretly rather proud!—to overhear two of the more cocky young male attendees accusing me of sexism, after I had explained to them all that it was my goal to have as close as possible to an equal number of boys and girls featured in leadership roles. Some of you will have read my previous columns on the conspicuous gender imbalances in this field, and in Britain especially.[18] I can only conclude that the two boys concerned are not TAO readers.

The rehearsals were hardly a model of British choral efficiency: organ shoes were constantly being put on or taken off (even when playing Byrd, in which pedals—heels or toes—should not be used at all); conductors had to climb over each other to reach the music stand; instructions on how to bring the choir in on an upbeat, or how to cut off consonants, or which direction the second beat of a four pattern goes, were interjected whenever necessary. The services were far from polished, and I will admit to having felt a minor sense of foreboding that the future of the English Choral Tradition seemed to be in some rather clumsy and inexperienced hands. But in the end, we made it through both services relatively unscathed, despite the occasional awkward liturgical pause. The tutors and congregation ignored it when the organist didn't quite make it upstairs in time for the Nunc dimittis, and when the conductor momentarily forgot about the Responses after the Creed, and instead we focused on and were moved by the unexpected atmosphere of worship that this "clumsy and inexperienced" new generation brought to the music of the ancient and beautiful service of Choral Evensong.

---

18. See December 2011 and July 2016 on pages 205 and 209 respectively.

Chapter 3

Trials and Tribulations

In the UK, choristerships, choral scholarships, and organ scholarships are awarded after a competitive annual audition process called "Trials" (Voice Trials, Choral Trials, Organ Trials, etc.). These can be trying times (literally) for both auditioners and auditionees, and in this chapter it may be obvious that for a couple of months of every year, I am understandably preoccupied with those processes. There is also advice for any potential applicants, especially those from outside the UK.

New Year, New Choir

Happy New Year! You are probably reading this in January, but I am writing it in October, at the end of the first two weeks of a new academical year in Cambridge. We have three eight-week terms here, with appropriately liturgical names: Michaelmas (October to December), Lent (January to March), and Easter (April to June). The four-month-long summer holiday (historically known as the 'Long Vacation') is now rather ominously referred to as the Research Term, the inevitable result of productivity-focussed trends in higher education.

Since most Cambridge undergraduate degrees last for three years, a chapel choir consisting of twenty-four students usually contains about eight first years ("freshers"). The stringent demands of the Cambridge admissions process mean that many good singers are rejected in favour of stronger academic applicants, and therefore the distribution of voice-parts in the choir can be skewed initially. My fellow directors of music and I have often been in the awkward position of having five new soprano choral scholars, a situation which creates unwanted and unexpected vacancies in the other sections of the choir, which often have to be filled with less experienced singers.

I have always held the (undoubtedly over-optimistic) view that every time one sits down to practise an instrument, or every time a choir gathers to rehearse, the standard should continue to rise, picking up where it left off at the end of the last rehearsal or practice session. (I blame my mother for imparting this slightly demented work ethic to me.) At the start of each Michaelmas Term, one of my main objectives is to achieve a continuity of progression with my choir, despite the long summer break and the arrival of new singers who are adjusting to a new academic regime and to life away from home. No matter how new the choir is at the beginning of the year, I do my utmost to ensure that it sings to a higher standard than that attained by the choir at the end of the preceding Easter Term.

Sometimes my hopes and ambitions are swiftly dashed: inevitably in a choir where the average age is only 19 or 20, there are vocal problems to be solved. The second- and third-years are often rusty after the summer break, while the first-years' voices need time to settle into the choir's intense schedule (about ten hours per week). The students are all young, and need to be encouraged to sing in a healthy, well-supported, and relaxed way. They need to notice when their voices are tired, and the freshers (in particular) need to be patient, and not seek to compete with the more experienced voices of their older peers.

Most of the new singers are surprised by the speed at which they are expected to learn significant quantities of new repertoire (at Selwyn we have three, and sometimes four, choral services every week). The first years need to master the dark art of accurate sight-reading as swiftly as possible (though some of them are reasonably competent to start with). The usual exercises are useful: singing music to the letter-names of the notes (though keys with a lot of black notes are a mouthful); remembering tonalities (not playing notes again after stopping for verbal instructions); reading words in rhythm; swapping parts in hymns; not rehearsing simpler pieces at all before performing them in the services. I encourage them to prepare music in advance so that time is not wasted in the rehearsals with the dull monotony of note learning.

There are also straight-forward practical difficulties. One of my new young tenors did not sing the second set of Responses particularly well last Tuesday, but this was simply because he didn't have the music in front of him. His experience in his school concert choir did not prepare him for the liturgical complexities of Choral Evensong, and he had forgotten about the Responses which follow the Creed. On top of all this, there are the more subtle choral issues: ensemble, tuning, clarity of text, sound colour, style, performance practice issues, and, overall, the need to sing in a musically coherent and convincing way.

Occasionally, when I have calmed down (usually with the aid of a gin-and-tonic!) after an unsatisfying or inconsistent service early in the Michaelmas Term, I can sometimes acknowledge that it is unreasonable to expect a young choir which contains several new singers to reach the highest performance standards. The desire for continuous improvement is surely unrealistic. Nonetheless, this doesn't stop me from striving for it every year, and I am sure that I am not the only choir director who suffers from this particular disorder. We should all attempt to achieve the highest possible standards, even if, in practice, we fail more often than we succeed. As the poet Robert Browning put it so succinctly (if not especially gender-neutrally): "A man's reach should exceed his grasp, or what's a heaven for?"[19]

---

19. Browning, Robert. 'Andrea del Sarto' published in *Men and Women* (1855)

July 2010

Sight-Reading: Sink or Swim?

As I write this, it is the beginning of the final term of the academical year in Cambridge, and we have just completed our first week of services after the Easter vacation. I eased my choir back into the routine gently, with some standard repertoire (Dyson *Mag & Nunc in D*, the Ireland *Te Deum in F*, Howells *Collegium Regale* Mass) and some repeats from earlier in the year (including music from our post-Christmas recording).

Yesterday, the first challenging new repertoire of the term appeared on the music list. The anthem was Byrd's 6-part *Haec dies*, which for some inexplicable reason I have not done for five or six years, so only one or two people in the choir actually knew it. Imagine my delight and surprise when they coped impressively with their first read-through. As you would expect, the lively 'et laetemur' section required a little work, but the rest of the piece came together in next to no time, and we even had an unexpected 15 minutes of rehearsal time remaining to look ahead to Tuesday's anthem, Josquin's magnificent setting of Psalm 91, *Qui habitat in adjutorio altissimi*, which is a 24-part canon: one part for each singer in my choir. This was a real test of how the singers' sight-reading skill had developed since those early October days at the start of the year. Even the weakest readers managed to reach the double bar-line at the same time as everyone else, and they were buzzing with pride at the magnitude of their achievement.

One of the things I hear most frequently from foreign conductors and singing teachers is that English choirs sight-sing more fluently than American and Continental choirs. I'm not entirely sure that this is true however. Of course, I was thrilled with our Josquin and Byrd rehearsals, and I daresay that if we'd had foreign visitors observing yesterday, they would have been impressed, but my singers are not particularly different from anyone else's. In fact, I think many people possess the skills needed to be able to sight-sing, even though they may not realise it, and even the weakest can improve considerably.

As a child, I found it all rather easy. I simply related my first instrument (the piano) to the vocal pitching of intervals, often by silently playing a passage on the desk while singing, and the right notes would usually come out of my mouth. I did not realise that what I was doing was considered difficult by many. I have also known many other instrumentalists who have made this sort of connection, and I like having some of them in my choir: their singing voices might sometimes be a little less polished, but they are usually fairly confident about getting the notes right.

Then there are those singers who have to be taught to sight-read. Some of the teaching methods I use include such things as rehearsing hymns and psalm chants by singing them to the letter-names of the notes (if I am feeling particularly demanding, I will ask them to transpose the exercise, and sing the new note names), refusing to give notes again after stopping for verbal instructions in order to encourage them to remember tonalities, reading the words of quick passages in rhythm (the aforementioned Byrd benefits from this activity), insisting on careful and accurate counting (95% of the battle in a piece like the Josquin is actually knowing which beat of the bar one is meant to be singing).

In England, sight-singing skills are often acquired due to a basic survival instinct: the music for the regular choral services has to be learnt and polished with startling rapidity. Although it is perhaps not the most pedagogically sound method, my singers certainly realise early on that they need to be able to sight-read well, in order to cope. In an ideal world, a combination of relaxed teaching and frantic necessity would be best: the theory is crucial, but it needs to be put into regular and frequent practice in order for the skill to become reliable.

This morning I re-read the UK Report I wrote in November 2009[20] in which I bewailed my new choir's inadequate sight-reading ability, which limited what I could concentrate on during choir practices. What was so gratifying about yesterday's rehearsal of *Haec Dies* was that the singers could progress rapidly from complete unfamiliarity to a polished, professional performance in the space of about 15 minutes, without the need to waste time with tedious note-bashing. I have no doubt that the skill and confidence that my young singers demonstrated yesterday is due to them having mastered the practical basics of effective sight-reading, and not to any mystical genetic advantage that comes from being English (though that is of course leaving aside those with perfect pitch which, to be fair, probably is a mystical genetic advantage, regardless of nationality).

---

20. January 2010 on page 67.

Cambridge Choral Scholarships

E very year in Cambridge we audition potential Choral Scholars, the (normally undergraduate) students who sing in one of the 22 college chapel choirs, in up to seven services a week during university term. The students learn the ins and outs of the liturgical trade while they study for their degree (which can be in any subject), and when they graduate, many will be involved with daily services as cathedral lay clerks, or else will sing in their local parish choirs as a respite from being a lawyer, teacher, or investment banker, thus perpetuating the great choral tradition of which the UK is justifiably proud. Not surprisingly, I often get queries from overseas about choral scholarships, so I thought it would be helpful for me to reflect upon the audition process, to give readers an idea of the sorts of things we are looking for.

Each year there are about 200 choral scholarship applicants competing for about six vacancies per annum in each of the choirs. Candidates can apply for as many colleges as they like, listing their choices in an order of preference, which allows the voice parts to be spread around: one well-known college invariably has enough first-choice soprano applicants to fill about seven symphony choruses, so plenty of them will be passed on to other colleges. Generally, though not always, the applicants have some choral experience, ranging from having been cathedral choristers (so having sung daily services throughout their childhood), to having only sung in their local town choral society (which means that their repertoire consists only of *Carmina Burana* and the most famous bits of *Messiah*).

The end of September (when I am writing this) is audition time, and the past two weeks have consisted of a rather fraught combination of arduous testing, interviewing, negotiating, late-night meetings, early morning emails, frantic phone-calls, and plenty of running around from the university Music Faculty to college chapels throughout the city. The days are long, and the process unavoidably convoluted. This year we have not been helped by one of the rainiest Septembers in recent times, causing auditioners and auditionees to arrive drenched and flustered. Historically, these weeks are called Choral Trials—and, in some years, the word "trials" is certainly appropriate.

During their short audition, candidates are asked to perform vocal exercises which explore their range, to sing a solo piece, and to endure sight-reading and aural tests. There are also numerous other considerations, foremost amongst which is academic potential—this is Cambridge, after all. I will deal with each of these in turn.

The vast majority of applicants are 17 years old, so we often have to make decisions based on as-yet-unrealised potential. We may find ourselves admitting a baritone who becomes a tenor in his second year, or a soprano who turns into a contralto the week before her arrival in Cambridge. Vocally, we see the full spectrum of abilities, from the nervous, breathy, untrained soprano who is accustomed to hiding behind the 45 other young women in her section, to the unexpectedly mature solo tenor, with polished technique and sophisticated personal presentation. There is also a predictably high number of "LCBs" (a.k.a. Light Calibre Baritones)[21], prevalent in the young men whose voices only changed a couple of years before their audition. Assessing their vocal potential (or lack thereof) can be somewhat hit-and-miss, though we try our best to investigate their capabilities without inflicting lasting damage.

The standard of their chosen solo pieces varies as much as their vocal abilities. Unfortunately, some candidates are not as well advised as others:

---

21. This very useful phrase was coined by Herbert Howells and appeared most notably at the end of the Agnus Dei in his *Collegium Regale* Communion setting (Novello, 1947).

at the age of 17, just because you *can* sing Mozart's *Exsultate jubilate* doesn't necessarily mean that you *should*. Generally speaking, though, we do get a sensible, if occasionally bland, selection of movements from Vivaldi's *Gloria*, plenty from the ubiquitous *24 Italian Songs and Arias* (surely more than 24 songs were composed in Italy between 1600 and 1750?), and even occasionally an inspired bit of Rubbra, Quilter, or Madeleine Dring, which always provides a refreshing break. Probably the two most frequent occurrences are *How beautiful are the feet* for the numerous sopranos, and *Where e'er you walk* for the LCBs.

As I have discussed in this column before, the ability to sight-read is crucial for Cambridge choral scholars, since they have to perform so frequently during a given week. In the auditions, we ask candidates to sing a passage of Renaissance polyphony (a section of a piece by Byrd or Palestrina, perhaps), normally in Latin. This reasonably straightforward music often reveals of a candidate's capability, despite its comparative harmonic simplicity. Some of us hardened old-hands will also ask candidates to read Kenneth Leighton or Lennox Berkeley, or pieces by other composers whose melodic lines are less predictable.

Aural tests at Cambridge are eminently practical. I remember as a child being taught to recognise intervals (usually by relating them to familiar tunes: does anyone actually know *My bonny lies over the ocean*, apart from as a way to recognise a major 6th?). Here, we ask them to generate the intervals themselves instead, which is much more realistic when it comes to sight-reading. So, for example, the auditioner might play a D, and say to the auditionee "please sing a B natural a major 6th above this D", and then "and below that B, an F natural". As an extension of the "sing the middle note of this chord" exercise (a trusted perennial favourite), we often continue with "the middle note that you are singing is an A, so please can you tell me what the other notes are"? These exercises are particularly good for demonstrating whether a candidate can hear with his or her inner ear, as opposed to just memorising the incipits from well-known nursery rhymes.

Obviously, no matter how musical a candidate is, if he or she is not at the appropriate academic standard to study at Cambridge, the ability to sing is irrelevant. For more detail, please see above, but suffice it to say that we are looking for absolutely top grades (the more A*s the better). Then there are also the unquantifiable qualities that make someone a good Choral Scholar: motivation, organisation, commitment, dedication, enthusiasm, and a good sense of humour. Few and far between are the candidates who meet all of these criteria. But then, we might encounter someone who will develop into the next Robert Tear, Simon Keenlyside, or Elin Manahan Thomas. And the excitement when you suspect that you have discovered a real talent is almost worth the misery of the Trials—except when it rains without ceasing during the whole week.

Choosing Cathedral Choristers

It is Voice Trials season around the UK—the time of year when cathedrals audition children for entry into their choirs for the following September. I recently spent a full day auditioning girls for Ely Cathedral Girls' Choir (ECGC), and I thought readers might be interested to know how cathedral choristers are selected.

ECGC was founded in 2006 (a relative new-comer to Ely's 1000-year old musical tradition), and consists of 18 girls ages 13 to 18 (in UK parlance, school Years 9 to 13, equivalent to grades 8 to 12). King's Ely is the only choir school where senior school girls receive the intense boarding school experience that junior school choristers receive elsewhere. Most cathedral boys' choirs, and several girls' choirs, consist of full boarders, ages 8 to 12 (school Years 4 to 8); a number of cathedrals have older girls' choirs, but do not provide boarding, or daily rehearsals. This should give you some idea as to the basic infrastructure. Consequently, in preparation for Voice Trials, I wrote to local churches, took part in school visits, and in particular, targeted the cathedrals whose girls have to leave their choirs after Year 8. I also met many potential applicants during the year, spoke to their parents about the commitment, gave the girls a pre-audition to help them prepare, showed them around the boarding house, and answered numerous questions about the duties of a cathedral chorister.

The Voice Trials day finally arrived, and I commuted to Ely even earlier than usual, to ensure that the house was tidy, that signs indicating rooms and venues were posted, that the coffee percolator was working, that application forms, reference letters, and other paperwork were in order, and that my proposed sight-reading test was challenging enough without being unmanageable. At about 0840, the first anxious candidates arrived (it was hard to tell whether the girls or their parents were more nervous). By 0915, the house common room was bursting with mummies, daddies, grannies, a singing teacher and a school registrar or two, as well as with ECGC staff and current choristers working hard to put the many 12-year-old girls and their various entourages at ease. Large pots of coffee and tea, along with the school's best home-made cookies helped everyone to relax, and conversation seemed to be flowing quite easily.

My assistant organist and I took the applicants to our song school for a proper warm-up and a short rehearsal. We sang an Epiphany-themed hymn, it being that time of year, and then learned the first few pages of a tuneful Magnificat for upper voices by Malcolm Archer. We were able to observe who coped well in ensemble, who learned quickly, who showed signs of being a natural leader, who had the confidence to make eye contact with me as I was conducting, and whether there were any indications of potentially problematical technical habits.

Then followed the most complex part of the day, an intricate timetable of simultaneously-scheduled solo song rehearsals, interviews with the House Mistress, meetings with the Principal and Headmaster, parental consultation sessions, and a rota for school lunch with current choristers. In the song rehearsals, my assistant checked tempos, balance, breathing, and other details with each of the girls. A wide range of repertoire was on offer, including the *Domine Deus* from Vivaldi's *Gloria*, *Se tu m'ami* attributed to Pergolesi, a *Panis angelicus* and a *Down by the Salley Gardens* or two, Fauré's lovely *En Prière*, Mozart's *Laudate Dominum*, and an absolutely delightful Elizabeth Poston carol about a dormouse. Interviews with the House Mistress concentrated on boarding: how would a girl see herself contributing to life in the house, how would she cope living away from home, how resilient was her sense of humour? Meetings with the Principal and the Headmaster concentrated on things academic: how would they balance cathedral duties with GCSE and A-level studies, what other extra-curricular activities did they do, and what was their understanding of priorities, what did they want to do at university? Finally, I had a fascinating time consulting with the girls' parents: were they typical 'Stage Mothers' who would send me a grumpy email every time their child missed out on a solo, were they the over-protective 'Helicopter Parents' who wouldn't be able to let go? Would they allow boarding house staff to be *in loco parentis*. I enjoyed being an amateur psychologist for a couple of hours.

After lunch came the all-important individual auditions. Each girl was allocated 15 minutes, and the audition panel consisted of me, my assistant organist, the school's Head of Vocal Studies, the House Mistress, and the school Principal, both of whom are also musicians. After the performance of their solo song, I took over at the keyboard to test vocal range and quality, and to do aural and sight-reading tests. After examining their ability to sing and identify intervals, pick out the top, middle, and bottom notes of various less-than-consonant chords, sing back melodies, and other similar exercises, I asked them to read aloud the Collect for Epiphany Sunday from the *Book of Common Prayer* (not many of them could correctly pronounce the word 'fruition', and none could define it), and then to sight-sing a section of an anthem by the obscure nineteenth-century English composer Sir William Sterndale Bennett, which fortunately none of them knew, even those who are current cathedral choristers—poor forgotten Sir William. In all these tests, I was looking for how quickly they responded aurally, whether they could work things out in their heads, what use they made of their varying levels of instrumental training to assist themselves, and how swiftly changes and improvements were made during the course of the audition.

After many long hours, with just a short break for the very hasty consumption of a sandwich, the selection process was finally completed. In making our decisions, we took into account every aspect of the day, including vocal potential, musical teachability, leadership skills, academic ambition, sense of humour, parental quirks, and crucially, whether or not the girl in question simply loved to sing. I was very fortunate this year, in being able to appoint five outstanding young choristers, including the current Head and Deputy Head girls of another major cathedral choir, who will finish their time there at the end of this academic year. They will arrive in September, to carry on the daily round of singing in the cathedral that has been going on since long before King Canute approached Ely by barge sometime in the early eleventh century and called out "Row nearer, my men, that we may hear these good monks sing"—I'm sure he'd have been just as pleased with the girls' choir these days!

January 2015

Auditioning for a Cambridge Choir

Like many of you, I spend a great deal of time assessing singers for places in my choirs. Recently I have auditioned an unexpectedly high number of overseas students whose choral backgrounds were slightly untypical, including a Finnish pop-singer, a Parisian singer-songwriter, a Spanish instrumentalist, and an American post-graduate with two degrees in Music. For all of them, some aspects of the audition process came as a surprise. Consequently, I thought that a description of a standard Oxbridge choral audition might be of use, in case you find yourself needing to prepare for one. Most auditions have four parts: the candidate sings a solo song (three to four minutes long) accompanied by one of my organ scholars; I take them through vocal exercises to determine range and timbre; I assess aural perception and sight-reading; then there is an informal interview. I will deal with each of these parts in turn.

I hear a surprising variety of solo songs, from simple folksongs to elaborate Baroque arias. If I'm honest, I prefer the former as a way of judging young voices. I advise candidates to sing something 'easier' than they might otherwise assume, so that even if they are nervous, they can still sing well. Besides, not all 17-year-olds are capable of singing coloratura as convincingly as they might think. One poor boy who auditioned for me earlier this year sang a Purcell aria with lengthy and complicated 16th-note runs. The look of achievement on his face at the end was almost as conspicuous as the tension in his neck during the performance. He was rather miffed when I asked him to sing a verse of a hymn as an alternative. On the other hand, the afore-mentioned Finnish pop-singer brought a beautiful unaccompanied Finnish folksong. Within three bars, I knew more about her natural voice than I would have learnt from three pages of unsuccessful virtuosity.

In the vocal exercises (scales, arpeggios), I listen for the quality and timbre of the voice, where *passaggi* lie, the extent of the range, where the sound is most resonant (often rather limited in 17- and 18-year old tenors and basses). I also look and listen for technical issues and bad habits, especially in those who have not had formal singing lessons. In the better developed voices, I like to hear depth, colour, and vibrato; in those which are less polished, I want to hear ease of production, and potential in the sound. In all cases the singer should enjoy the physicality of singing—they should relish what it *feels* like to use their voices well. My Spanish instrumentalist, a bass with a sonorous low register, is just discovering this resonance, and it wouldn't surprise me to see him give up the viola in favour of singing.

Oxbridge-style ear tests are the thing which disconcert people the most, especially those from foreign climes, regardless of the number of Music degrees they possess. Indeed, I remember being surprised myself at how different they are from those that I had learned. The exercise which most often trips up the unaware auditionee (and especially those from North America) is the identification of intervals. As a child, I was taught intervals in the following way: familiar tunes were applied to every combination of two notes in order to classify them; at first one learned to identify intervals played one note at a time; the advanced student could recognise 'My bonny lies over the ocean' when the two notes were played simultaneously. It was more like stamp-collecting than musicianship. Here in the UK, the exercise involves not so much the identification of an interval, but rather its creation: the candidate is given a named note, and asked to sing up or down a named interval, to another named note. So, for example: "This note *[auditioner plays]* is a 'D'. Please sing up a perfect fifth to an A *[candidate sings]*; and below that A, please sing down a major third to an F natural *[etc.]*." This is so much more musical than being able to spot 'Here comes the bride' out of context.

The singing-back-of-melodies also has its twists. Our melodies are rarely straightforward tonally, and the starting note, often different from the finishing note, is not repeated at the end of the playing. Here's an example of a particularly awkward 'melody' to sing in tune:

After the candidate has sung the melody, I give the name of the first note, and then ask him/her to identify the other notes, and the intervals between them. One of my favourites is this little gem:

In the second example here, I expect musically astute candidates to identify the third note as a G sharp (rather than an A flat), to be able to state the melody's key, and to recognize the important difference between a major third and a diminished fourth.

We also ask candidates to sing the top, middle, and bottom notes of various cluster chords, usually involving three notes, but sometimes five, or seven. One of my favourite trick questions is to ask young basses to sing the bottom note of a straight-forward first inversion major triad, inspired of course by Duruflé's *Ubi caritas*.

The sight-reading test usually takes two forms: firstly, a Renaissance motet in Latin (Byrd, Palestrina, and the like), in which the candidate sings his/her part while I play the other three parts on the piano; secondly, something less obviously tonal, without any assistance from the piano beyond the first pitch. I have an obscure but perfect piece of Benjamin Britten which I use for this task.

In the informal interview at the end of the audition, with a potentially successful candidate, I will discuss commitment, organisational skills, and what is expected of members of my choir. For the less fortunate ones, the discussion will centre on what other options might be available to them—one hopes that these will be other choral options, but I have been known to suggest rowing *in extremis*!

I hope that this is a helpful précis of an Oxbridge choral audition. All of these tests can be prepared for in advance of course, and I would advise any of you who might be coming over to the UK to study, or who are preparing students for an English choral audition, to think along these lines when practising. Not being disconcerted by what the auditioner is asking for in the first place will greatly help any auditionee to give the right answer.

Cathedral Organists by the Numbers

In last month's column (above) I wrote about assessing singers, so I thought I would focus this month on the task of assessing potential organists. This subject has been in my mind since I recently found myself auditioning candidates for the position of Assistant Organist to Ely Cathedral Girls' Choir, which I direct. There had been expressions of interest in the post from England, Scotland, Ireland, America, New Zealand, and Australia, and in the end, we had a gratifyingly strong field from which to choose. Consequently, I thought readers might be interested know what I and my colleagues usually looking for when shortlisting and interviewing for a position such as this, in case you encounter someone who is considering applying for a cathedral job in the UK. In fact, I have decided to make this is a two-part column, and, next month, I will offer detailed specifics about the application procedure, auditions, and interviews.

I will begin, though, by giving a broad overview of the various positions which come available periodically. All cathedrals have at least two full-time organists, and several have three, or even four. With up to eight choral services per week, and even more during peak liturgical seasons, cathedral organists certainly earn their keep. The posts' titles are multifarious, so for the sake of clarity, I will refer to them by the informal numerical labels that are commonly used in the UK. Like most things in Britain, these posts are ordered hierarchically (note the absence of the egalitarian title "Associate", which is common in the States).

> Number 1: Organist / Director of Music / Master of the Choristers / Master of Music
>
> Number 2: Assistant Director of Music / Sub Organist / Assistant Organist
>
> Number 3: Sub Assistant Organist / Assistant Sub Organist / Second Assistant
>
> Number 4: Organ Scholar (a.k.a. General Dogsbody)

Predictably, musical duties are shared amongst the music staff in about as many ways as there are cathedrals in the UK. Generally (though not exclusively), the Number 1 conducts the choir in the majority of services, while the Numbers 2, 3, and 4 accompany at the organ in rotation. In several cathedrals, the Number 2 directs the girl choristers (which all but a handful of cathedrals now have), and/or the voluntary choir (amateur adult ensembles found in about three-quarters of cathedrals).

Choir practices are also divided between the organists, especially in cathedrals where girls' and boys' rehearsals take place simultaneously but separately. A common model sees the Number 1 taking boys' practices on their own from the piano, while the Number 2 leads the girls' practice, and the Numbers 3 and 4 share the training of the youngest children (probationers). In most cathedrals, the professional adult lay clerks rehearse for about 15 minutes before each service, with whoever is conducting the service itself. Administrative duties are also suitably apportioned: the Number 1 is in overall charge, the Number 2 might take responsibility for visiting choirs, the Number 3 for the organ recital series, and the Number 4 attends to the choir library.

It is obvious from this broad general outline that a cathedral organist requires many skills: playing the organ, training choristers, and being a competent administrator are all aspects of the various jobs. It is crucial to note, however, that the balance and emphasis of each position is different at each cathedral, and the post of Sub Assistant Organist at one place is not necessarily the same as that of Assistant Sub Organist at another. Therefore anyone considering applying for a cathedral organist position *must* research carefully exactly what that position entails at that particular cathedral, in order to ensure that it is an appropriate role for him/her.

In some cathedrals, for example, the Number 4 spends much of his/her time making coffee and turning pages, perhaps only plays one service a week, and learns while observing the higher Numbers at work. In another case, the Number 3 might be required to play for five or six services per week, so professional competence and experience belie the number of subordinating adjectives in the official job title. Someone who has just completed a major Oxbridge-type organ scholarship, and who has been accompanying four or five services per week for a few years, is not going to be challenged in an observational Number 4 post. Conversely, someone who has completed an Organ Performance degree at a conservatoire, and whose solo repertoire playing is outstanding, but whose choral accompaniment skills are less well developed, is likely to be overwhelmed by a six-services-a-week Number 3 post, no matter how many competitions she/he has won. Needless to say, an applicant who pitches his/her own strengths and experience at the right sort of position will have a much higher chance of being shortlisted.

The position at Ely provides a good case-study to illustrate the need for advance research before an application is made. That particular musical hierarchy is rather quirky, since the girls' choir has its own dedicated music staff. So the boys' choir has a Number 1 and a Number 2, and the girls' choir also has a Number 1 and a Number 2. The cathedral's Number 1 is in overall charge, but whenever the girls are singing, the girls' choir Number 1 (a.k.a. me) is very much in control. The role of Assistant Organist to the Girls' Choir could be placed somewhere in between a typical Number 2 and a typical Number 3 (insofar as any of these positions can be called 'typical'). Although it is intended to be a first serious job for a young organist, it is not for the faint-hearted: the present incumbent played more services in his first two weeks at Ely, than a friend of his did in his first two *terms* as a Number 3 (Organ Scholar) at one of the most ecclesiastically important cathedrals in the Anglican Communion. In addition, since I am away from Ely from time to time, my Assistant needs to be a skilled and imaginative choral conductor, and also a competent administrator. Not surprisingly, our shortlist consisted of the people who appeared on paper to have the strongest combination of those skills, and who had obviously read the Further Particulars in detail, and who therefore understood the nature of this particular cathedral organist post.

I hope that this has given you an idea of the various types of cathedral organist positions available, and the sorts of skills required by those who hold them, and whetted your appetite for more details about the application procedure, auditions, and interviews. If you're feeling at all discouraged about the requirements, remember the old adage "the closest to perfection a person ever comes is when she/he fills out a job application form." So, hopefully you will now read the *Church Times* classified adverts online each Friday with reinvigorated intensity and deepened appreciation. And don't forget to tune in next month to find out just what you have to endure if you are lucky enough to be called for an audition.

Application Forms and Auditions

Last month (above) I provided information about cathedral organist positions in the UK, and discussed how important it is to research what is involved if you (or one of your students) are considering applying for such a post. This month's column considers the technical aspects of the process—application forms, auditions, and interviews.

In most cathedrals, the paperwork includes an application form, a covering letter, and two or three references (it is customary that one should be a cleric). 'Supporting Material' (CDs, videos, programmes, other musical paraphernalia) is often actively discouraged. The application form is usually generic, covering everything found on a CV/résumé. Indeed, it is often specified that the latter should not be included at all. For procedural consistency, child-protection, and safeguarding, the same application form is completed by everyone applying for a cathedral position, from emptying rubbish bins to preaching sermons. The covering letter, a maximum of about 800 words, should explain why the candidate has applied and how he/she is particularly suited to the post in question. Needless to say, those applicants who appear most suitable on paper are most likely to be shortlisted.

The above undoubtedly sounds familiar, but it is in the interviews and auditions that the differences between the North American process and its UK counterpart are most clearly manifest. While in North America, an organist search might take five weeks, with five different candidates running a church's music for five successive weekends, in the UK all shortlisted candidates are auditioned and interviewed on the same day. Indeed, social interaction with one's competitors is often part of the 'fun'. Working out a rota for the auditions requires a degree in Event Planning: five candidates and the various panels of assessors must be rotated around a schedule including organ practice, playing audition, choir rehearsal, spoken interviews, meals, social time, and some 'down time'. Despite occasional moments of social awkwardness, completing the process in the space of a day or two, instead of over five weeks, has its advantages.

The organ-playing audition for a Number 2, 3, or 4 usually includes the performance of two contrasting solo works of the candidate's choice, one of which must be Bach, with an overall time limit of 10 to 12 minutes. Candidates are then asked to demonstrate a variety of keyboard skills (e.g., sight-reading, transposition, improvisation, score-reading). The most imaginative tests combine these skills: "the candidate is invited to play the final verse of this hymn (presented in open score) down a tone; it should be followed by an improvised extension of between 75 and 90 seconds in length". Candidates are also asked to play an accompaniment or two, of which they may only be informed a few days in advance. For the Ely post discussed in last month's column, candidates had to prepare Peter Aston's *G major Magnificat* for upper voices (a fiddly but well-written accompaniment) and the applicants received the score just four days before their auditions. A cathedral organist in the UK must be a 'quick study'—they should never actually be sight-reading during a service, but they rarely have time to polish.

The other main aspect of the musical assessment is a c.20-minute choir practice, usually with the trebles (girls or boys) alone, though for a Number 1 appointment, a full choir practice might also be required. The rehearsal with the trebles is taken by the candidate on his/her own, from the piano, which gives the assessors a chance to determine whether the applicant suffers from Keyboard Bashing Syndrome. Unfortunately, organists who have no piano training are often afflicted with such maladies. He/she might be asked to work on two pieces, one that the children know, and one that they do not know. This gives the assessors the opportunity to observe whether the candidate can work at a musically sophisticated level (on phrasing, tuning, diction, colour, vocal technique, etc.), in the familiar work, and also at the more basic level of teaching notes in the unfamiliar piece. I am particularly interested in observing *how* a candidate teaches notes: I look for those who have conscious pedagogical methodology, and do not simply subscribe to the "this is how it goes, sing it back to me" school of sight-reading.

The spoken interviews normally last about 30 minutes each, and are designed to find out more about the candidates' personalities and working habits. The general interview might include obvious questions like "discuss the role of music in liturgy", as well as more probing queries like "what are your weaknesses?" The legally-required safeguarding interview is likely to include scenarios requiring a difficult decision to be made about a vulnerable individual. It goes without saying that appropriate and professional procedure must be understood and followed at all times.

There is no doubt that the selection process for these positions is arduous, both for the candidates and for the assessors. However, this should not put you off if your skills really do match a specific set of Further Particulars. There are a number of foreigners, Canadians, New Zealanders, Australians, Europeans, and Americans, contributing to cathedral music-making in the UK, and if you fit the Person Specification for a particular position, then please do send in your completed generic application form and your 800-word manifesto. Even the complexities of obtaining a visa, should you be successful in your application, should not discourage you if you are determined to become an organist in the UK.

January 2016

Another New Start

A happy new year to you all! I am sitting down to write this just a few weeks into Michaelmas Term (the first of Cambridge's three academical terms). This year saw an enormous change in Selwyn College Chapel Choir, with over 65% of the singers new in October. Since most degrees here last for three years, only a third of the choir should change every year, but last year circumstances conspired against me, with the result that the leavers outnumbered the returners for the first time in my many years as director of music. Not surprisingly, it has resulted in an exhilarating first few weeks of term, as the numerous freshers (Cambridge's term for first-year students) have struggled valiantly to find their collective musical feet.

At this time of year, I often wonder how long it will take the new version of the choir to reach the dizzying artistic heights that last year's group had managed to achieve. Freshers are thrown in at the proverbial deep end, to "sight-read or swim", and the learning curve is steep, especially when we have significant external commitments early in term. I remember toasting a particularly vertiginous such slope after singing Evensong at St Paul's Cathedral in Week 3 a few years ago.

Here I must mention that, for many years, I have been blessed with a choir that can sight-read well. There was one particularly notable epoch when eleven of the 26 singers had perfect pitch, and they were even conveniently well-distributed across all the sections. That group successfully managed a liturgical performance of the Frank Martin *Mass for Double Choir* on just 60 minutes rehearsal time, in the middle of university examinations. For this feat, I was the marvel and envy of a number of my colleagues in other college chapels. Sadly, those students have long since graduated, so such musical extravagance is less easily accomplished these days.

In addition, despite the Michaelmas Term's undoubted choral *frisson*, I am becoming increasingly dissatisfied with the inevitable drop in standard between the end of one academical year and the beginning of the next. Instead of relishing October's exhilaration of large volumes of music being prepared for performance on one hour's rehearsal, I find myself yearning for the polish and finesse of July. The old choir understood my musical intention when I raised an eyebrow, or wiggled my little finger, or indeed, simply made eye contact with one of the cantoris altos. By contrast, the new choir looks terrified and overwhelmed, and freshers avoid eye contact with me at all costs, despite the fact that this year's large new intake includes a number of good sight-readers.

And so, this year I am trying something different: all singers must arrive in chapel with the notes learned in advance. My choir librarian ensures that music is put out well in advance, and one of the tech-savvy basses has put together a Spotify and YouTube playlist of most of this term's music list. (This is obviously a method of learning notes which was not available to older generations of musicians like me, but the current cohort of overworked Cambridge students is grateful for it.) In addition, the majority of choir members have pianos in their college rooms, and/or access to music practice rooms. I have even suggested that instead of working only on solo repertoire in their singing lessons, they might usefully take some of the more vocally demanding choral music to their teachers. Last week's chapel repertoire included Byrd's *Laudibus in sanctis* and Philip Stopford's *Truro Service*, both of which present significant technical challenges on which their singing teachers could provide valuable guidance.

This new regime is working well so far, though not surprisingly, it has both advantages and disadvantages. On the plus side, I have been able to focus on details such as sound, diction, phrasing, and style much earlier in the year than usual. The new version of the choir is beginning to cohere as a single musical instrument, and even most of the freshers are responding well to my direction. On the other hand, their individual sight-reading skills are not being stretched and improved as they were in the past, and there has had to be a shift in attitude to accommodate this new methodology. Fortunately, the returners have supported the change unanimously, and of course, the newcomers have never known anything different. They did need to learn how much preparation was needed: one of the altos began by attempting to memorise three services of Choral Evensong each week, whereas one of the basses merely listened to a You-Tube clip in the background before rehearsal. Best practice probably lies somewhere between these two extremes, and the singers are learning to judge for themselves how much time is required in order to arrive adequately, but not overly, prepared.

Despite these glitches, I am convinced that this is a more professional way of preparing for chapel services, even if their sight-reading improves less rapidly. I think even my former perfect-pitchers, many of whom are now professional musicians, would agree that it is a positive innovation. With the notes prepared in advance, we are working on more subtle musical details, and the choir are singing with conviction and freedom even though it is only Week 4. As the poet Samuel Taylor Coleridge is reputed to have said, "He who is best prepared can best serve his moment of inspiration."[22]

---

22. . . . though there is no actual evidence that he did say this.

December 2016

Trios and Trials

As I write this in early October, we have just completed Cambridge's annual round of organ scholarship auditions. In previous *UK Reports*, I have written about Choral Scholarships,[23] but not about the process by which we admit undergraduate organ scholars, so I thought you might be interested to read about the trials to which we subject these poor unsuspecting applicants who are often high school pupils in Year 13 (the equivalent of Grade 12). They spend four days in Cambridge participating in a rigorous round of auditions, interviews, and written assessments, with the goal of winning an organ scholarship and an undergraduate place to study their chosen academic subject (not necessarily Music). Candidates may apply to all colleges, listing them in preference order, and they can apply to both Cambridge and Oxford in the same year. Those candidates who apply to Cambridge via the normal academic route can only list one College and they cannot apply to both universities.

As well as undergoing academic assessment, organ scholar applicants endure strenuous musical tests. For the formal organ auditions, they select one of four prescribed Bach trios:

- Trio in E flat major BWV 525 (first movement)
- Trio in E minor BWV 528 (first movement)

---

23. See December 2010 and January 2015 on pages 73 and 81 respectively.

• Trio on 'Herr Jesu Christ, dich zu uns wend' BWV 655
• Trio on 'Nun komm der Heiden heiland' BWV 660

These options have been in place for many years. Occasionally the directors of music consider changing them, but we invariably return to the fact that the mental composure and physical coordination required to play a Bach trio are simply unsurpassed by anything else in the repertoire. A flawless BWV 655 at age 17 bodes well for a Duruflé *Requiem* as a second-year undergraduate. In addition to the trio, candidates bring a second, contrasting piece of their own choosing.

The formal audition also consists of keyboard tests: sight-reading, score-reading, and transposition. The sight-reading is on three staves, with an occasional manual change, or "add Great to Pedal" instruction. It is (roughly) of ARCO (AAGO/ARCCO) standard. Perfection is not expected (and is rarely achieved) but some ability to cope with the overall shape of the extract, even for a less-experienced candidate, gives a sense of how long it might take that person to learn a new accompaniment or voluntary. The score-reading test is in four-part G- and F-clefs, and demonstrates the candidates' potential as accompanists for choral rehearsals.

Transposition is consistently the most demanding exercise, despite the fact that it is a skill which organists are expected to have. Its potential is obvious: one may need to accompany a young singer whose song is in an unsuitable key, or choose to adjust the Office Hymn to suit the subsequent Magnificat. However, few Oxbridge directors of music require their organ scholars to transpose on a daily basis. In a small number of colleges, it is more common, but rarely (if ever) without advance preparation. In the majority of chapels it is seldom demanded, and a candidate's inability to transpose may be an indication of a different weakness altogether, particularly as teenagers generally take up the organ later now than they did a generation ago. In one second audition, I found that a candidate could not play the hymn fluently in the key it was written in, let alone in a different key. Running before you can walk is unwise

As part of the formal assessment, candidates direct a seven-minute choir practice. They are assigned a short anthem to conduct, and an ad-hoc choir is assembled. Although many of the candidates have had a fair amount of choral experience as singers and accompanists, they generally have little or no proficiency as choral conductors. The choir is a somewhat motley crew of current organ scholars and postgraduate students. Although they (usually) get most of the notes right, their sound, tuning, ensemble, diction, and musicianship always require improvement and polish. Unfortunately, most candidates are so inexperienced that we rarely hear anything more profound than an occasional comment on dynamics, quite apart from whether or not they can beat a four pattern clearly. Obviously, those who end up with organ scholarships become more experienced and nuanced choral trainers after a couple of years working under a professional director of music. The UK's notorious throw-them-in-at-the-deep-end approach to choral training is still the dominant pedagogical *modus operandi*.

In addition, the candidates also take a variety of written assessments, including aural tests, harmonisation of a Bach chorale, and various other subject-specific academic tests. A number of one-on-one interviews with leading intellectual specialists in their chosen field will also be part of the process. The procedure is both exhaustive and exhausting. That most of them then board a train for Oxford and do it all again during the second half of the week is testament to the resilience of youth!

After the auditions and interviews, decisions are made during lengthy and intense meetings. Academic and musical considerations are taken into account, and we deliberate carefully about every candidate. Successful elections will also include academic conditions (the need for the candidate to achieve appropriate grades in their end-of-year school exams), and, all being well, a full year later, they will arrive in Cambridge (or Oxford) to take up their organ scholarship, at the beginning of their undergraduate career. Hopefully, at that point, they feel that the undeniably demanding audition process was well worth the time and effort.

Chapter 4

Concerts, Cathedrals, and Compact Discs

This chapter brings together columns which consider the pros and cons of the recording industry, radio broadcasting, and concert performances, as well as visits to unfamiliar venues to sing for new audiences and congregations. In particular, there is reference to these activities' relevance for liturgical choirs, whose singers may be more accustomed to the heat-and-serve variety of regular service singing than the careful preparation of repertoire for a recording or broadcast.

April 2010

Some Reasons for Recording

Early in an unusually chilly early January, my choir met in Selwyn College Chapel during their Christmas vacation for an intense and tiring (though stimulating and rewarding) week of recording. Cambridge chapel choirs continue to release countless CDs each year, despite the fact that the classical music recording industry is apparently on its last legs. Why is it that so many of us are still willing to give up entire weeks of our lives to create yet another CD for an already saturated market, with little prospect of breaking even financially, let alone making a profit? Are the musical benefits gained from recording worth the financial risk and the sheer exhaustion?

In Cambridge, a tiny city with a population of only about 110,000, there are approximately 65 choral ensembles, both community- and university-based (i.e., both "town" and "gown"), including some of the most famous choirs in the world. Not surprisingly therefore, there is a certain amount of healthy competition, and emphasising the size and quality of one's respective CD back-catalogue is a seemingly unavoidable part of the territorial posturing rituals. Many choirs try to convince Cambridge's last remaining classical music record shop, Heffer's Sound, to display a gigantic reproduction of their latest CD cover in the front window, and success in this is deemed to be a noteworthy coup, a sign of superiority, despite the fact that most people either order CDs online these days, or else download MP3s and save considerable amounts of space on their shelves at home.

Of course, we continue to make recordings for less superficial reasons than these. The vast majority of the choirs in Cambridge are primarily liturgical, and therefore they rarely have time to polish music to full 'concert' standard. Although the members of a typical college chapel choir spend approximately eight to ten hours per week singing together, a huge proportion of this time is spent sight-reading Choral Evensong, with varying degrees of impressiveness. The luxury of lengthy rehearsals, and the frequent repetition involved in the recording process, provide a welcome opportunity to work comprehensively on the music, polishing details in a way that we would otherwise seldom experience. There is also an educational benefit: members of the choir learn key transferable skills such as the art of silent page-turning and how to suppress hiccoughs, as well as more musical techniques like the discipline required to reproduce accurate tuning, precise ensemble, and faultless diction, over and over again—especially when a car alarm outside, or a helicopter circling overhead, seem intent on ruining otherwise perfect takes. The improvement both in the choir as a whole, and in the individual singers, is usually conspicuous after only a few days of such meticulous and concentrated work.

The choice of repertoire for a CD also provides an insight into a given choir's primary purpose and motivation. Perhaps at the behest of a college's Development Office (always keen to entice elderly alumni into parting with their money), a chapel choir may release a recording of tried and tested perennially popular anthems, all of which have been recorded hundreds of times before (*O for the Wings of a Dove* anyone?); or else, inspired by the many pretty postcards of Cambridge in the snow, the searing heat of mid-July may seem the ideal conditions in which to record yet another CD of only the best-known Christmas carols. By contrast, though, some choirs take pride in offering recordings of lesser-known works by lesser-known composers (whether dead or alive). The university and college libraries are full of intriguing, unedited manuscripts, just waiting for a musicologist's care and attention to enable them to spring from a dusty MS to a shiny CD in a single bound. Contemporary composers are often keen to have their choral music performed and recorded by Cambridge choirs, where quasi-professional singing expertise is obtainable, but without the forbidding Musicians' Union price-tag. Indeed, the CD that Selwyn Choir was recording in those freezing January days consisted of liturgical choral works by contemporary composer Paul Edwards (b. 1955), who has spent his life composing music for the Anglican church. His best-known work, a Christmas carol called *No small wonder* has rather overshadowed the rest of his beautiful, technically sophisticated compositions which are well-crafted for the voice, and certainly deserve to be far better known. It would be lovely if the CD (when it is released) helped to spread awareness of this exquisite repertoire and to foster interest in Edwards' work.

So, I would like to believe that the week Selwyn Choir spent in the cold, (re)recording take after take with the noisy chapel heating turned off, was extremely worthwhile. Perhaps the fact that we poor humble church musicians are unlikely to become internationally rich and famous as a result of our CD sales is not as important as is the knowledge that our choirs benefit in less tangible ways from the discipline of focussing so single-mindedly on producing a recording which seeks to strive towards a perfection that is (and should be) always unattainable. And if I manage to ensure that a huge picture of the cover of Selwyn's Paul Edwards CD appears in a shop window somewhere in Cambridge, then that will merely be an additional bonus.

June 2010

Entertaining Angels

At least once a term I allow Selwyn Choir to escape for a day from the ivory tower of the university to sing in a church or cathedral somewhere in the real world. I also regularly invite other choirs to sing in Selwyn, either jointly with us, or as deputies when we are away. These distinct duties of being a guest and a host can sometimes alternate with alarming rapidity, and over one slightly harried weekend last term, the members of Selwyn Choir were visitors and hosts in rather swift succession.

On the Saturday, we travelled to Gloucestershire to sing Evensong in Tewkesbury Abbey at the invitation of an elderly Selwyn alumnus. He sang in the college choir in the 1950s, and he generously organised our entire trip, including taking all thirty of us out to dinner in an excellent local pub after the service. I found myself in the blissful (and unusual) position of being able to focus solely on music making. With the help of the Tewkesbury parish office, our kind host sent me the appointed psalms and hymns, booked the church hall for robing, fixed a time with the verger to take us through the procession, co-ordinated tea and biscuits, pre-ordered our chosen meals at the pub, and even arranged for the vicar (another Selwyn alumnus) to take time off from his well-earned Sabbatical in order to be there for our visit.

The very next day, the roles were reversed. Back in Selwyn, an alumna of the college brought her large London-based children's choir to join us for Evensong. The 50 children (ranging in age from seven to 18) were accompanied by about 100 groupies (parents, siblings, friends, etc.), and somehow we had to squeeze them all into the chapel, along with our regular congregation. In addition, there were subtle negotiations with the college catering department which enabled our visitors to be fed and watered, changing rooms were booked, extra service leaflets were photocopied, a sacristan took the visitors through their processional paces, additional chapel wardens were on duty, and seats were reserved for attending dignitaries (including two composers whose works we were singing, namely the visiting choir's patron John Rutter, and Selwyn alumnus Grayston Ives, who was also preaching the sermon). I enjoyed the whole occasion very much, and the choirs sang impressively, but I have to admit to being relieved when it was over.

Next month, Selwyn Choir will sing services in Westminster Abbey, where we will enjoy again the luxury of being visitors. The vergers will practice the processions with us, the Abbey organists will play for us, the refectory staff will provide us with refreshments, and the coach driver will brave traffic in the centre of London for our sakes. Just two weeks later, we will in turn host a visiting university choir from Edmonton, Alberta. I only hope that my singers will be able to welcome them warmly, despite the looming presence of end-of-year academic examinations. And so the pattern of guest and host alternates throughout the year.

The administrative headaches that are necessarily involved in arranging these sorts of events are often tiresome, and the planning is unquestionably time-consuming. I have often groaned at the mere thought of having to make sure that the necessary arrangements are in place. However, I usually manage to convince myself that, though the emailing, phoning, and double-checking are undeniably irksome, the musical and social rewards are significant. Singing in an unfamiliar venue, to an unfamiliar audience, invariably raises performance levels. Singers learn to adjust quickly to different acoustics, and organists to new instruments. In joint services, everyone benefits from encountering the technique of a different conductor, while the conductors usually enjoy being able to explore the possibilities offered by new singers. A drink or a meal after the music making invariably provides the opportunity to meet musical and clerical colleagues, as well as congregation or audience members, and it is during these times that future projects (e.g., services, concerts, and recordings) are discussed and planned. In the summer season, when the list of administrative hassles can include finding host family accommodation for up to thirty people, the visitors' debt of gratitude should be particularly high. In September, I will be taking Selwyn Choir to Ontario and Québec (which is not really feasible as a day trip) and we will be particularly grateful to any Canadians who are kind enough to make their spare bedrooms available for a few days.

Benjamin Franklin, in his great wisdom, observed that "guests, like fish, begin to smell after three days".[24] That may be true (though sometimes it can take less time than that!), but I prefer the verse from Hebrews 13: "Do not neglect to show hospitality to strangers, for thereby some have entertained angels unawares".[25] The giving and receiving of hospitality as part of the annual pattern of worship for choirs is of considerable importance. It is certainly worth the effort, both musically and spiritually. However, when hosting a gathered choral throng, it is not necessary to find every moment of the whole event inexpressibly enjoyable. As that old anonymous saying puts it, "hospitality is making your guests feel at home, even if you wish they were!"

---

24. Franklin, Benjamin. *Poor Richard's Almanack*. Philadelphia, 18thC.
25. Hebrews 13: 2

May 2012

Learning from
Collective Music-Making

As I begin this column, I am seated in the fan-vaulted splendour of King's College Chapel, listening to the final rehearsal for the annual orchestral-choral extravaganza put on by the Cambridge University Musical Society (CUMS), which, having been founded 170 years ago, is one of the world's oldest and most distinguished university music societies. The music being prepared for performance is Debussy's luscious early work for women's voices and orchestra, *La damoiselle élue*. While the women rehearse, the men quietly await their turn at the back of the chapel. The full combined forces are performing the whole of the third act of Wagner's *Parsifal*—a change from Choral Evensong, to be sure!

Admission to the Society's first orchestra, "CUMS1", is by (extremely) competitive audition at the beginning of each academical year, and all members have to re-audition every year, which keeps the standards impressively high. The orchestra's principal conductors have included Sir Charles Villiers Stanford, Sir David Willcocks, and Sir Stephen Cleobury, and amongst previous guest conductors are numbered Britten, Dvořák, Kodály, and Tchaikovsky—so there is a not insubstantial weight of history for its players to bear in mind. Each year, the orchestra works with five or six of the best college chapel choirs, to put on a performance in King's of some of the most iconic works in the repertoire. Over the past few years, we have performed the likes of Britten's *War Requiem*, Mozart's *C minor Mass*, Brahms *Ein Deutches Requiem*, Elgar's *Dream of Gerontius*, and other celebrated classics, none of which could be performed by any of the choirs on their own. Eminent Cambridge alumni are invited to return to their alma mater to conduct these performances. Recent conductors have included Christopher Robinson, David Hill, and Sir Richard Armstrong. This year's unusual programme is being directed by Sir Mark Elder, while next year we will perform Beethoven's *Missa Solemnis* under the baton of Sir Roger Norrington. The concerts provide wonderful opportunities for the young singers and players who range in age from 18 to 21.

It is not just the conductors who are University alumni with impressive international reputations: the professional soloists also often include those who have come through the ranks of the musical traditions of the University. In addition to an Oxbridge graduate or two amongst this evening's soloists, the role of Parsifal is being sung by New Zealand-born, Juilliard-graduate Simon O'Neill, undoubtedly one of the finest Heldentenors in the operatic world today. The 19-year old aspiring tenor choral scholars behind him may never reach those heady professional heights, but they can learn much about technique, musicianship, and stamina from observing O'Neill at work.

An invitation to sing in the choir for one of these concerts is a highly coveted honour. Although CUMS has a symphony chorus (along with four symphony orchestras, a chamber orchestra, a wind orchestra, and a chamber choir), the CUMS Chorus is a so-called town-and-gown ensemble, with membership consisting of 200 volunteer singers of all ages, and varying degrees of vocal proficiency ('twas ever thus with symphony choruses, of course). Using a collection of the best of Cambridge's choral scholars for these performances brings an extraordinarily skilled yet youthful vibrancy to the choral sound, giving it an energy and focus which is rarely heard in a large symphony chorus. This year's chosen performers are the mixed chapel choirs of Clare, Gonville & Caius, Jesus, and Selwyn, along with the men of King's, and a selection of hand-picked members of the inter-collegiate University Chamber Choir.

Not surprisingly, the logistics of mounting a project like this are considerable, especially given that every college has completely independent (and often conflicting) rehearsal schedules. There are also the students' intense academic timetables to take into account, not to mention the issues of booking rehearsal venues, soloists, and the guest conductor him/herself. The orchestra and combined choirs generally rehearse two or three times on their own, with rehearsal conductor and a chorus master respectively, in different participating colleges or in the Music Faculty, before the guest conductor arrives. All rehearsals are compulsory, though this is less easy to patrol than the policy-makers might think. And we don't always get it right—we had too few rehearsals for the *War Requiem*, and have had too many for this year's Debussy/Wagner venture. Practicalities have also proved difficult at times: on the day of this year's first rehearsal in King's Chapel, all of the singers had had a full day of lectures and supervisions, followed immediately by Evensong in their own chapels until about 7:15pm, and then a full rehearsal for this concert, from 7:30pm. When the chorus rehearsal overran, the ability of the singers to appreciate artistic endeavour at the expense of such basics as food and drink was somewhat compromised, and resulted in a fair amount of disgruntlement.

Practical logistics and physical privation aside, these performances are certainly one of the highlights of the University's musical year, and are inevitably sold out. The standards are invariably high, and the professionalism expected of the undergraduates causes them to mature as young musicians in ways that even they themselves recognise. The combination of rigorous rehearsal, eminent guest conductors, renowned soloists, highly talented and intelligent young players and singers, a magnificent venue, a well-educated audience with professional expectations, and, of course, truly great music, really does foster a remarkable fervour and intensity of purpose.

One hopes that the young musicians involved in this year's performance will appreciate the opportunity that they have been given. Certainly, the youthful voices of the singers are not mature enough to cope easily with the demands required of a Wagner opera chorus. That kind of vocal robustness necessitates utterly secure technique and years of hard work. Nonetheless, in preparing for this concert, they will have gained valuable insight into the world of professional music-making and, who knows, in 20 or 30 years times, some of them may be back in Cambridge for another such concert, but this time as the conductor or as one of the soloists.

June 2015

A JAM Session

E ach year since 2002, when the Lent Term ends in Cambridge, Selwyn
Choir has stayed in residence for an extra week to give a concert in
London for an organisation called the John Armitage Memorial Trust
(JAM). Now in its 15th season, JAM is a charity that promotes the composition and performance of new music. It has gone from rather humble beginnings in its founder's kitchen, to being one of the UK's most
respected advocates of living composers.

JAM was founded in 2000 by Edward Armitage, now chair of Trustees, in memory of his father, John, who had taken early retirement from
a successful career in advertising in order to return to the real love of his
life—music. John went back to university in his 60s to study composition,
but very sadly, he died of cancer before completing his degree. As a mature
student, he had too often found himself restricted from submitting music
to competitions, since the majority have age limits (usually under 30).
When his son formed the Trust, he remembered this frustration, and to
this day, JAM remains one of the few national competitions to which any
composers over the age of 18 can submit music. The only restriction is
that composers must be living, studying, or have been born in the UK.

John played the trumpet, and had always loved choral and organ
music, so Edward chose brass, organ, and choir as JAM's primary musical
forces. From the beginning, JAM has programmed an annual commission

111

from an established composer, alongside works submitted by student, amateur, and less-well-known composers. While the bigger names tend to attract the audience, the smaller names benefit greatly from the networking opportunities. The established composers who have been commissioned include Jonathan Dove, Judith Bingham, Paul Patterson, Gabriel Jackson, Tarik O'Regan, Giles Swayne, Thea Musgrave, and the late John McCabe. JAM has also been responsible for launching the careers of composers: Paul Mealor and Phillip Cooke first submitted to JAM as students, and subsequently were commissioned as well-established composers. All of the composers benefit musically of course. JAM's principal conductor, Nicholas Cleobury (for whom I function as chorus master), is known internationally for his work in the new music world. The performances are consistently of an impressively high standard; concerts are recorded professionally, and the recordings can be used freely by performers, composers, and JAM itself to promote their work and JAM's mission.

Edward put together an extraordinary team early in JAM's time, engaging outstanding professional singers, players, and conductors, as well as teachers, composers, and performers to judge the submitted works. It is a testament to his enthusiasm, charisma, and his vision, that although the team has expanded substantially over the years, and although the Trust's schedule has increased from one concert per year to about 20 (including a week-long festival and active outreach/education programme), nearly everyone who was involved from the early days is still involved today.

As anyone who has premièred a new work will know, these events are not without challenges as well as rewards. This year's March concert provided a few cases in point. Composers—even the most experienced and established ones—don't always get it right. So for example, one of the submitted pieces, in 3/4 time and marked "Andante, quarter-note = 62" felt stodgy and heavy in rehearsal. I experimented with various possibilities, and we eventually settled on quarter-note = 86, and the piece came alive. With a little trepidation, we sang it for the composer, and fortunately the change was approved enthusiastically. Balance between voices and brass is always a concern too, especially in lively ecclesiastical acoustics. In one of this year's works, although doubling the choral parts by the brass may have helped the choir to pitch the difficult intervals, it meant that occasionally the singers were obliterated entirely. Exotic time signatures and needlessly complex rhythmic patterns are also a familiar feature of much contemporary music, and precision is crucial in performance. One of my choir's favourite jokes is: "How many JAM composers does it take to change a light-bulb?" Answer: "Seven in the time of four."

From time to time one discovers a composer who, born too late in a world too old, delights in reinventing 1960s-style experiments with graphic scores and aleatoric techniques. In one such work this year (which, to be fair, was extremely effective in the concert), the composer mixed up the poem's phonemes in an improvisatory manner, such that nothing was comprehensible until about three minutes into the piece. Unfortunately, getting through rehearsal with any semblance of gravity was something of a trial for my undergraduates.

Challenges aside, our relationship with JAM has been without doubt one of the most profitable and rewarding collaborations of my time at Selwyn. The singers have benefited immeasurably from the musical discipline required to prepare and perform two or three programmes each year consisting entirely of new music. We have also made commercial recordings for a number of the composers we have met through JAM, and personally, I am constantly inspired and humbled by Edward's commitment to this scheme, which was sketched out on the back of an envelope 15 years ago, and is now thriving. Since its inception, JAM has performed about 75 new works, many of which have entered the standard choral, brass, and organ repertoires, and that is a legacy of which I am sure John himself would have been justifiably proud.

February 2017

BBC Radio 3 Choral Evensong

A particular highlight for UK choral foundations is an invitation to broadcast Choral Evensong live on BBC Radio 3 on a Wednesday afternoon. My colleagues and I recently broadcast from Ely Cathedral, and the service marked the 90th birthday of composer Arthur Wills. Wills spent much of his career as Director of Music at Ely, and he is still a faithful member of the congregation on Sunday mornings.[26]

For our broadcast, the introit, responses, canticles, and voluntary were by Arthur, and the anthem was *O pray for the peace of Jerusalem* by Howells, because it was just before Armistice Day (11 November). We also sang an Office Hymn and a congregational hymn, and the psalms appointed for the ninth evening (47, 48, 49). If truth be told, these were not entirely unchallenging: in the Coverdale translation, used in most cathedrals, the final word of verse five of psalm 47 was amusingly apt on 9 November 2016 (do look it up).[27] Fortunately, we managed to sing it without losing our composure. The service was a celebration of someone who had devoted his life and work to the cathedral, and it was appropriate that we could share it with the nation, and indeed the world, by means of "the wireless" (as Wills still calls it).

---

26. Arthur died in 2020 at the age of 94.
27. God is gone up with a merry noise; and the Lord with the sound of the trump. Psalm 47: 5. Coverdale translation. Antwerp, 1535.

Choral Evensong is the longest running outside broadcast in BBC history. It was first heard during the "National Programme" in October 1926, and came from Westminster Abbey. It continued as a regular weekly fixture from the Abbey for ten years, after which St Paul's Cathedral and York Minster were included in the roster. The programme moved to the BBC's classical music station, Radio 3, in 1981. Choral Evensong visits nearly 100 different cathedrals, abbeys, churches, and chapels each year, including a small number outside of the UK (St Thomas Fifth Avenue in New York City has been featured four times), and it is one of the most frequently requested programmes on the BBC's listen-again service. With the Wednesday live broadcast, a Sunday repeat, and worldwide online availability, it is reckoned that the number of listeners regularly approaches a quarter of a million.

Despite constant funding cuts imposed on the BBC (a publicly-funded service, with no advertisements), Choral Evensong has remained intact, though producers insist that musical standards within the worship are kept as high as possible. As one of its longest-serving producers has said, it is not impossible that a concert with the Berlin Philharmonic Orchestra conducted by Simon Rattle might follow immediately in the schedule, and the juxtaposition of the latter with an under-rehearsed or untidy choral service would be undesirable. In general, the repertoire consists of standard musical fare, often with a local twist (as in our Arthur-Wills-fest at Ely), though occasionally listeners hoping for a Stanfordesque or Purcellian comfort zone are challenged. For example, a service is broadcast by a professional choir every year from the London Festival of Contemporary Church Music, where the repertoire consists entirely of brand new works by living composers. There have been services of Jazz and Blues Evensong, Choral Vespers from Spain's Montserrat Abbey, and Orthodox Vespers from the cathedral in St Petersburg. Despite this adventurous programming, the focus is always upon creating a service of worship, and not a concert. They spend as much care on the details of rehearsing the lesson readers and the clergy's prayers as they do on the music, as I was reminded in Ely last month.

Originally, the programme existed to allow members of the public to feel as if they were participating in the regular liturgical life of wherever the broadcast was emanating from, but this aspiration is not without complications. For example, a fly-on-the-wall in Ely Cathedral on a normal Wednesday would find only the girl choristers on duty, singing upper-voice repertoire including a great deal of plainsong. Instead, listeners on that particular Wednesday found girls, boys, and men singing, two organists and two conductors, the entire Chapter in residence, and all the proverbial bells and whistles primed and ready to demonstrate the cathedral's music at its most impressive. Every week there are grumbles on social media about this excess, and concerned listeners moan that they are no longer participating in just a regular weekday service. However, the reasons for this are built into the infrastructure of the radio scheduling. The time slot allocated to Choral Evensong is 60 minutes—we never sing introits on weekdays in Ely, nor any hymns other than a choir-only plainsong office hymn. The service rarely takes more than 40 minutes, including the organ voluntary, so needing to fill in a further 20 minutes inevitably leads to a more substantial service than a regular Wednesday would demand.

Notwithstanding these niggles, BBC Radio 3's Choral Evensong continues to be popular, and is also a very good way of motivating a choir to give of its best, in order to ensure a future invitation. The BBC website explains the programme's enduring popularity as follows: "there is an atmosphere of great stillness when people are uplifted by the sheer beauty of choral singing. The heritage of the English choral tradition is unique and it is greatly valued. Throughout weekly broadcasts, hundreds of thousands can share this unparalleled experience." As the London Evening Standard put it earlier this year when the programme celebrated its 90th anniversary, "Thank God for the BBC's longest running show, [. . .] Choral Evensong: nearly as old as God himself."[28]

---

28. London *Evening Standard*. November 2001.

September 2021

Trolling Right Back at You.

There is a renowned UK singer-songwriter named James Blunt, who is particularly well known for his self-deprecating Twitter responses to trolling followers. For example:

> Troll: "James Blunt has an annoying face and a highly irritating voice."
>
> JB: "And no mortgage."

Or,

> Troll: "I must be one of only two people who genuinely likes every James Blunt song. The other being him."
>
> JB: "Nope, you're on your own, mate."

In the choral trolling world, "The Choir" section of the BBC Radio 3 forum (http://www.for3.org/forums/forum.php) poses plenty of opportunities for similarly imaginative replies. This is the forum where armchair experts wax lyrical about all things choral, and especially the live broadcasts of Choral Evensong on Radio 3 which occur every Wednesday at 3:30pm.[29]

---

29. For a brief history of Radio 3 Choral Evensong, the BBC's longest-running outside broadcast, see my UK Report from February 2017 above.

The broadcast last week came from the chapel of Selwyn College, Cambridge, and was directed by Yours Truly. It was the choir's first live broadcast—we had only ever done pre-recorded services in the past. The service went very well, and the choir sang music by Eleanor Daley, Herbert Brewer, Rani Arbo, and myself, extremely beautifully. I was very proud of them, and thankfully, the vast majority of the feedback was gratifyingly positive.

One anonymous comment on the aforementioned forum struck me, however. It reads as follows: "Anthem caught the ear. Good and well-sustained. As for the rest, unadventurous. Bit slow. [. . .] elsewhere competent [. . .]". As trolling goes, this is pretty mild, although 'competent' in this forum certainly intends to damn with faint praise. The author, a certain "DracoM" is a frequent, vocal, and often negative contributor, so I have advised the choir to ignore the comment.

Nonetheless, when it came to writing this column a few days later, that comment lingered in my mind. The writer's subtle ability to undermine confidence aptly reflects the literary inspiration for his/her screen name. What if someone else reads this and believes it? What if a potential choral scholar sees it and decides not to apply? What if we are never again invited to broadcast a live service? It's all terribly imprecise as well—exactly what was "a bit slow": the reading of the second lesson? the third verse of Psalm 147? the whole of the Magnificat? Of course, wasting time considering answers to these questions is manifestly absurd, but that is the consequence of such small-minded, thoughtless flippancy, especially when expressed anonymously to anyone who has made themselves vulnerable by stepping up in front of an audience (or in this case, a microphone).

Regardless of one's perceived idea of the quality, context is always important. What DracoM didn't know when he glibly expressed his dissatisfaction is that 65% of this year's choir are first-years with no professional recording or broadcasting experience beyond Selwyn's livestreaming system; that they have sung two metres apart from each other all year, and have had to learn their choral craft without the help of their older peers; that most of them finished their year-end examinations just 36 hours before the BBC arrived; that four of them were in self-isolation, having been notified by the legally-binding Covid contact-tracing app; that one of the soloists had Covid (not due to choir, I hasten to add) and was in bed; that until three hours before the broadcast, there was a very real risk that three further perfectly healthy senior choral scholars would be put into immediate self-isolation by a non-choir friend's pending Covid test result. So, even if we had actually sung everything a bit slow and the repertoire choice been unadventurous, there might well have been a legitimate explanation for that. In addition, I would have been grateful for the description "competent", regardless of how it was intended.

As it happens, I am persuaded that our broadcast was very definitely not sub-par (indeed, it's really very good, even if I do say so myself!). We found an ideal balance between old and new repertoire; everything went at exactly the tempo I set; and the choral and vocal technique on display, particularly in the lengthy daily psalmody, was "competent" in all the right senses of the word. Many of the lovely emails I received commented on the fact that the broadcast felt like an act of worship, not a concert, and several indicated how much they appreciated the new music that we introduced.

And so, if I were James Blunt, how should I respond? An old episode of the Muppet Show comes to mind:

Statler: "Hey, you old fool, you slept through the show."
Waldorf: "Who's a fool? You watched it."

Here's my version:

DracoM: "Unadventurous. Bit slow."
SEAM: "Who's unadventurous? You listened to it!"

Whether posting such a riposte would make me feel better or not is a moot point. Musicians are creative beings, and the need to play, sing, conduct, and compose is what defines our existence. But we are also out-of-shape, exhausted, and trying to do whatever we can in exceptionally challenging circumstances. Stepping up to the microphone/camera/stage nourishes us, but also makes us vulnerable. We are recovering from a crisis unprecedented in our lifetimes. The performing arts, and choral singing in particular, have struggled more than many other sectors of society. Be grateful for what is offered, and be kind with your anonymous comments, even if you were underwhelmed by someone's performance. Unless you are their teacher or their employer, they don't need to know.

October 2010

Sunbathing on a Tropical Beach?

As I write, the sun is shining brightly, and has been doing so here constantly here for well over a month (yes, honestly!). The grass is withered and parched, and even native Brits are looking atypically tanned. The question on everyone's lips is "Where are you going on your summer holidays?" If truth be told, I don't normally take summer holidays. Or at least, when I do travel to exotic places, I always seem to find myself accompanied by about 30 extra people. I am referring of course, to the dreaded Choir Tour. Thanks to such expeditions, I have had the privilege of performing throughout the UK, across most of mainland Europe, and in New Zealand, Israel and Palestine, and North America. Although I have usually managed to snatch a little time for sight-seeing on these journeys, none of them has had quite the relaxing and restorative effect that a week on a beach in the south of France might have offered.

Choir Tours are particularly on my mind just now, as I am about to embark on two of them: first to Paris with Ely Cathedral Girls' Choir, and then, shortly thereafter, to Ontario and Québec with the Choir of Selwyn College, Cambridge. Not surprisingly, I have spent many months preparing for these expeditions. Airlines have been pitted off against each other to see which can offer the best prices, and which can guarantee not to be on strike in August and September. The internet has been trawled thoroughly to compare the cost of hired coaches, Greyhound buses, public trains, metro systems, taxis, etc., and the resulting combination of the least expensive modes of transport will make us feel as if we are starring in the next instalment of the 1980s comedy classic 'Planes, Trains, and Automobiles'. Sight-seeing attractions have been investigated: can the already stretched tour budget can manage a communal trip up the Eiffel Tower or a ride on Niagara's Maid of the Mist? Thankfully, Google has also been agreeably forthcoming when asked to search for such phrases as "Paris for free" or "Cheap things to do in Toronto".

Accommodation with the Ely girls in Paris is reasonably hassle-free, since we are staying in a budget hotel quite near the centre. The only really serious considerations concerned the complex problem of room sharing: which of the girls were most likely to squabble if they were confined to a small shared space for more than 30 minutes? In Canada, Selwyn Choir will be staying in host families most of the time. This allows us to meet real people, and to experience ordinary life in a foreign country. On the other hand, difficult allergies and intricate dietary requirements will (I am sure) create complications for our long-suffering hosts. Personally, I already pity the poor person who will be tasked with providing gluten-, nut-, and dairy-free vegetarian meals in a dustless environment with no cats or dogs or pineapples (!) in the immediate vicinity. And even if all of these potential perils are manoeuvred, the potent combination of jet-lag and over-excitement is rarely conducive to civilised dinner-table conversation with strangers. Nonetheless, we are, of course, *exceedingly* grateful to our hosts, since there is no way that we could afford to come to Canada without their generosity.

So far I could be describing any sort of group trip away. But what is it that makes choir tours so significant? Not only do the members of the group travel, socialise, sleep, eat, and sight-see in each other's company, but they also rehearse and sing together every day, considerably enhancing their communal life while they are away. The discipline of this regular practice invariably improves the quality of the performances, achieving the kind of focused and sustained improvement that is hard to accomplish in the middle of term when there are so many other preoccupations and distractions. Not infrequently, the intensity of the collective musical experience turns an ordinary group vacation into something far more profound and worthwhile than a pleasant, though ultimately purposeless, week in a sunny tourist resort.

Therefore, whisper it quietly, but I do actually enjoy choir tours, and I don't normally feel as if I'm having a proper holiday if I haven't got 30 hangers-on relying on me to issue orders. In truth, I get rather bored sitting on beaches, and the adrenaline provided by public performances keeps my "vacation" time interesting. And there's the added challenge of singing services in unfamiliar venues, with unexpected liturgical quirks, and often in a variety of foreign languages. I will never forget the thrill of a Mass in the Czech Republic many years ago, wondering if I could determine correctly when to start the Sanctus. You don't get that sort of kick from gently perspiring under a palm tree.

Organising a holiday for two is relatively easy with the help of the internet. Organising a choir tour, however, is a logistical nightmare, and would not be possible without the dedicated assistance of a host of selfless people abroad. In conclusion then, I would just like to express my thanks to all of those in France and Canada who have helped make this year's summer "vacation" so enjoyable. If only the poor dears knew what they had let themselves in for . . .

Chapter 5

The Guest Clinician
Will See You Now

Many choirs invite visiting clinicians to work with them once or twice a year, and residential summer programmes often have a special guest conductor. These are memorable events for the participants and for the visiting musician, often involving international collaborations. I have learned much from the many friends I have made on these sorts of excursions, and this chapter brings together the columns written shortly after these sorts of trips.

New York, New York

The title of this month's column should really read 'US Report' since my summer included two weeks in New York City, where I directed the annual Girl Chorister Course at St Thomas Church Fifth Avenue. 36 girls (ages 12 to 18) from 15 states and 28 cathedrals/churches spent nine days living in the St Thomas Choir School, which is located just south of Central Park. For nearly a century, this famous boarding school has provided trebles for the church's internationally-acclaimed choir of men and boys. Unfortunately for 51% of the population, neither the school nor its wonderful choir admit girls, so this summer course provides a welcome opportunity for talented young women to participate in the liturgy at St Thomas.

The course basically seeks to replicate the boys' daily experience: the girls reside in the school, share rooms, eat meals in the dining hall, attend music theory classes, encounter some of the city's legendary attractions, and, most importantly, sing together. Up to four hours a day are spent in intensive rehearsals, preparing for two upper-voice Choral Evensongs during the week, and one full Sunday Eucharist, with the gentlemen of the St Thomas Choir. In addition, the girls gather each night in the high-ceilinged school library to sing the ancient Gregorian Office of Compline, sharing the chanting of plainsong psalms, canticles, and antiphons, and the reading of lessons and prayers.

The course staff consists of a house mother, an administrator, a nurse, a priest, a singing teacher, an activities leader, an organist, a theory teacher, and the musical director. Two of us are responsible for the course's musical direction, in alternating years: coincidentally, we have the same first name and we are both Trustees of the Royal College of Organists. Sarah Baldock (sometime director of music at Chichester Cathedral) directs the girls in the years which are divisible by two, and I direct them in those which are not, prompting the dubious but convenient nicknames "Even Sarah" and "Odd Sarah".

This year's choral repertoire included music by British composers from the 16th to the 21st centuries. The girls were required to prepare the music in advance, so that we could move swiftly beyond the dull basics of note-learning, and focus on the more interesting tasks of polishing phrasing, singing with line, attending to diction and tuning, listening critically, responding to gesture, modifying sound quality, and reflecting upon the implications of stylistic performance practice. We also spent a good deal of time concentrating on more humdrum but equally necessary practicalities: encouraging professional behaviour in rehearsals; marking copies effectively; processing confidently in church; ensuring that cassocks and surplices were hung straight; that flat, smart, polished black shoes and black socks were worn in church; that hair was tied neatly in a bun off the face and shoulders; and that coloured fingernail polish and retro 1970s-style eye makeup were removed.

Since the girls represented a wide geographical area, certain pronunciation modifications were necessary to achieve unanimity. I prefer a low back vowel in 'God' to ensure that the omnipotent, omniscient deity is distinguished from 'Gad', who was merely the first son of Jacob by Leah's slave-girl Zilpah. Occasional vowels needed to be pronounced more carefully by all (/idʒɪpt/ 'Ee-jipped' rather than /idʒəpt/ 'Ee-jupped). We worked on correct singing enunciation of consonants—for example removing the rhotic /ɔʳ/ from 'Lord', and learning to hear the difference between /d/ (which is voiced) and /t/ (which is not), to avoid that odd Anglo-German quirk 'Thanks be to Gott'. Imagine my delight when, after seeing *The Phantom of the Opera* on Broadway, no fewer than six of the girls commented on Christine's word-final-voiced-alveolar-plosives when she sang 'inside my mind'!

This year's repertoire also allowed much variation in sound and style. A fuller, richer sound, with warm vibrato was appropriate for Parry and Bairstow; we found a colder, calmer colour for the austere opening of James MacMillan's masterful anthem *A new song*; the tongue-in-cheek jollity of Bryan Kelly's *Jamaican Canticles* required bright and sparkling tone. A semi-chorus of more experienced girls performed John Shepherd's *In manus tuas (I)*, and we worked on shaping and articulating the lengthy melismata, listening to the interweaving of counterpoint, and having confidence to swap parts freely from those learned in advance. Over the course of the nine days, the girls' critical capacity and their performance skills improved immeasurably, (and some were impressive to begin with, thanks to the obviously excellent training that many of them are receiving from some of you who are reading this!), and I was delighted with the high standard they reached in a short space of time.

Lest you think that these girls come to New York City only to work like little choral slaves for nine days, let me reassure you that there is ample leisure time as well. We began the week with a photo scavenger hunt, traipsing through mid-town Manhattan posing as Rockettes at Radio City and with the doorman outside the "Eloise Hotel", bathing our hot feet in the Columbus Circle fountain, and impersonating Audrey Hepburn eating her breakfast at Tiffany's. We attended the aforementioned Broadway musical, went boating in Central Park, and enjoyed fabulous views of the city skyline, the Brooklyn Bridge, and the Statue of Liberty from a speed boat in the harbour. Notwithstanding these various activities, the highlight for many I am sure was shopping on Fifth Avenue after the final rehearsal! So, if you haven't sent girls to this course before, I urge you to consider doing so. They participate in exceptional music-making in an extraordinary building in the centre of one of the world's most exhilarating cities. About 70% of the girls return each year, which is surely testament to how outstanding the course is.

Of course, where girls sing liturgically when they become adults is still a fraught question in the UK, and the subject generates heated debate.

Although nearly every cathedral now has a girls' choir, there is still no accepted place for women in 'mainstream' cathedral choirs, apart from one alto at Peterborough (a former Selwyn choral scholar, in fact) who has recently become the first woman employed as a full-time lay-clerk in an English cathedral. Needless to say, her appointment was controversial. However, it is worth emphasising that both US and UK girls are increasingly well catered for chorally, as children and as teenagers, both in their home parishes and in cathedrals—and at St Thomas during the summer. That in itself is a huge improvement on what was available to women of my generation when we were in our teens.

A Ceremony of Carols

This column will appear in print at just around the time that the musical world will mark the 100th anniversary of the birth of Benjamin Britten, one of England's most significant composers. Britten was born in the east-coast fishing port of Lowestoft, Suffolk, in 1913, on 22 November, the feast of St Cecilia, patron saint of music and musicians (which also happens to be my own birthday). Therefore the focus of this column is both seasonally and geographically appropriate. Britten's much-loved Christmas masterpiece for upper voices and harp, *A Ceremony of Carols*, has strong North American associations: Benjamin Britten and Peter Pears had moved to the States a few months before the outbreak of the Second World War in 1939, for a variety of musical and political reasons. They returned to England in 1942 via Halifax, Nova Scotia, where Britten is said to have purchased an anthology of English medieval poetry. On the journey across the Atlantic, he set a number of the poems for treble voices, collating them upon his return into the work we now know as *A Ceremony of Carols*. His choice of harp as the accompanying instrument is attributed to an earlier (unfilled) commission to write a harp concerto. Although he had only learned about the instrument from a written teaching manual, the *Ceremony*'s harp part is impressively idiomatic and imaginative.

Last summer, in distinctly un-Christmassy 100-degree July weather, I spent a week in the small town of Madison, Indiana. The occasion was the

ABRSM National Summer Harp Academy, under the artistic direction of renowned harpist Carol McClure. The course took place at the summit of the Clifty Falls State Park, overlooking the majestic Ohio River, with breathtaking views in all directions. Over 50 students, ranging in age from eight to just under 80, assembled for a week of intense musical training under the tutelage of no fewer than nine professional harpists, led by the Czech Republic's Jana Boušková, one of the world's most distinguished performers. Although the majority of those gathered were harpists, there were enough players (students and staff) to make up a small string ensemble; there were also a few pianists, several singers, and a trombonist or two, one of whom was Carol's multi-talented husband Wes Ramsay, who is a performer, composer, arranger, producer, publisher, and teacher [and who also happens to be the publisher of this volume of essays].

I was honoured to be invited to participate as a specialist choral conductor. My brief was to turn a subset of the harpists into a choir, with a view to performing the whole of Britten's *Ceremony* at the end of the week. The singers included a range of the students on the course, children, teenagers, and adults, who sang with varying degrees of confidence and polish, which was an appropriate combination given Britten's well-documented interest in writing for children and amateur performers.

What was particularly unusual about the way this performance was envisaged and rehearsed, was that the choir members were also all learning the harp accompaniments as part of the week's musical tasks, and therefore we had to approach the work from the point of view of both singer and player. Indeed, when we came to the performance itself, we had a different accompanist for each movement, with singers moving from their place in the choir to slip onto the stool of an awaiting instrument. Two harps were set up for the performance so that the various *attacca* movements could be negotiated without interruption, despite a change in player.

Considering the work from the perspective of both singer and player, provided illumination and clarification on many levels. For example, we discussed the need for harpists to understand the poetry: the opening chords in 'Wolcum Yole!' need to be phrased as if they were singing the word 'Wolcum', with its unaccented second syllable; the trembling trills in 'In freezing winter night' represent the shivering of the child; the harp part's rifle-like figuration reflects the battle imagery in Robert Southwell's 'This little babe'; the harp creates a spinning-wheel effect in the middle section of 'As dew in Aprille' depicting the common image of Mary at her spinning wheel during the Annunciation; the power-chords in 'Adam lay i-bounden' accompany the choir's enthusiastic shouts of "Thanks be to God" (*Deo gratias*). Conversely, the singers need to be aware of their harpists: every choir's tendency to sing behind the beat at "Candelmesse, Quene of bliss" in 'Wolcum Yole' causes dread for harpists, since their continuous eighth-note figuration becomes impossible if the singers drag; the alternations between 6/4 and 3/2 time in 'Balulalow' need to be sung rhythmically if the harp's cradle-rocking figuration is to remain uninterrupted; all choirs are prone to rushing through 'This little babe', a favourite movement, but the accompaniment is likely to prompt an acute case of Repetitive Strain Injury if it is allowed to run away. The fact that the choir members for this performance were all harpists as well as singers allowed us to work in great detail on the relationship between the vocal parts and their accompaniment.

For me personally, one of the real highlights of the course was having my first (and thus far, only) harp lesson. After a week of convincing both singers and players of the value of a comprehensive understanding of the work, it became clear that my own horizons needed expanding. Carol McClure took me aside, made me do all kinds of hand-position exercises, sat me down at a beautiful ebony grand concert harp, and allowed me to pluck out 'Twinkle, twinkle little star'. By the end of 15 minutes I had learned every harpist's favourite *glissando*, that at the end of 'Adam lay i-bounden' which leads into the 'Recessional' (though, truth be told, I didn't always land completely convincingly on the top A at the end).

Like any residential summer music course, the ABRSM National Summer Harp Academy aimed to provide its participants with intense musical discipline, rigour, and perspective. They certainly achieved these goals on every level, and with particular success in the imaginative and detailed way in which we were able to work on the *Ceremony of Carols*. Upon his return to the UK, Britten allegedly stated that America had "all the faults of Europe and none of the attractions"—perhaps he might have felt differently if he'd had the opportunity to spent a week overlooking that lovely view of the Ohio River!

February 2016

A Weekend in London (Ontario)

I recently travelled to Canada for a brief (four-day) trip to direct the second annual Choristers' Festival at Metropolitan United Church in London, Ontario. This event was the initiative of the Met's visionary director of music, Gregg Redner. Gregg was educated both at Juilliard in the US and at Exeter University in the UK. The Met has an accomplished adult choir, with a long and illustrious history, and recently Gregg has established a children's choir, which now boasts nearly 20 choristers who rehearse three times a week, and who are mastering the art of singing.

As you may have surmised from my opening sentence, the Choristers' Festival is a relatively new venture. It celebrates the significant role that children play in liturgical choral music, and allows choristers throughout the region to interact, both musically and socially. The Festival has grown enormously since its inception in 2014: in its first year, about 40 children participated; in its second year, there were more than 90 girls and boys, ranging in age from six to 16, who came with their directors from across southern Ontario. Our schedule included a full day of rehearsals, talks, workshops, and meals together, and ended with a worship service. I also had the opportunity to work with the Met Choristers on their own, and was impressed to observe their developing musicianship and professionalism.

For their repertoire, I was invited to choose four anthems for upper voices and organ. There were also hymns and psalms to prepare for the service. The first Festival's choral repertoire had been limited to unison works, as Gregg was wisely being conservative about attendance and ability. I was permitted some two-part repertoire this year, and I chose music representing four different liturgical seasons, in the hopes that the various participating choirs could use the music again later in the year. For Advent we had C. V. Stanford's masterful *A Song of Peace* from his Bible Songs, Op. 113. Lent was represented by Simon Lole's lovely two-part anthem *The Father's Love*. In addition we had Peter Aston's tuneful Pentecost work *I give you a new commandment* and Mendelssohn's beautiful 'O rest in the Lord' from *Elijah*, which is suitable for most occasions.

I have no doubt that many of you have found yourselves in the position of being a "Guest Clinician" for a workshop such as this, and I wanted to reflect upon the challenges of rapidly trying to mould a group of unfamiliar singers into a choir that is ready to perform in public in a short space of time. For me, one of the main disadvantages is an entirely unmusical one: they had all learnt my name before I arrived, whereas I was entirely reliant on over 90 name badges. When they all put their various liturgical robes on, covering up their name tags, I felt somewhat adrift when it came to nomenclature.

Such a large group of children will inevitably display a huge variety of abilities. The participants in this year's Choristers' Festival were in various categories such as "six-years-old-and-can't-quite-match-pitch-yet-but-looks-cute-in-a-cassock-and-ruff" to "16-and-will-probably-major-in-vocal-performance-at-university", so it was a challenge to keep them all engaged during rehearsal. My repertoire choices assisted me, purely by accident, if truth be told. Although it is in unison, and therefore was meant to be one of the "easier" pieces, the intense dramatic scope of Stanford's *A Song of Peace* was ideal for the teenagers, whereas the simple canonic two-part melodic lines of the Peter Aston were ideal for the younger children.

It is always difficult to know what to expect in terms of advance preparation for such events, and this can add to the challenge of preparing a concert or service in a limited period of time. All of the choirs involved were given the music several weeks earlier, and were asked to prepare it. Gregg's Met Choristers knew the music nearly from memory. By contrast, one of the other groups were rather less assured, since they learn music primarily by rote (a rather short-sighted way of teaching choral singers which might be the subject of a future column). Although they had all been sent word sheets, which had duly been learnt, combining the words with the notes proved to be a demanding task at times. The differing understanding of basic choral technique is also unpredictable: some singers knew perfectly well what "put the final consonant on the tied eighth-note" meant; to others, that instruction was incomprehensible.

Of course, there is also much joy to be had in jumbling together a large group of singers from several different places and asking them to rise to the challenge of a professional performance. In this case, despite a few rough corners, I was delighted with the results, and I hope that the children enjoyed themselves as much as I did.

I've always thought that the phrase "Guest Clinician" sounded rather anatomical, but the given the need for quick diagnosis in unfamiliar people of choral issues, combined with the prescription of musical restoratives, it is perhaps an apt description of the role that we play in these situations. I would just like to finish with congratulations to Gregg, to his supportive Pastor Jeff, and to his able organ scholar, Catherine, for their vision, their enthusiasm, and the warmth of their welcome. If you direct a children's choir in the vicinity, do get in touch with them about the third annual Choristers' Festival next year!

RSCM Charlotte

It will come as no surprise to some of you that this column has a North American flavor [sic]. As I write, I have just returned from North Carolina, where I was music director for the RSCM America Charlotte course. The RSCM (Royal School of Church Music) was founded by Sir Sydney Nicholson in 1927 as the School of English Church Music. It consisted of a training college for church musicians, and an association of affiliated churches committed to maintaining high standards of liturgical music. After suspending operations during World War II, the association was revived in 1945, with its royal charter granted by King George VI. When the training college closed in 1974, the RSCM set up regional branches overseas, and it now boasts nearly 7,500 affiliated churches, organisations, and individuals internationally, about 650 of which are in the States. Among the many benefits, the Voice for Life training programme is particularly popular, as it provides a rigorous framework for training choir members of all ages. Vocal production, music theory, and liturgical context are examined at various levels, and successful singers wear coloured ribbons over their vestments to indicate their achievement.

Eleven summer training courses are run by RSCM America every year, and they accept various combinations of singers: girl and boy trebles; teen girls and boys with changing voices; adult altos, tenors, and basses. University-age organ and conducting scholars are welcome at many courses as well. North Carolina's Charlotte course began in 2004, and the 2016 course had over 100 participants, including 53 girls and boys under the age of 18. There were also two organ scholars and an organist, two administrators, several pastoral staff members who doubled as section leaders and rehearsal conductors, a nurse, and a chaplain. I had to learn a lot of names very quickly.

We were resident in the beautiful campus of Queens University, Charlotte, whose early-20th-century red-brick colonial-style buildings were particularly lovely at sunrise (I know this thanks to jet-lag). We rehearsed daily in the neo-classical Myers Park Baptist Church, known locally as the nicest Episcopal church in Charlotte. Its divided east-end quire, generous acoustic, high altar, vaulted ceiling, and graceful cruciform shape may explain this liturgical misnomer. We even had incense at Evensong on the final day. Our daily routine began at 7:45am with Eucharist, at which the trebles and teens read lessons and psalms, with varying degrees of bleary-eyed fluency. After an excellent breakfast (I didn't have the courage to try "Cheesy Grits" despite assurances that they were a local delicacy) there followed three hours of rehearsals and theory classes. Afternoon activities for the adults consisted of seminars discussing such things as care of the young voice, music technology, and Voice for Life resources, while the under-18s played games and went swimming. Two more hours of rehearsal were followed by an adapted version of Evensong in which we sang whatever we had been working on that day. We abandoned all liturgical scruples and substituted Mass movements for the Canticles on one occasion. After the children were tucked up in their dorms, the adults enjoyed some convivial social time.

If you were to ask the participants what they will remember most about this year's course, I reckon that they would respond with "the repertoire". I love great music, and I never choose mediocre fillers (Sterndale Bennett in A flat, anyone?) nor dumbed-down cutesy children's music (butterflies and bunny rabbits are best left outdoors, IMHO), even though this means that I neglect some standard repertoire. I also often struggle to combine ambition with realism. Although I knew that the skill levels of the participants would vary widely, I still chose a music list that many an English cathedral would baulk at. The theme was 20th-century settings of 17th-century metaphysical poetry:

Ralph Vaughan Williams—Mass in G

Herbert Howells—Evening Canticles in B minor

Kenneth Leighton—Preces and Responses

John Ritchie—Lord, when the sense of thy sweet grace (Richard Crashaw)

Kenneth Leighton—Drop, drop slow tears (Phineas Fletcher)

W. H. Harris (three-part teen girls)—King of Glory, King of Peace (George Herbert)

W. H. Harris (arranged by me for two-part teen boys)—The Call (George Herbert)

Anthony Piccolo (trebles)—O hear us, Lord (John Donne)

Gerald Finzi—Lo, the full final sacrifice (Richard Crashaw)

All on one day. Yes, really.

It is an ambitious list of masterpieces, I admit. Our chaplain brought the texts alive in his wonderful teaching, and the choir rose magnificently to the challenge, singing absolutely beautifully in the Sunday services. When questioned, the overall favourite of the trebles was the Finzi: they loved the great tunes; they all learnt the meaning of the words allegory, sacrifice, and oxymoron; and they could probably even deliver an academic paper on the medieval image of the self-wounding pelican. It seems to me so important that we should never treat children as if they were children, especially when introducing them to liturgical music. The 12-part unaccompanied Vaughan Williams, the tuning traumas of the Leighton, the inconvenient five-four bars in the Howells, all paled into insignificance for me, when I glimpsed one of the 10-year-old trebles grinning in eager anticipation two beats before "rich, royal food" in the Finzi.

The RSCM was established to maintain the highest standards of liturgical music-making. This applies both to the composition and to the performance thereof. Life is, quite simply, too short to sing rubbish music.

Making Music in
Moorhead, Minnesota

Earlier this year, I travelled to Minnesota to spend a few days at Concordia College in Moorhead. I had a fascinating and enjoyable time, teaching, lecturing, playing, conducting, socialising, and even preaching a sermon. The visit provided me with the valuable opportunity to observe and learn about an unfamiliar (to me) musical heritage, and I hope my input gave the students and faculty a fresh perspective as well.

The Lutheran choral tradition is a relatively unknown phenomenon in the UK. That such a wealth of exceptional choral singing grew up in the middle of prairie grasslands is as endearing as it is baffling. Even a routine Google search attests that Minnesota has a "national reputation" for choral excellence, and certainly some of its professional choirs (particularly VocalEssence) have reputations that extend far beyond America's borders. In general, however, the tradition is a well-kept secret, and I was amazed to see the many hundreds of students singing in Concordia's numerous outstanding choirs.

The choral structures of Concordia and Oxbridge are distinct in many ways, despite the fact that the student singers are roughly the same age and at a similar stage in their education. An Oxbridge chapel choir rarely numbers above 26 members, while there are 80 to 100 singers in the various choirs at Concordia and other such institutions. Although the weekly rehearsal commitment is similar (between eight and twelve hours per week, depending on the choir) an Oxbridge chapel choir "performs" (liturgically) several times per week, whereas the Lutheran choirs sing in public far less frequently. Even Concordia's so-called Chapel Choir rarely contributes to the college's daily chapel services.

I observed that the choirs in this particular American tradition spend many weeks learning and rehearsing a single programme, polishing and memorising the music. By contrast, in Oxbridge, we churn through large swathes of repertoire every week, sight-reading in pre-service rehearsals on a near-daily basis. Not surprisingly, the quality of performance also differs. In many an Oxbridge chapel, "rough around the edges" might be considered a compliment, especially early in the year, while "woefully under-rehearsed" might be a more accurate description in some cases. On the other hand, Concordia's choirs' performances are polished, sophisti-cated, and professional. Indeed, I worried at times that they were actually *over*-rehearsed. The opportunity for spontaneous music-making seemed remote, and risk-taking was actively discouraged. At its worst, this can produce music that is studied and soulless.

There is a commonly-held belief in Britain that American choirs can-not sight-read, and therefore require many weeks of preparation. Not-withstanding the fact that most of the singers I met at Concordia actually *do* read rather well, this maxim is not without some truth—and potential weaknesses of this kind are compounded by the choirs' infrastructures. Large choirs rarely enable weaker readers to develop independence. A soprano in a section of 35 doesn't need to acquire musical confidence; but in a section of eight, she will need to find her feet very quickly indeed. In addition, the lack of performance experience has a significant effect on the learning speed (quite apart from reading ability). If there is no need to prepare an anthem for performance for another six weeks, there is no urgency. On the other hand, if Evensong begins in 45 minutes, there is urgency aplenty! And before anyone raises the "we-don't-have-the-cathedral-chorister-tradition-so-their-previous-experience-isn't-comparable" argument, I would like to add that the vast majority of the students in a normal Oxbridge chapel choir (perhaps excluding the likes of King's, St John's, or New College) will have had very similar experience in their elementary and high-school choirs to any singers at a place like Concordia. Nowadays, most will have attended a state-maintained (i.e., not private) school, and sung in an unauditioned choir which prepared one concert programme per term, most likely taught by rote and sung from memory. Some might also have sung in parish choirs where as teenagers they halved the average age in the stalls. Many will have had instrumental lessons, but few singing lessons. Most of them learn nearly all high-level choral skills—including sight-reading ability—at university, both by specific teaching from their directors, and also through osmosis, and indeed, necessity.

I return now to the "woefully under-rehearsed" (a.k.a. "rough around the edges") singing which is regularly heard in Oxbridge chapels. It goes without saying that this is musically unsatisfying for the singers and the conductors, despite definite long-term gain in sight-reading fluency and public performance confidence. Fortunately, tours and recordings outside of term allow time to rehearse things properly. Thanks to my experience in Concordia, I will be asking Selwyn Choir to memorise a good deal of our tour programme (we will be in California in July) in the hopes that we are able to present the kind of polished and professional performances that I was fortunate enough to hear from the choirs in Moorhead.

I will also, however, expect them to respond when I take musical risks: just because we have rehearsed and memorised a passage one way doesn't mean that we will perform it the same way every time. Different acoustics will require adjustments of tempo, dynamic, and vocal colour, and I might well find unexpected new places for *rubato* simply to suit to my own mood. After all, memorised or not, that is what live music-making is about—otherwise one might as well stay at home and listen to a recording from the comfort of one's living room.

June 2018

Clinician-ing in Kentucky

Earlier this year I took a brief journey across the pond to direct the music at an Episcopal parish church in Kentucky for a weekend in Lent. Although the term "Choral Clinician" has always sounded rather anatomical to me, it is an apt word to describe the visiting conductor who sees an unfamiliar choir just once, and is asked to offer diagnoses, recommend solutions, give advice, and provide a second opinion. It can be particularly fruitful for both metaphorical doctor and patient if the encounter is international, since that allows for comparing and contrasting different traditions.

I worked with two of the church's numerous choirs, the Parish Choir, with 12 paid section-leads as well as volunteers, and the Evensong Choir, which includes various local semi-professional musicians drawn from the wider community. In both groups there was also a hand-picked selection of some of the best of the Treble Choir's younger singers, both boys and girls. The adults in the choirs were relatively young, and all of the singers were accomplished, polished, and impressively well prepared for my visit. As well as the obvious investment that the parish has made in personnel, the church's musical facilities were remarkable by UK standards. Most English cathedrals and major London parish churches have only half as many paid adult singers; very few UK churches have anything resembling their luxurious rehearsal room; hardly any have two organs, let alone three grand pianos; none, as far as I know, has its own set of orchestral timpani!

The weekend's repertoire, chosen collaboratively by me and the church's director of music, included some works with a Cambridge University connection: Howells' *Collegium Regale* (King's College) setting of the Eucharist; Stanford's *Beati quorum via* (written for Trinity College); Gabriel Jackson's lovely *Tewkesbury Magnificat and Nunc dimittis* (composed for the 75th birthday of a Selwyn College alumnus). In addition we sang Anthony Piccolo's imaginative and demanding *Preces and Responses*, and Henry Balfour Gardiner's legendary *Evening Hymn*. Wikipedia ruefully notes that the fame of this piece rather overshadows the rest of HBG's output, which includes various major orchestral works. While Balfour Gardiner may be thought of in some circles as a "one-anthem-wonder", it's a fine piece to be remembered for. We also sang an unknown, very early and slightly odd setting of words by St Ephraim (c. 306-373) for SATB choir and organ by the eminent Scottish composer, James MacMillan. Although I admire his music greatly, this particular work left me somewhat dubious. I actually made a couple of impromptu changes (don't tell Boosey and Hawkes) in order to try to make it more convincing.

As indicated above, one of the interesting aspects of this sort of collaboration is the comparison of national traditions. What was most notable in the excellent Kentucky choirs as opposed to most comparable British choirs was the presence of a now-rather-outdated vibratoless style of singing. The Tallis Scholars popularised this approach in the 1980s, and one or two high-profile contemporary choirs have revived it thanks primarily to Baltic and Scandinavian choral influences. However the vast majority of UK chamber, cathedral, and collegiate choirs allow—and indeed encourage—full and healthy vibrato-rich singing. In the Kentucky choirs, several of the section leads had received substantial solo singing instruction, but it seemed to me that they were intentionally not using that training in a choral context. When I invited them to sing more fully, with real resonance, the tenors in particular (who were outstanding, by UK or US standards) were delighted. The sopranos took more convincing, though they were all relatively young. I had to reassure them that naturally-produced vibrato would not adversely affect either tuning or ensemble. After some cajoling, I managed to persuade them to sing fully and healthily, which substantially improved both their dynamic range and the vibrancy of the overall sound. This sort of full-bodied, connected sound, in which singers use their full voices in a choral setting, whilst still listening as collaborative musicians, is commonly encountered in the UK (and especially in the cathedral tradition). I am convinced that good ensemble singing does not require markedly different vocal technique from good solo singing.

When I do these sorts of workshops—in any country—I often spend a disproportionate amount of time dealing with word-final unstressed syllables. Since the word "scattered" contains a stressed syllable followed by an unstressed syllable (SCAT-tered), the second one must be sung more quietly than the first, as happen naturally in speech. As I'm sure you know, choirs often neglect this linguistic nicety (how often have you had to say "less *terd* please"?). Interestingly and highly unusually, these particular choirs had been so drilled in the art of "phrasing off" that the final syllable was often completely inaudible and incomprehensible. It was surprisingly refreshing to have to ask for "more *terd*" in places!

After I had directed two gratifyingly well-sung services (and played an organ recital) we retired to the director of music's home for refreshment. A delicious supper was followed by spontaneous entertainment in the form of songs from musicals, jazz standards, opera choruses (not always with the composers' intended libretti), and a memorable rendition of 'Ich grolle nicht' from Schumann's *Dichterliebe* by the afore-mentioned tenor section. Although British choirs socialise after services, there was a warmth and artlessness to the evening that was, in my experience, distinctly North American. I was very grateful to have participated in this enjoyable cultural exchange.

June 2019

A Weekend on Lake Erie

Earlier this year I took a brief trip to Cleveland, Ohio for a weekend, in order to play an organ recital and direct a diocesan "Treblefest", a gathering of young choristers from across an extended geographical/ecclesiastical area for a day-long workshop and Evensong. Although taking three days out in the middle of term in the UK had a fairly adverse effect on my inboxes, I had a musically fulfilling time on this flying visit.

The weekend was hosted by Cleveland's Trinity Episcopal Cathedral and by St Paul's Episcopal Church in the inner-ring suburb of Cleveland Heights. Upon arrival, I was collected by Richard Nelson, Professor Emeritus of Music Theory at the Cleveland Institute of Music (CIM), and Director of Children's and Youth Choirs at St Paul's. Rick and I first met several years ago at St Thomas Fifth Avenue in New York City, as he regularly sends girls to the annual Girl Chorister Course of which I am a former director. I stayed at a lovely early-twentieth century boutique hotel near the university (I recommend Glidden House—definitely one of the best breakfasts I have ever eaten).

During the trip, I was struck by just how interconnected the musical world is. Although I had very little free time, I made it a priority to pay a visit to the CIM, a revered institution whose reputation I have known all my life. I was greeted in the foyer by a poster advertising a concert to be given by violinist Malcolm Lowe, who taught my younger brother at the New England Conservatory 20 years ago. The first thing I saw on my visit to the library was the March issue of this august publication [TAO], lying open at the page on which my Cambridge MMus student Christiana Howell's 'UK Report' appeared. I was staying just a stone's throw from Severance Hall, the home of the Cleveland Orchestra, whose Brahms and Beethoven piano concerto recordings with George Szell and Leon Fleisher (with whom I studied 30 years ago) I wore thin with count-less repeated playings as a teenager. That evening I dined with the director of music at St Paul's, the extraordinary Karel Paukert, whose list of friends and colleagues reads like a veritable 'International Who's Who' of the musical world. I was fascinated by his anecdotes about having played and adjudicated with most of the globe's great musicians, including two of my beloved former teachers, neither of whom is still with us, David Sanger and Marek Jablonski. Even in those first few hours, the trip had taken on the form of a nostalgic pilgrimage, and not just a business trip or another freelance gig.

The next day I enjoyed the rare luxury of an uninterrupted six hours organ practice, which took place on St Paul's fabulous 1952 Holtkamp III/47. The instrument is versatile and colourful, and I much enjoyed play-ing it. My programme consisted of music by Bach, Langlais, Vaughan Williams, Franck, and Cecilia McDowall (an anti-Brexit selection from a nationality point of view, with some attempt at gender diversity, as per the promise I made in April's UK Report)[30] and the organ coped successfully with the many and varied styles required. This day of much-appreciated musical solitude was followed by the arrival of 48 girls and boys, ranging in age from six to 16, who travelled from across the region to spend the day singing for me. We had three hours rehearsal time to prepare for Cho-ral Evensong, at which the very supportive diocesan Bishop was the can-tor (that's unusual even in the UK). The music consisted of Simon Lole's *St David's Service* for unison treble voices and organ, my own setting of George Herbert's wonderful poem *Love bade me welcome* (an arrange-ment for two-part treble voices and organ of a lyrical melody composed by a retired Anglican cleric in the Ely diocese). As an aside, both of these

---

30. See April 2019 on page 179.

works are published by Encore Publications, an excellent liturgical music publisher located near Tunbridge Wells, Kent. The introit was Mendelssohn's solo aria 'I will sing of thy great mercies, O Lord' from his oratorio *St Paul*, which works beautifully as a unison anthem, and there were also the requisite liturgical items such as hymns, psalms, and responses.

As I'm sure many readers know, intense day-long workshops or this sort are exhausting for a conductor. The careful balancing of one's 'animateur' side with that of the serious artist is a tiring task, especially with jet lag, and when faced with a sea of unfamiliar faces. In addition, in a group of this age-range, one needs to encourage the diffident and nervous six-year-olds, appeal to the ever-so-cool pre-teens, and cajole the occasionally over-confident high-school pupils, all whilst simultaneously entertaining the visiting conductors observing from the sidelines, clipboards in hand. I was much in need of the G&T which awaited me in the pub after Evensong with members of the local AGO Chapter.

Notwithstanding the over-burgeoning inboxes which greeted my return to the UK, I was delighted to be invited to Cleveland. The children sang beautifully (they even watched me some of the time), the organ was a joy to play (even if I did have to fly across the Atlantic to achieve uninterrupted practice time), and the generous welcome of my hosts was gratefully received. That I was able to recall with gratitude wonderful teachers of my youth, while also forging new musical connections, was an added bonus.

Chapter 6

Composition, Counterpoint, and Choosing Music

From new repertoire to correctly-prepared suspensions, from the much-loved old standards to the expansion of the canon, you will find here a collection of my many columns which have focussed on all things related to choosing liturgical music, perusing new works by young composers, and honing technical skills.

Matching Words and Music

O ne of a conductor's most significant responsibilities is the selection of repertoire. As well as weighing up the musical options, serious consideration needs to be given to liturgical, practical, financial, and educational issues, to name but a few. I also try to incorporate sensible requests from the choir.

Cambridge's academical year consists of three liturgically-named eight-week terms: Michaelmas (October to December), Lent (January to March), and Easter (April to June). In most of the college chapels, music lists are published a term at a time, a convention that necessarily induces liturgical whiplash every vacation. Last week I spent the first few days of Christmas choosing Lenten music, reflecting upon the respective merits of such Passiontide gems as Victoria's *Vere languores* and Leighton's *Solus ad victimam* while the jolly sounds of the *Sussex Carol* emanated from my CD player. By the time March comes round, I'll be choosing Easter and Ascension music in the middle of Holy Week (trying desperately to avoid reading all the "Alleluias").

Despite these complications, my prime concern in choosing a music list has always been liturgical. I am fastidious to a fault in attempting to ensure that the music complements the lessons, and consequently I spend hours reading the sections of the Bible that the lectionary has appointed for the coming term. I experience a pathological satisfaction when a service is completely coherent, both thematically and musically. Indeed, one of the reasons that I welcome input from the choir is to try to encourage them to think about the music in the same way. I indicate the themes of the coming season (for example, Epiphany, Candlemas, Lent) and ask them for requests. I hope that this makes them think about the words in their favourite pieces, as well as simply musical considerations such as the number of suspensions or ninth chords, the presence of English cadences, the frequent occurrence of loud high notes, or whatever else warms the musical cockles of undergraduate hearts.

There are, of course, many obvious connections for the coming Lent term's music list: for Candlemas, a choice can be made between numerous settings of *Senex puerum portabat*; the Conversion of St Paul (25 January) necessitates the inclusion of specifically themed anthems and hymns. Once the options have been narrowed liturgically, the other aforementioned considerations come into play: musical (which of the "Senex" settings do I fancy this year—Palestrina, Victoria, Byrd in four or five parts?), practical (can my young tenors cope with that high B flat? if the piece is not in our repertoire will we have time to learn it? if the piece is longer than six minutes, will we be late for dinner in hall?), financial (if we don't own copies, can we afford to purchase a set?), educational (would Schütz's *Saul, Saul, was verfolgst du mich* provide a good vehicle to teach this year's choir about Baroque style? would the congregation benefit from learning this obscure but lyrical new hymn?).

My liturgical scruples are often sorely tested on more ordinary days, however, especially when the *lectio continuo* appoints lessons which seem out of place at a particular time of year. Next term, just a few days before Ash Wednesday, the second lesson recounts the resurrection of Christ. Last year, we heard about the Magi's journey to Bethlehem rather early, in the middle of November. On those occasions, I try to find more subtle connections with the readings. For the first of these two anomalies, I have chosen Finzi's *Welcome, sweet and sacred feast*, the Richard Crashaw text for which is a reflection on sacrifice, death, and rebirth. Conveniently, one of my choir members requested this piece as well, so I can present my entirely autocratic selection as if it were a caring and thoughtful response to the suggestions of my singers. The kings' appearance in November was satisfactorily paired with Jonathan Dove's masterful *Seek him that maketh the seven stars* which is not an explicitly Epiphany anthem, but which nonetheless reflects upon our desire to seek God, with the astronomical imagery an added coincidence.

Music, although always merely the servant of the liturgy, can nevertheless profoundly illuminate the themes and messages of the lessons, often shedding new light upon them. I hope that just occasionally the choir and congregation might notice (and perhaps even be moved by) the kinds of liturgical and musical connections that we directors of music spend long hours devising. It is not always an easy task, though, and I have to admit to having been stumped by one instance in next term's music list: one of the readings at evensong is from 1 Corinthians 11, the notorious passage in which St Paul exhorts women to be both veiled and silent in church. After much deliberation, I chose the hymn "Jesus, these eyes have never seen" (389 in the New English Hymnal), which contains a reference to seeing God through a veil. If anyone spots this clever allusion and compliments me on it after that particular service, I hereby solemnly promise that I won't reply until I am safely outside the chapel. . . .

So You Want to Write a Fugue

Thus begins the legendary work for SATB voices and piano by the great Canadian pianist Glenn Gould (1932-1982), which I sang as a member of the Ontario Youth Choir many years ago. Gould demonstrates extraordinary technical wizardry and compositional skill in this epic piece, as well as the occasional lapse of good taste. As organists, we play a lot of fugues, but these days not many of us have the urge to write one.

As a teenager enjoying Gould's humorous pastiche, I certainly never envisaged myself writing a fugue. Upon arrival in Cambridge, however, where the composition of fugue was, and continues to be, a compulsory component of an undergraduate Music degree, I soon found myself immersed in the study of this fundamental contrapuntal discipline. Now, several years later, I am on the other side, teaching and examining the current students. As I write, we have just completed the examination season here, and I have spent the past few weeks assessing the fugues written by undergraduates. Inevitably, I was moved to brood upon the role and purpose of this archaic and perhaps antiquated art-form, which for some reason we continue to consider a crucial part of a basic musical education.

Music students in Cambridge enjoy the luxury of weekly small group lessons (called 'supervisions') with a specialist supervisor. Indeed, harmony and counterpoint are considered such important specialist techniques that they are taught in individual supervisions. In the first year of a three-year degree, all undergraduates are taught fugal exposition. Their initial study includes detailed review of dissonance and how to treat it correctly (suspensions, accented and unaccented passing notes, 6/4 chords, etc.); lengthy reflections on tonal and real answers; consideration of, and responses to, prominent dominants; negotiation with, and neutralisation of, modulations; composition of invertible countersubjects and codettas; implementation of redundant entries, and so on. The students also undertake in-depth analysis of the *Well-Tempered Clavier*'s expositions, although (if truth be told), JSB didn't always obey all the rules (see, for example, the F# minor fugue in Book One, where the exposition proceeds in the order Subject, Answer, Subject, *Subject*).

Having mastered the exposition, students go on in the second year to learn how to write the rest of a fugue. They scrutinise structure and overall shape; they learn to navigate sequential modulations through the circle of fifths (and other progressions) between middle entries of the subject in related keys; they discover the perils of modulating too far sharp-wards or flat-wards; they quickly ascertain the usefulness of triple-invertible counterpoint in spinning out the number of bars they are able to present to their supervisors. Once these more basic compositional skills are mastered, the real fun begins, as they begin to experiment with devices like augmentation, diminution, inversion, retrograde, stretto, pedal point, aposiopesis, and other such esoteric musical trickery. At the end of the year, each student is required to submit a fugue as part of a portfolio of pastiche tonal compositions.

In the final year, those who wish to continue studying fugue are tested in the most traditional of ways. Supervisors expect their charges to write one complete fugue on a subject of their own choosing, for each weekly supervision. Assessment of success is based on balancing musical flair and technical dexterity, while dealing with the specific motivic, harmonic, stylistic, and structural challenges and implications of each subject. At the end of the year, the examination (on which the mark for the entire course is based) consists of a four-hour written exam, with a choice of five subjects, a pencil, an eraser, and a pad of manuscript paper. Access to a keyboard is not permitted. Now, if that isn't archaic, I don't know what is.

Archaic or not, the questions remain: is fugue still a useful discipline to teach, and what transferable skills can be gleaned from the arduous learning process? Of course, there are pedagogical benefits. I frequently make use of the abilities I acquired as an undergraduate when I now teach my own students. However, I realise that I also benefited at a less direct level. I regularly write descants, and make arrangements for my choir: in these practical tasks, the lessons I learned about treating dissonance correctly are fundamental. If I am writing an entire piece, an appreciation of the structural constraints of a fugue help me not to wander away from the musical argument, and the development of my own inner ear through the study of fugue as an examined discipline has proved invaluable. Needless to say, an understanding of a fugue's construction aids performance as well. I recently learned Brahms' *Fugue in A flat minor* (WoO 8) for organ, which is a tour-de-force of contrapuntal ingenuity (although some Cambridge examiners might look askance upon the statement of the answer in inversion in the exposition!)—I am sure that my appreciation of its qualities, and my ability to communicate both the detail and the whole to an audience is much keener now than it would have been before I had the courage to write a fugue myself.

In some of the episodic material in Glenn Gould's aforementioned fugue, he sets the words "so just forget the rules and write one". Personally, I would caution you against following this whimsical advice too literally. On the contrary, I am convinced that only a deep and considered understanding of the rules can enlighten both the composition and performance of fugues. It is not enough simply to have the urge to write one—and it is evident from Gould's masterpiece that he knew this too.

Unsolicited Submissions

In the brief lull after Holy Week and Easter, I accomplished something long overdue. On top of the piano in my room in Selwyn College, there is something which I call my "composer pile". It consists of music sent to me by composers, and their agents and publishers, who hope that I might be willing to perform their works with the chapel choir. This Easter Week, astonishingly, I actually managed to reach the bottom of the pile for the first time since last summer.

Selwyn Choir has carved out something of a niche for itself as performers of new music over the years. Under the auspices of London's John Armitage Memorial Trust, we have premièred major works by a host of established composers, including the likes of Jonathan Dove, Paul Patterson, Gabriel Jackson, Judith Bingham, John McCabe, and Tarik O'Regan. In addition, we have brought several new names to the attention of UK audiences, not the least of whom is Paul Mealor, who, although unknown at the moment, will probably be an international superstar by the time you read this, having been commissioned to write a motet for a certain royal wedding. We have also recorded a number of CDs of music by living composers including Colin Mawby, Paul Spicer, Paul Edwards, and Gary Higginson, as well as a cover CD for *Choir and Organ* magazine which featured the music of about twenty young composers. We also perform new liturgical choral music frequently in services, and it is a particular joy when the composer is able to be with us in person for these occasions. Indeed, I had a very pleasant High Table dinner in our college dining hall recently with Cecilia McDowall, after singing her superb Easter anthem *Regina coeli* in Evensong.

It is Selwyn Choir's frequent participation in these musical activities that leads to the existence of my "composer pile". Over the past week, I have divided the scores into three sub-piles: the "shred-and-recycle-asap-for-the-benefit-of-humanity" pile, the "file-for-long-term-storage" pile, and the "actually-this-looks-rather-interesting" pile. So, I found myself reflecting upon what it is that turns an emailed PDF score from a nervous but hopeful young composer, or a "Sample Only" stamped copy from a pushy agent or publisher, into a listing on a service sheet? Or, perhaps more worryingly for the composers, what is it that consigns something to the dreaded shred-and-recycle pile? As well as the indefinable but unavoidable matter of my own personal taste, I consider a number of issues, both practical and intangible.

On a purely practical level, length is crucial: if a setting of the Magnificat is so epic as to last for twenty minutes, we will be late for that High Table dinner. The accompaniment is also important: at Selwyn, we only have an organ available—an accompaniment labelled "harmonium, drums, handbells, and two melody instruments" is not really feasible here. I look for vocally idiomatic writing: an over-abundance of off-the-voice special-effects oo-ings and ah-ings is physiologically tiresome for singers. An understanding of passaggi, vowel formation, and the technical capabilities of the human voice need to have been taken into account. Idiomatic organ writing is a consideration as well. One anthem by an established UK composer (who will remain nameless) opened with a 32nd-note chromatic pedal scale at *Allegro Vivace*, to be played with alternating feet, while simultaneously closing the swell box. That one quickly found its way to the shred-and-recycle pile.

The less tangible considerations are of course more interesting, though also harder to justify. I look for a challenge for the singers and the congregation, and I'm afraid that I enthusiastically shred and recycle anything saccharine, vacuous, pointlessly simplistic, or unimaginative. Conversely, pieces that are unnecessarily obtuse rarely impress me: although my choir members are skilled readers, accustomed to the demands of modern avant-garde choral music, if something is so rhythmically and/or harmonically complex that the musical reward is inversely proportional to the amount of rehearsal time required to master it, then it will not be programmed. Composers need to remember that liturgical choirs, especially those in the UK, prepare services on a very limited amount of rehearsal time (for example, we prepared Cecilia McDowall's anthem from scratch in a total of 25 minutes rehearsal time, which is 15 minutes longer than I normally allocate to the anthem).

My composer pile on an envelope, drawn by 15-year-old Anoushka Sharp. Reprinted with permission.

Personally, I also like to see contrapuntal proficiency: I want to know that the composer understands the correct treatment of dissonance, and doesn't simply plonk down cluster-chords unthinkingly or ignorantly. I like to see a coherent and convincing structure: for example, the highest note in the soprano part, or the 'best' chord in the piece, should be motivated, and occur somewhere significant (the Golden Section, for example), and not appear seemingly by accident in the third bar. Word setting is also crucial: I frequently shred pieces by composers who carelessly apply musical accents to unstressed syl-LA-bles (especially if the language is their mother-tongue). As for the choice of text, my musical adaptation of the old saying "it was a brave man who first ate an oyster" is "it was a brave man who thought that the world needed another setting of John Donne's 'Bring us, O Lord God'". Even another "Drop, drop slow tears" is dangerous: is it good enough to be prioritised on a music list above William Walton, Kenneth Leighton, *and* Orlando Gibbons? If you are competing against an established masterpiece, tread carefully.

Despite sounding rather hard to please, I do love receiving sample scores of new music, and even if it takes me longer than it should to get through the pile, the excitement of finding an undiscovered gem, especially one that might actually enter the repertoire and stay there, always keeps me going. So, if you are a young composer who knows how to choose and set liturgical words, write suspensions and use second-inversion chords correctly, highlight the Golden Section in a work, compose idiomatically for the organ and for the voice—not to mention keeping your musical and emotional expression disciplined enough that it lasts only five minutes—please send me your work. There's an empty space on my piano at the moment, and plenty of High Table dinners waiting to be enjoyed!

September 2011

But Everyone Knows That

That distinctly British institution, the BBC, is rightly celebrated for the quality of its programmes. Some pander to mainstream interests; others focus on the quirky and niche. Given this, I should not have been surprised when I chanced upon a documentary about the composer Charles Hubert Hastings Parry (1848–1918). While Parry is an unexpected subject for prime-time TV, even more remarkable was that the programme was presented by none other than HRH Prince Charles, The Prince of Wales. During the broadcast, Prince Charles discussed the composer's life and music, interviewed academics and performers, and attended rehearsals and concerts. One particular highlight was the pianist and scholar David Owen Norris's perceptive and concise analysis of what is arguably Parry's best-known tune, *Jerusalem* (to William Blake's words "And did those feet in ancient time").

On the day after I watched this documentary, we held our final service of the year in Selwyn College Chapel. Some months earlier (and long before the Royal Wedding in April!), as I was devising the term's music list, I succumbed to a graduating choral scholar's repeated petitions to include Parry's *I was glad* for his last service. This anthem is one of those pieces that everyone knows, therefore I programme it only every few years in order to avoid boredom. Imagine my surprise, then, when I arrived at the rehearsal to discover that about 80% of the choir had never sung it, and indeed, those who hadn't watched the Royal Wedding hadn't even heard of it!

I tried to reassure myself that this was merely an anomaly, but then I had a similar experience at a concert in Ely Cathedral. Billed as an evening of classical favourites, the programme included such well-known pot-boilers as Vivaldi's *Gloria*, Handel's *Zadok the Priest*, and Bach's *Jesu, joy of man's desiring*. The cathedral's Director of Music and I dutifully swallowed our pride before sharing the conducting of these popular classics. Most of the capacity audience loved it, but, afterwards, there was a vociferous objection from one audience member, who complained because he didn't recognise any of the music.

These experiences prompted me to puzzle over the following question: in 2011, which pieces (if any) can safely be classified as belonging to the canon of choral music? I was not shocked that members of Selwyn choir hadn't sung *I was glad* (they are still students, after all), but I certainly didn't expect so many of them not even to know of its existence. They all had a fair amount of choral experience before arriving at Cambridge, so I assumed that they had sung at least some of what I consider to be "standard repertoire". Seemingly, my concept of what constitutes "standard repertoire" is out-dated. So, while they didn't know Parry's *I was glad*, they were thrilled to sing Morten Lauridsen's popular Christmas motet *O magnum mysterium* last December. The times are indeed a-changing.

The media play a role in popularising music, of course. The aforementioned royal wedding has helped to invigorate the career of Paul Mealor, whose commissioned anthem *Ubi caritas* received a healthy audience of over two billion for its première. The Widor *Toccata* has become a favourite recessional with couples due to various televised post-war royal weddings. Music can also enter the public consciousness when it is used in television commercials. Indeed, *Jesu joy of man's desiring* was played on the world's longest xylophone in an advertisement for a Japanese mobile phone company, which "went viral" on YouTube a few months ago (though obviously our disgruntled friend in Ely hasn't seen that one). And here in the UK, Parry's *Jerusalem* has the status of an unofficial national anthem, mainly thanks to cricket and rugby fans "singing" it during matches.

The question remains, though: is there still a body of music that "everyone knows"? In a programme of popular choral classics, *Jesu, joy* and *Zadok* would come close to the top of my list, along with the Vivaldi *Gloria*. Handel's *Messiah* and Fauré's *Requiem* would feature too, with the Mozart *Requiem* in contention (so long as I was sure that the audience was old enough to have seen the film *Amadeus*). Comfortingly, a quick Google search for "famous choral music" produces a recommended Top Ten which includes a number of these works. However, coming in at number seven on this list is Josquin's *Missa Pange Lingua*—undoubtedly a great work, but do members of the general public really hum snippets of it while they are showering in the morning?

Obviously it is partly our responsibility to educate. I choose a broad range of repertoire at Selwyn so that when my singers leave, they have encountered at least a little of everything. I will probably start programming the so-called classics more frequently though, after this Parry experience. A fusty and dogmatic view would dictate that choristers should learn the tradition for its own inherent merit. By contrast, a more forward-looking teacher understands that they need to know the tradition in order that additions to it are placed in context: if one has never sung plainchant, then one cannot understand the foundation of the Duruflé *Requiem*. At the end of Mealor's *Ubi caritas* the quotation of the plainchant (and by implication of Duruflé's motet), is meaningless unless both the chant and the Duruflé are familiar. Similarly, Lauridsen's *O magnum mysterium* can't be fully appreciated without a secure knowledge of the settings of the same text by Victoria, Palestrina, Gabrieli, and Poulenc.

Surely, in this age of instantly-accessible information, our knowledge of the repertoire should be greater than ever? As a teenager I saved for weeks, in order to afford the box set of an early Alfred Brendel Beethoven Piano Sonata cycle. When I finally owned it, I wore out the cassettes with repeated listening, since I was convinced that in order to be a musician, I needed to know those works. If it had been possible in the 1980s simply to perform a Google search for "Brendel Beethoven", I would probably not have listened as attentively as I did. The difficulty of acquiring the knowledge was part of the inspiration and the motivation. Recordings had to be tracked down, ordered from shops, and were often only obtained after weeks of impatient waiting. Today, allegedly experienced choral musicians not only do not know the likes of *I was glad* (let alone the Vivaldi *Gloria)*—even though numerous recordings are available instantly and free—but (and this is worse) they seem to feel no shame that they do not know it.

As for the audiences, of course it is even harder to predict what they will and won't know. It would seem though, that even some of what I always assumed "everyone knew" is no longer known. Indeed, in some ways I rather envy my cantankerous friend in Ely who has never heard the great classics. I would love to be able to hear them again for the first time, in order to re-appreciate their power, beauty, and significance.

One, Two, Three,
Find Your Own Music!

Like many of you, I am a member of various Facebook groups for organists and choir directors. Recently I have noticed a sharp increase in the number of posts from choral conductors asking for advice on repertoire for their choirs. The questions are often posed in the form of a challenge: "I need a short, fun piece for a middle school choir with 43 teenage sopranos and six young bari-tenors; must be secular and jolly. One, Two, Three, GO!" Although I never accept these (slightly patronising) challenges myself, I do sometimes read the suggestions and responses. I have been observing this popular recent trend in social media behaviour for about six months now, on both sides of the Atlantic, so I thought I would muse upon the implications it has for our choral programming, and what it says about our "research methods" these days.

Firstly, it is obvious from the copious numbers of replies that many members of these forums have a great deal of experience and an impressive and comprehensive knowledge of the repertoire. Also they evidently have both the time and the enthusiasm to share that knowledge with those posing the questions, many of whom appear to be at relatively early stages in their careers. The magnanimity of the replies is encouraging, and group members' willingness to share their experiences with their younger colleagues is, of course, laudable. It is also the case that when the search terms include such specific constraints as the afore-mentioned "43 teenage sopranos and six young bari-tenors" the know-how of older colleagues can be incredibly useful, especially in finding non-standard works, or particularly successful, if obscure, arrangements.

The comments make for fascinating reading. I have certainly learned the names of a number of choral arrangers of pop songs, for example, which is a genre I willingly admit to having neglected in my career thus far, mainly because it is rarely liturgically appropriate for a weekday Choral Evensong. Predictably, in this age of unashamed self-promotion, only infrequently does a post go by without at least one self-assured composer contributing a link to one of his or her compositions which allegedly suits the specified criteria perfectly. There are also plenty of inadvertently amusing responses: Benjamin Britten's *Ceremony of Carols* is not really ideal for an elderly community choir of mixed voices; neither Paul Mealor nor Francis Poulenc were appropriate suggestions for someone who specifically requested something "straightforward, with little dissonance, and no *divisi*". In sum, I enjoy reading these posts, partly for my own benefit, and partly for the entertainment value.

However, I do worry that the current generation of young choir directors may not be learning to research repertoire independently, in the way familiar to those of us who grew up before the invention of social media. I recall a reaction which provides some context for my unease: one memorable reply to a particular "One, Two, Three, GO" challenge was "One, Two, Three, You can do all my work for me". This critic was shot down rather unceremoniously in the subsequent comments, which remarked on his lack of generosity, his misunderstanding of this forum as a munificent community of shared knowledge, his inappropriate grumpiness, etc., etc.. If I'm honest though, I was not unsympathetic to his reaction. A recent post from someone looking for "sacred European Romantic era music for mixed chorus" springs to mind: the individual concerned was subsequently astonished to learn that there was a large body of works by the likes of Brahms, Mendelssohn, and Fauré, of which he had been completely unaware.

The internet enables swift and easy access to vast amounts of standard repertoire (scores and recordings), yet people seem increasingly disinclined to explore these works for themselves, preferring to rely instead on recommendations from others. It is the lack of self-motivation and natural curiosity that alarms me. I recall many hours spent as a student playing through (say) the whole of Byrd's *Cantiones Sacrae*, and manually looking up entries for obscure composers in *The New Grove Dictionary of Music and Musicians*. Therefore I can be forgiven (I hope) for finding it baffling that some directors of music seem content to display publicly some of the larger gaps in their knowledge of basic repertoire.

At the risk of sounding old-fashioned, I prefer choral conductors to be independent in choosing music, rather than simply relying on the generosity of their e-friends. It has never been easier to find out what the standard repertoire is, and Facebook may not always be the best option. A simple Google search brings up any number of resources, all of which could save public embarrassment (Brahms, Mendelssohn, and Fauré are hardly obscure composers, nor is their choral music insignificant). Huge numbers of scores are available on cpdl.org and imslp.org, and recordings are available on YouTube and Spotify. Don't wait to be told what to do: be self-sufficient, courageous, and imaginative. Having said that, though, I haven't actually had the courage to post this on any of the forums I belong to—yet!

Nonetheless, it is true that the repertoire-request posts are undoubtedly some of the most popular, and participation in them is widespread and obviously much appreciated. I expect (and indeed hope) that by reflecting upon these matters here I will provoke a number of angry Letters-to-the-Editor. I look forward to reading them. So, ready? One, Two, Three, GO!

January 2017

Highest Praises

I was recently invited to rehearse a local school choir of unchanged girls'
and boys' voices in Years 5 to 8 (equivalent to North American Grades
4 to 7). The children are auditioned informally on joining, rehearse twice
a week, and perform in chapel services and termly concerts. The teacher
who invited me was keen to inform me that although they didn't read
music, they could sing in several parts. I will admit that this information
filled me with less enthusiasm than she anticipated.

I was asked to rehearse one of the pieces on their repertoire list for
the term. I had been specifically charged with improving confidence and
vocal sound, so I looked for music which would allow me to concentrate
on those aspects of their singing. Unfortunately, it quickly became apparent that none of the pieces was going to reveal anything useful about their
voices or their musical potential. My concerns ranged from vocal range
through musical quality and style, and although I risk sounding elitist
(which may well be one of my failings) I was concerned that my own skills
were unlikely to be of much use, even though I was invited precisely to
showcase those skills.

This experience prompted me to reflect upon what conductors should
consider when choosing repertoire for children's choirs, and how the
music a choir sings is inseparable from the quality and nature of the
sound the singers produce. I realise that there are mitigating factors,

especially in schools, including the need to accommodate music from different traditions, and a variety of faiths (or none), but our task to encourage high-quality choral singing does not have to be compromised by these constraints.

The first and most significant concern must be that of range. Treble (i.e., unchanged) voices should be taught as young as possible to use their head voice in a healthy way. Example (a) shows the ranges and average tessituras that I was asked to choose from in the scenario above, whereas example (b) shows an appropriate range and average tessitura for treble voices at this age.

(a)

(b)

There is a worry that children don't want to sing serious music in their head voice, since pop culture dictates that belting vacuous songs of questionable merit leads to stardom. Surely, discouraging this falsehood by choosing good music for our young singers is one of our most important challenges.

We must also avoid repertoire which is incorrectly categorised as being for "upper voices" rather than women's choir (i.e., sopranos and altos). Children should not sing real alto parts, but directors should choose music for trebles or sopranos, either equal parts, or with S1 and S2 parts as appropriate. Once girls' voices start to develop during high school, and the many mezzos and occasional contraltos begin to emerge, SSAA repertoire will be of great use, but at the elementary/junior school level, it is usually unwise to programme it.

As I mentioned above, their conductor took great pride in her choir's ability to sing in parts. I would far rather hear a children's choir sing in unison, with a well-produced *legato* sound, than in any number of complicated parts, whether of appropriate ranges or otherwise. Indeed, in order to work on confidence and vocal sound, as I had been instructed, the fewer parts the better. So many excellent unison pieces exist, and there are any number of solo songs which can be sung chorally. Even with a so-called professional children's choir, unison singing is invaluable.

Choosing high-quality, well-written repertoire by skilled and imaginative composers who understand how to write for children is also crucial. Avoid platitudinous or patronising poetry—children can (and should) be taught to read and understand sophisticated texts as well as any adults. Teach them to have good taste in well-crafted repertoire. Pop Songs and Easy Listening (even when clothed in the guise of classical music) are fine in small doses, but there are still a few vestiges of significance in Bach, Mendelssohn, and Howells as well. Look, for example, at the simpler Handel and Mozart arias, 20th-century song (Vaughan Williams, Ireland, Copland) or the unison works, both sacred and secular, by the likes of Britten, Holst, Bairstow, Fauré, and Stanford. These are all excellent unison repertoire (stylistically, technically, and vocally) for a middle-school-age treble choirs. There are also a number of useful treble voice liturgical anthologies published by Novello (the 'High Praise' volumes)[31] and the RSCM (the English anthem collections).[32]

Last, but far from least, *teach them to read*. It would be inexcusable to send a child to school for five years to have them only able to recite things that they had learned by rote. Why is this acceptable in a choral situation? Teaching children to read music is not impossible,[33] and, as with any language, the earlier they start learning, the easier it will be for them—and for their teachers.

In the end, you'll be relieved to know that my rehearsal with the aforementioned school choir was successful. After warm-up exercises which concentrated on improving vocal sound, I taught them a new hymn tune (not by rote), and then I worked on performance confidence in the most competently-composed of their pieces—but the melody only (not the alto parts), and I transposed it up a minor third.

---

31. High Praise Vols I & 2, Novello & Co. London, 1998 and 2004
32. The English Anthem Collection Vol. 2, RSCM, Salisbury. 1995.
33. See March 2013 on page 10 for an example of my own practice.

December 2019

Last-Minute Arrangements

Well, the Silly Season has arrived—indeed, it's possible that you aren't even reading this until after Epiphany. Advent and Christmas in our business are hard work. If your December is anything like mine, you'll rarely see your house in daylight, you'll often arrive home several hours after your partner/spouse/roommate/children (delete as appropriate) has/have gone to bed, but you'll nonetheless need at least another hour yourself to wind down before you are able to sleep, your body buzzing with adrenaline, and your head spinning with festive fragments of the music you have just conducted, sung, or played.

As a rule, Americans tend to do their music programming a lot further in advance than Brits. I am always rather disconcerted by the late-summer Facebook posts from my organist friends in the States proudly advertising music lists for the whole of the forthcoming year. In Cambridge, our music lists are usually published three times a year in order to coincide with the three academic terms; cathedrals' music lists are normally announced monthly; large parish churches often appear in liturgical chunks (e.g., "Michaelmas Day to Advent" or "Ash Wednesday to Passiontide").

What is reassuringly consistent across many of the UK's liturgical institutions' published music lists is that the specifics of the big services (Advent Processions, Epiphany Carol Services, etc.) are left until much later to plan in detail. So although my Michaelmas Term music list indicates exactly which psalm chant we are using on the Tuesday in Week Seven, and music is changed only *in extremis* (e.g., the entire bass section has gone down with the flu, so you have to sing Philip Moore's Second Service rather than his Third, and you really hope that no-one notices), for what are arguably the most popular services of the term, the choir's various appearances for Advent and Christmas, the music list simply says "Advent Procession with Carols" or "College Carol Services". I am free to leave the specifics of these significant events until either the photocopying of the service sheet or the need to rehearse the choir are looming uncomfortably.

Choral Eucharist 6:30pm	CANTICLES	A hymn for St Cecilia – Malcolm Archer	When in our music – Engelberg
Eve of St Cecilia	VOLUNTARY	Resurrection Fanfare – June Nixon	
Sunday 24 November	INTROIT	Crown of roses – Tchaikovsky	PSALM
Choral Evensong 6pm	RESPONSES	Sumsion	24 – Tone VIII.1
CHRIST THE KING	CANTICLES	Sarah MacDonald in A flat	SP
Sunday next before Advent	ANTHEM	The Lord reigns – Richard Allain	254 – Paderborn
	VOLUNTARY	Hymne d'action de grâce (Te Deum) – Langlais	267 – Guiting Power
Tuesday 26 November	RESPONSES	Sumsion	PSALM
Choral Evensong 6:30pm	CANTICLES	Stanford in B flat	3 – SEAM after Purcell
	ANTHEM	Round me falls the night – Annabel Rooney	
	VOLUNTARY	Rockingham – Parry	
Thursday 28 November	RESPONSES	Sumsion	PSALM
Choral Evensong 6:30pm	CANTICLES	Rachel Portman in G	80 – Peterson
	ANTHEM	O radiant dawn – James MacMillan	NEH
	VOLUNTARY	Conditor alme siderum – Dupré	6 – Bristol
Sunday 1 December 6pm			
ADVENT SUNDAY	ADVENT PROCESSION WITH CAROLS		
Tuesday 3 December	RESPONSES	Byrd	PSALM
Choral Evensong 6:30pm	CANTICLES	Sixth Service – Weelkes	82 – Martin
	ANTHEM	Rorate coeli – Byrd	
	VOLUNTARY	Cannaris (Suite in D minor) – Elisabeth Jacquet de la Guerre	
Thursday 5 December 6:45pm			
Sunday 8 December 6pm	COLLEGE CAROL SERVICES *(ticketed)*		
Tuesday 10 December 7pm			

Canon Hugh Shilson-Thomas MA *Dean of Chapel & Chaplain*   The Revd Roger Revell MA ThM *Assistant Chaplain*
Sarah MacDonald MA FRCO ARSCM *Director of Music*   John Trotter DMA *Visiting Bye-Fellow in Music*
Michael Stephens-Jones ARCO *Senior Organ Scholar* | Yvette Murphy *Junior Organ Scholar* | Matthew Nicholls BA MMus *Student-on-attachment*

Last year, I chose a programme for our carol services and concerts which was unashamedly European—a sort of Anti-Brexit-Carol-fest, if you like. I chose a selection of my favourite Old World carols in a selection of languages, including English, Latin, French, German, and Spanish. I then looked for appropriate arrangements: they needed to be for unaccompanied mixed voices (one of our venues had no keyboard instrument); our rehearsal time, in typical UK fashion, was extremely limited (difficult esoteric/academic arrangements were therefore impractical). As you all know, there is far too much musical choice available at any time of the year, let alone at Christmas. However, despite the fact that publishers, composers, and arrangers had sent me literally hundreds of new carols to peruse, I actually couldn't find what I needed, with the various constraints adequately met. And so I had to resort to producing unaccompanied, SATB not-too-difficult-but-still-interesting-and-singable arrangements of *Riu, riu chiu, Quelle est cette odeur agréable*, and the medieval English carol *Gaudete*, before the following Wednesday. Fortunately, these traditional carols are all in the public domain, so were fair game from an arranging point of view.

As a teenager and university student, I was never one of those people to whom harmony and counterpoint came easily, either on paper or at the keyboard. I had to work hard to develop any fluency, but when I found myself faced with the need to produce three arrangements in 72 hours, I was grateful for the rigour of my very old-fashioned Cambridge degree, since these sorts of last-minute arrangements require technique. I have realised over the years that composition and arranging are not fundamentally about inspiration, or mysticism, or genius. Instead they are about technique, rigour, and constraints. The more of the latter there are, the fewer options there are, and therefore the task is easier.

So, despite the fact that there is already too much music out there, if you find yourself needing to arrange or compose something that doesn't exist yet, don't be afraid—but first, make sure that you have honed your technique. You need to study harmony and counterpoint; learn how to manipulate and develop pre-existing material; ensure that stressed linguistic syllables occur on strong musical beats; handle dissonances correctly; be able to prepare/strike/resolve a suspension; know when—and more importantly, when not—to use second inversion (or 6/4) chords; structure pieces coherently; allow external constraints to provide positive inspiration for your creativity. And in the UK especially, you need to be able to work quickly.

The late Sir David Willcocks (1919–2015) was an extraordinary technician, and around the world we especially associate his arrangements and descants with Christmas. His arrangement of *Tomorrow shall be my Dancing Day*[34] was a very fine example of technique at work—and quickly: the copies, still purple and wet from the mimeograph machine, arrived in front of the choristers and choral scholars just minutes before that year's live radio broadcast of 'Nine Lessons and Carols'. Perhaps we can't all hope to be quite as imaginative as Sir David, but we can certainly work hard to ensure that our technique is sound, and that when we are stuck, we can fill gaps quickly and efficiently. A very merry last-minute-arranging to you all!

---

34. in *Carols for Choirs 2*, ed. David Willcocks and John Rutter. Oxford. 1970.

July 2021

A Promulgation of Publishers

Earlier this year, I was commissioned to compose a hymn to words by Justin Welby, the Archbishop of Canterbury. The text, from a BBC interview where he reflected on the pandemic, grief, hope, and the resurrection, required minimal adaptation to render them into a rhymed, metrical poem, designed for congregational singing. The tune ('Hope', 7676 with refrain) is tuneful and memorable, and its first recording received many favourable comments on social media and YouTube, for which I was grateful. It is published by Encore Publications, one of the UK's most highly-respected independent liturgical music publishers, and is available in an inexpensive edition for choir (with harmony and descant) and congregation (with a license for printing in orders of service). Here ends the opportunistic plug. . . .

In fact, an unexpected barrier to the hymn's performance in the States actually gave me the idea for this month's column. One of my American friends wanted to use the hymn for an online reading session with his state choral directors' association. However, he was told that the (large, well-known, international) distributor responsible for providing repertoire for that session "would not work with Encore". While this is probably shorthand for "we don't have time to negotiate with a small unknown publisher, for the sake of one short piece," it did nonetheless sound unhelpfully limiting, given the wealth of repertoire available from

Encore which is ideally suited to liturgies of all denominations. And so I thought I would spend a column introducing TAO readers to a selection of independent choral and organ music publishers in the UK, and particularly those who publish music by the many musicians like myself who write practical liturgical music on a daily basis. I hope that this might help some of the excellent music available here to make its way over the pond, where I have no doubt it would be both useful and appreciated by church musicians and congregations alike.

Firstly, it is important to remember that just because a publishing house isn't represented by a major distributor doesn't mean that they don't publish excellent music. (Conversely, just because a publisher *is* represented by a distributor it does not necessarily follow that every piece they promote is of good quality.) Many small independent publishers don't have the resources to sell their wares aggressively, even in non-pandemic times. They may have only two or three members of staff, all of whom are specialist musicians, music engravers and type-setters, and often composers themselves. They don't employ someone to send daily marketing emails around the world, or to maintain a high-profile social media presence. Indeed, aggressive marketing campaigns are sometimes associated with inadequate editions (typos, missing accidentals, impractical page-turns, low-quality production values), if a company's priority appears to be profit rather than quality of product.

Below is a suggested list of independent UK publishers, all of whom specialise in choral and organ music, promoting particularly the music of contemporary composers and church musicians. I've listed one additional interesting feature for each. Look them up and order some perusal copies, which will enable you to judge production value as well as musical quality. Normally it shouldn't take more than a week to 10 days for a set of copies to be shipped across the Atlantic, and many of the publishers can also provide sample PDFs by email (though in my experience, choir members prefer to sing from a real copy rather than a photocopy, even when the latter is legally purchased and produced from a publisher-provided PDF). There has been something of a "second renaissance" in choral music recently, with many contemporary composers turning their hands to writing for choirs. Those who are church musicians themselves also understand the need to write practical music that is effective liturgically, and can be performed well by amateur singers on limited rehearsal time. This list is certainly not exhaustive, but it aims to give readers an idea of the options:

Banks Music Publications, Yorkshire; established 1972
—https://www.banksmusicpublications.co.uk/
  • also has a print-to-order service for many out-of-print choral titles

Chichester Music Press, Hampshire; established 2003
—http://chichestermusicpress.co.uk/
  • also has a "print personalised manuscript paper" feature for those who still write by hand

Encore Publications, Kent; established 1992
—https://www.encorepublications.com/
  • publishes many works heard at major royal and national occasions, including James Vivian's new arrangement of 'Eternal Father, strong to save' sung at the funeral of HRH the Duke of Edinburgh

Kevin Mayhew, Suffolk; established 1976
—https://www.kevinmayhew.com/
  • vast catalogue of hymns, choral, organ music, as well as devotional and theological books

Multitude of Voyces, Wiltshire; established 2017
—https://www.multitudeofvoyces.co.uk/
  • not-for-profit charity which publishes the ground-breaking and acclaimed anthologies of liturgical choral music by women composers

RSCM Press, Wiltshire; established 1927
—https://www.rscm.org.uk/our-resources/music-publishing/
  • extensive liturgical resources including hymns, anthems, service music with composers represented from the renaissance to the present day

There are also the larger publishing houses such as Boosey & Hawkes, Chester, Faber, Novello, OUP, Peters, and Stainer & Bell which publish much of the received canon of liturgical music, as well as the music of their own living "house composers". Most of these do have agreements with major international distributors, so their music is easier to source outside the UK. In addition, there are also many very fine composers who choose to self-publish.

I hope this has piqued your curiosity, and that you find some wonderful music that might have been overlooked by the big distributors. (And as an added bonus for me, maybe you might even like to look at my new hymn!)

Chapter 7

'Very Few Female Composers'

In this chapter you will find a selection of essays dedicated to expanding the canon, in particular with reference to the inclusion of music by female composers, both historical and contemporary, in liturgical music lists. The publication of Multitude of Voyces' groundbreaking anthologies, as well as a number of other initiatives by organisations such as the Women's Sacred Music Project, A Great Host of Composers, and my own series with Selah Publishing, will (I hope) put to bed the erroneous notion that female composers either do not exist, or that their music is difficult to find/programme/sing.

April 2019

"Very Few Female Composers . . ."

In 2016, a 17-year-old British student in Year 12 (equivalent to Grade 11) realised that the listening syllabus for her A-level Music exam consisted of 63 pieces from the western classical canon written entirely by male composers. A disappointing response to her letter to the chair of the examining body ("Given that female composers were not prominent in the western classical tradition (or others for that matter), there would be very few female composers that could be included.")[35] spurred her on to write to the then parliamentary Education Secretary, and to initiate a major online petition. In response to the significant media attention that her actions prompted, that syllabus has now changed, and 12 of the 63 composers are women—just under 20%.

A year or so later, BBC Radio 3 (the UK's primary classical music station) began to scrutinise their programming list more closely, partly in response to composer Judith Bingham's regular trawling through playlists. Despite 24-7 broadcasting, entire weeks could pass without a single woman composer being broadcast. Agents and publishers have not helped. A quick count of three of the UK's biggest music publishers gives percentages of women amongst their "house composers" as follows: 19%, 12%,

---

35. https://www.theguardian.com/education/2015/dec/16/a-level-music-female-composers-students-campaign-jessy-mccabe-edexcel

8%[36]—and that's just publishing houses that deal with living composers. Even allowing for historical and cultural discouragement (think of Fanny Mendelssohn, who had to publish her own music under her brother's name[37]) the imbalance is notable. There have been equal numbers of students studying music (including composition) to degree level at UK universities for several decades now, so the continued lack of representation is perplexing.

In the Lent Term 2019, a group of Cambridge undergraduates organised the Cambridge Female Composers Festival.[38] The entire university was involved, with collegiate, community, and university choirs, orchestras, instrumentalists, and singers participating in concerts, recitals, and services throughout the term. There were also lectures, pre-concert talks, and a composition workshop and competition, as well as a fascinating "blog" with contributions from musicians around the university on a variety of topics.[39]

The concerts during the festival included a wide variety of styles and performers. I was honoured to conduct the launch concert, which included two large-scale works by Lili Boulanger (1893–1918) the first woman to win the prestigious Prix de Rome: the *Vielle prière Bouddhique*, and her monumental setting of Psalm 130, *Du fond de l'abîme*. Choral works by four contemporary British composers were also featured, namely Judith Weir (b.1954), Judith Bingham (b.1952), Hannah Kendall (b.1984), and Cecilia McDowall (b.1951). I also accompanied one of my choral scholars in a recital which included songs by Clara Schumann (1819–1896), Elizabeth Poston (1905–1987), Madeleine Dring (1923–1977), and Lili's older sister Nadia Boulanger (1887–1979). In addition, performances across Cambridge included a cantata by Elisabeth Jacquet de la Guerre (1665–1729), a string quartet by Florence Price (1887–1953), a recital of Moroccan Jewish women's

36. Oxford University Press, Edition Peters, and Boosey & Hawkes, calculated in February 2019

37. https://en.wikipedia.org/wiki/Fanny_Mendelssohn

38. This was renamed the Minerva Festival in 2020, after the Roman goddess of wisdom and justice.

39. https://www.minervafestival.com/

traditional songs, a piano recital featuring repertoire by Germaine Tailleferre (1892–1983) and Amy Beach (1867–1944), orchestral music by Joan Tower (b.1938) and Cécile Chaminade (1857–1944), and an organ recital with music by Sofia Gubaidulina (b.1931) and two current Cambridge undergraduates.

The liturgical contribution to the festival will probably be of particular interest to readers of this report. Several college chapels, including my own, agreed to host a special service of Choral Evensong or Choral Eucharist which included only women composers. In addition, one college choir managed to ensure that there was at least one woman composer featured in every single service they sang this term. The fact that I am impressed by this feat, despite being a published female composer myself, says something about the well-established gender bias. Finding anthems and solo organ music was relatively straightforward. The more functional liturgical works were rather less easy to source. There are a number of canticle settings, a handful of mass settings, and four published sets of Preces and Responses for mixed voices. Interestingly, the place where we all struggled most was with that most esoteric of compositional genres, the Anglican psalm chant. It turns out that I myself am one of the few living female composer to have written any. According to the National Archive of Anglican Chant, there are a number of 19th-century chants by women, but if they were published, they appeared under the composer's husband's name.

This festival has raised real awareness in Cambridge, a university which is still significantly male-dominated, especially in the musical sphere. I am not a crusader for this cause. Ironically, I am perfectly capable of unwittingly writing an entire term's music list with only male composers on it—but I intend to be more careful in future. Perhaps I could encourage you to do the same. Next time you need a setting of "Ascendens Christus in altum" why not programme Raffaella (Victoria) Aleotti (c.1570–c.1646), rather than Palestrina? Or how about the lovely "The Holly and the Ivy" arrangement by June Nixon (b.1942) rather than one by John Rutter? It is so much easier to do this now, as so many young musicians, both male and female, are researching this field and publicising their findings, not to mention mounting ambitious festivals in age-old institutions like this one. If we, the older generations are able to help and inspire up-and-coming generations with our own programming, then perhaps fewer gifted female composers will have to publish under their brothers' or husbands' names in future.

Silent in the Churches Part I

There is an unexpected irony in the title of the next three columns, since nearly everyone is "silent in the churches" as I write (spring 2020—you'll remember it, I expect). I contemplated abandoning the series and writing instead about the potential psychological and musical effects of a hypothetical global pandemic, but I preferred the illusion of normality that was provided by discussing the historical neglect of female composers on liturgical music lists.

This month's report is the first in a three-part mini-series based on a lecture I gave recently in Cambridge. The subject, which has become an unexpected specialism for me, is that of liturgical choral music by women. I hope that this will address the frequent requests on social media for related resources. Whilst I am delighted to see these recurring queries, there is an element of reinventing the wheel every time the same links have to be provided again and again. The comments indicate a growing interest in this topic, but also a lack of knowledge about how to find repertoire. In each of these columns, I will introduce selected composers in detail, and provide pointers for independent research.

The title of my lecture was gently though intentionally provocative. I chose a quotation from 1 Corinthians 14—"silent in the churches". In the NRSV, verse 34 reads as follows: "Women should be silent in the churches. For they are not permitted to speak, but should be subordinate, as the law also says". This sentence (and others like it) has been used for centuries to justify the church's refusal to allow women to contribute to public worship. Ironically, most scholars agree that this particular passage was not written by St Paul at all, but was a later interpolation by a different writer or scribe.[40] Amongst various grammatical and exegetical propositions substantiating this claim is the indisputable fact that in several important early sources, verses 34–35 appear in the margins or at the end of the chapter, rather than between verses 33 and 36. Nonetheless, whether it is strictly Pauline or not, the use of such passages as ammunition over two thousand years for the suppression of women in the church is undisputed.

More recently, although there has been a rise in the visible presence of women in liturgical leadership, both clerical and musical, there is one place where they are still noticeably neglected, namely on music lists. Recent research in Oxford University found that in the 2018-19 academical year, just 2.02% of the music sung in their college chapels was by female composers—slightly lower than the percentage of works by William Byrd that were sung in the Michaelmas (first) Term alone. The three choral foundations, each of which sings seven services a week, managed only one piece each by a woman, out of a total of about 1750 named composers programmed liturgically over the year. A similar study is currently ongoing in UK cathedrals—it remains to be seen whether they fare any better. I would like to think that were such a survey taken of Cambridge chapels, we might demonstrate rather more diversity than Oxford, and this would owe significant credit to the annual student-run festival celebrating female and non-binary composers.

Western classical music originates in the sacred monophonic music of the Roman church, now known as Gregorian Chant, which developed gradually over the church's first millennium. The various repertoires which were received and standardised during the reign of Pope Gregory I (hence "Gregorian") include multifarious musical, liturgical,

40. For a comprehensive and clear summary of the research, see this post from the University of Edinburgh's former Professor of New Testament Language, Literature, and Theology, Professor Larry Hurtado (1943-2019): https://larryhurtado.wordpress.com/2017/09/23/paul-and-1-corinthians-1434-35/.

and geographical influences. As well as the many traditional melodies, there were individual composers of sacred monophony, the most famous of whom was—perhaps surprisingly—a woman, namely Hildegard von Bingen (1098–1179). Hildegard was a German Benedictine abbess, mystic, philosopher, composer, and visionary. During her lifetime, she founded two monasteries, invented a language, and wrote medicinal, theological, and liturgical texts, as well as being a prolific composer. Over 150 of her musical works have survived, including individual songs and liturgical drama. She was canonised by the pope in 2012. Hildegard's music is melodically wide-ranging and highly melismatic, and she set her own words. It is widely available in its original monophonic form, and is very effective sung by a soloist over a simple choral drone (in fifths and octaves). Modern transcriptions of her works can be found on the website of the Hildegard Society.[41]

It is generally accepted that the development of polyphony in 12th-century Notre Dame marks the official birth of the western classical canon. The genre developed over the next few centuries, flourishing in particular during the 1500s and 1600s. Much of the repertoire was written to be sung in monasteries, cathedrals, and Oxbridge chapels, all of which were, of course, entirely male. However, there was also a wealth of polyphony written by nuns for use in convents, much of which is only being rediscovered and edited now. In many cases, if it was published during the composer's lifetime, it was done so anonymously, which makes it harder to source and attribute.

Some of this repertoire has a small compass (the measurement of the interval from the lowest note of the bottom part to the highest note of the top part) which seems to restrict it to performance by women's voices only (i.e., it could never appear on mainstream liturgical music lists). This is the case with the male monastic composers' repertoire too of course, and yet Palestrina's *Missa Aeterna Christi munera* (for example) which has a limited compass indicating that it should be sung by men's voices (i.e., ATB), is often performed by full SATB choirs. Leonora d'Este (1515–1575), daughter of the notorious Lucrezia Borgia, wrote glorious florid polyphony, and

41. http://www.hildegard-society.org/p/music.html#Manuscripts

although her music is particularly suitable to women's choirs, some judicious transposition can open it up to mixed choirs as well. Editions of her music can be obtained from Professor Laurie Stras at the University of Southampton. Musica Secreta's stunning recording "Lucrezia Borgia's daughter" is available on Spotify.[42] One composer whose music is readily available on cpdl.org in modern editions suitable for mixed-voice choirs is Raphaella Alleotti (c.1570–c.1546).[43] Her anthems are both beautiful and technically fluent, and provide a refreshing alternative to Palestrina and Victoria.

I hope this has pointed you in the direction of some useful resources for the first 1500 years of church music. Tune in next month for coverage of the 17th, 18th and 19th centuries; the July column will address the 20th and 21st centuries.

Where to Start: A List of Anthologies and Resources

MULTITUDE OF VOYCES ANTHOLOGIES
(distributed by Stainer & Bell; available through Cliff Hill Music)
    1—SATB anthems (publ. 2019)
    2—SSA anthems (publ. April 2020)
    3—Christmas music (publ. November 2020)
    4—Music for Lent and Holy Week (forthcoming 2023)

THE SARAH MACDONALD CHORAL SERIES (Selah Publishing Co., Inc., Pittsburgh)
12-15 titles every January and June, inaugurated January 2020

GOOGLE SPREADSHEET (hosted by @oneequalmusic on Twitter)
https://docs.google.com/spreadsheets/d/1J8soqFKyeDAx4G9b2vxVT21Oy4qsb57SCv4014BLdRg/edit#gid=1207640246

FEMALE COMPOSER SEARCH (on cpdl.org)
http://www1.cpdl.org/wiki/index.php/Category:Women_composers

---

42. https://open.spotify.com/album/09cGO09uvbIuQVvdmnKalG
43. http://www1.cpdl.org/wiki/index.php/Sacrae_cantiones_(Raffaella_Aleotti)

A GREAT HOST OF COMPOSERS
https://www.greathostcomposers.org

AMPLIFY FEMALE COMPOSERS
https://www.amplifyfemalecomposers.org

June 2020

Silent in the Churches Part II

C ontinuing on from last month, which dealt with female liturgical
composers of the early church through the Renaissance, in this
month's I will consider the 17th through the 19th centuries.

A rich source for unearthing forgotten compositions by women is
the archives of European convents. The number of such works now readily available on cpdl.org and imslp.org is increasing rapidly, as academic
study in this field is popular. For example, Maria Xaveria Peruchona's
(1652–c.1709) music, published in Milan in 1675, is florid, virtuosic, and
Baroque, and extremely enjoyable to sing. A basic modern transcription
can be found on imslp.org, and a scholarly performing edition of one
of her anthems is available in the Multitude of Voyces anthology distributed by Stainer and Bell.[44] The beautiful works of Chiara Margarita
Cozzolani (1602–c.1677) and Isabella Leonarda (1620–1704) are available in editions suitable for mixed voices on cpdl.org. A number of works
by Caterina Assandra (1590–1618) which can be found on imslp.org
are appropriate for upper voices. Like the well-known treble duets and
trios by Dering, Couperin, and Marcello which were immortalised by
Oxford University Press in the 1970s,[45] the two- and three-part pieces

---

44. https://stainer.co.uk/shop/mov1/
45. *Anthems for Choirs 2*. ed. Philip Ledger. Oxford. 1973.

in Assandra's 1609 collection are scored for equal voices with continuo accompaniment (suitable for the organ or the piano), and are easily as musically satisfying as the ubiquitous *Give ear unto me*.

When asked to list female composers of classical music, even non-specialists name Clara Schumann (wife of the more famous Robert), and Fanny Mendelssohn (sister of the more famous Felix). Fanny was a prodigiously gifted pianist as a child, and apparently could play much of the *Well-Tempered Clavier* from memory by the age of just 13. A number of her early compositions were published under her younger brother's name. She was educated at the Sing-Akademie in Berlin, whose leader once paid her the highest of all compliments: in a letter to the poet Goethe, he wrote that "she plays like a man".[46] Unfortunately, despite her significant gift, Fanny, as a woman was not allowed to have a career, and her potential was undoubtedly never fully realised. Her father put this very succinctly to her in a letter in 1820: "Music will perhaps become his [i.e., Felix's] profession, while for you it can and must be only an ornament."[47] Although the majority of her music was instrumental or secular song, the Lieder with sacred texts lend themselves well to SATB arrangement, or to unison children's voices, or to solo performance where that occurs in the liturgy.

A little later in the 19th century, two extraordinary sisters were born in Paris: Nadia (1887–1979) and Lili Boulanger (1893–1918). Lili was the first woman to win the prestigious Prix de Rome, and Nadia was arguably the most influential teacher of the 20th century (her numerous students included Daniel Barenboim, Lennox Berkeley, Aaron Copland, Ástor Piazzolla, Walter Piston, John Eliot Gardiner, Gerre Hancock, and Philip Glass).[48] Much of their music can be found on imslp.org (though Nadia's is not yet in the public domain in Canada or Europe), and I would particularly commend to you Lili's *Pie Jesu* and Nadia's *Prière* or *Cantique*, the former of which can be sung as a unison anthem by treble voices

---

46. Carl Friedrich Zelter to Johann Wolfgang von Goethe. February 1831. Referenced in Todd, R. Larry. *Fanny Hensel: the other Mendelssohn*. Oxford 2009.

47. Letter from Abraham Mendelssohn Bartholdy to Fanny Mendelssohn on 16 July 1820. Published in Hensel, Mendelssohn, et al. *The Mendelssohn Family (1729-1847 from Letters and Journals*. New York 1881.

48. https://en.wikipedia.org/wiki/Nadia_Boulanger

and organ, and the latter two of which would both work well with a solo professional soloist and piano.

Meanwhile in England, the time of Victoriana and Edwardiana was in full swing, as the likes of Stanford, Elgar, and Vaughan Williams made their indelible mark on liturgical music lists of the next 150 years. During the 20th century, women such as Ethel Smyth (1858–1944), Elizabeth Poston (1905–1987), and Imogen Holst (1907–1984), in the UK, and Amy Beach (1867–1944), Florence Price (1899–1952), and Undine Smith Moore (1904–1989) contributed significantly to their musical landscapes, but only Elizabeth Poston's definitive setting of *Jesus Christ the Apple Tree* (1967) entered the canon. The majority of these women's music languishes in county archives, and Florence Price's music came perilously close to being lost completely.[49]

Many of these women were prodigiously talented musicians at very young ages. Many of them were also hampered in their careers by attitudes similar to that which held back Fanny Mendelssohn. After Amy Beach's marriage at the age of 18, she was forced to limit her public appearances, and much of her further development as a composer was of necessity self-taught, as her husband objected to her studying with a tutor. Imogen Holst was another composer with a more-famous male relative (her father, Gustav). She is remembered merely as an administrator and writer, despite being an accomplished and award-winning composer and conductor, and most of her music remains unedited and unperformed. Beautiful, practical, singable liturgical works by each these women, as well as Fanny Mendelssohn, Clara Schumann, and Lili Boulanger, (and many more) can be found in the anthologies published by Multitude of Voyces.[50] If you haven't already ordered them for your choirs, I urge you to do so. Tune in next month for a discussion of that rare and important thing: the Living (Female) Composer.

49. https://en.wikipedia.org/wiki/Florence_Price#Rediscovery_of_works
50. https://stainer.co.uk/shop/mov1/

August 2020

Silent in the Churches Part III

A s some of you know, I am an inveterate Completer-Finisher. Having set out to write a three-column series on where to find liturgical
choral music written by women, I am determined to see out the task, and
not even a global pandemic posing an existential threat to our health, our
livelihoods, and even our entire field will stop me. I have faith that we
will be singing again at some point soon (how can any of us do anything
other than have faith at this time?), so this column will eventually have
a practical purpose as well as satisfying my awkward character quirks.
The past two columns dealt with historical composers; this one addresses
contemporary composers.

Until relatively recently, music history was hampered by the vestiges
of the influential E. T. A. Hoffmann (1776–1822), who opined early in
the 19th century that instrumental music (or absolute) music was superior
to vocal (or programmatic) music, since it did not require the assistance
of another art (words).[51] Indeed, the phrase "not just a choral composer"
is still used as an apologia both about and by those whose primary output has been choral music (and you can, of course, substitute the word
"conductor" for "composer"). Perhaps in attempt to counter this, a school
of rather impractical choral music arose during the middle of the 20th

---

51. Hoffmann, Ernst Theodor Amadeus, first published in *Allgemeine Musikalische Zei-
tung* (xii. Jahrgang, No. 40, July 4, 1810)

century, with vocally difficult, aurally challenging, and sometimes esoteric repertoire suitable only for professional adult choirs, and which wasn't written to enhance divine worship. Consequently, the number of living composers on the average parish music list was usually vanishingly small.

Fortunately, over the past few decades, choral composition has experienced something of a second renaissance with the emergence of the so-called Choral Ecstatic Style. This genre "has captured the imagination of church- and concert-goers, . . . [and] can be summarised as timeless, spacious, and rapturous, with an innate depth of visionary and transcendental spirituality. These features have led to the simple, but apposite, description of the 'Ecstatic Style'."[52] There is now a large repertoire of choral music, which is beautiful, liturgically effective, skilfully and imaginatively written, and—most importantly—singable on limited rehearsal time. The musical language could be described as pan-consonant, though our definition of 'consonance' has expanded somewhat since the music of early-16th century England to which that term is normally applied. For the likes of Robert Fayrfax (1464–1521) and John Taverner (1490–1545) fifths, thirds, sixths, and octaves combining to create what we now think of as major or minor triads delimited consonance. In the contemporary idiom, composers take liberties, deploying lush, colourful harmonies with non-traditional added-chord notes, often influenced by jazz. The music is also characterised by a regular use of silence and space, which makes it particularly effective liturgically, and in large resonant acoustics. Although it isn't all slow-moving and meditative, the music has been categorised under the affectionate term "Holy Minimalists" (think of the late John Tavener (1944–2013), whose name is not infrequently confused with that of his Tudor predecessor).

By now, I expect you'll have noticed that I have only mentioned male composers thus far. This is deliberate, and is intended to put the column into context—and yes, I am aware of the irony in this sentence. The fact that it remains necessary to contextualise this topic in such a way is unfortunate: it's Fanny Mendelssohn, Clara Schumann, and Imogen Holst all

---

52. Gary Cole, liner notes for Regent Records "Eternal Ecstasy", REGCD REGCD427, Choir of Selwyn College, Cambridge, 2015

over again. Unfortunately, it is still the case that the highest profile names in contemporary composition are male. It would be wonderful if at least 51% of the most commonly-heard names were female or non-binary; if it weren't considered an insurmountable challenge to "name ten female composers" on Twitter (posted most recently in May 2020); if there weren't the need for Facebook posts asking "where can I find sacred choral music by female composers" (posted most recently in February 2020). I hope it will not surprise you to know that there are plenty of outstanding female composers who are writing music which is extremely beautiful, effective, and performable. See below for a personal and definitely not comprehensive list of names to investigate as a starting point at least.

I would like to conclude this three-column series with the following thought: lest there be any concern, I'm all in favour of dead white men, and I don't object at all to the western classical canon—or our niche fraction of it, the Anglican liturgical choral canon—as it has been received and passed on. However, there is a great deal of wonderful but neglected repertoire out there which deserves to be unearthed, researched, edited, and, most importantly, performed. I hope that eventually these overlooked female composers will find their places on liturgical music lists alongside— i.e., not replacing—Palestrina, Brahms, Stanford, and Leighton. On the other hand, if eventually some of the more forgettable workmanlike fare which makes regular appearances on liturgical music lists (Charles Hylton Stewart in F, C. S. Lang in C) is replaced by something better by a woman, then surely that is a good thing. It would be refreshing to see a gradual rebalancing of liturgical music lists everywhere, giving voice to generations of women who have been "silent in the churches" for far too long.

Where to Start: A List of Contemporary Composers

This is an anything-but-exhaustive list of names who fill all of the following criteria:

- they are living female composers
- they write sacred liturgical choral and/or organ music
- I have performed their music or have personal knowledge of it

If a name is not on this list, it is merely because I have yet to discover and programme their music. It seemed that a list of people to look up would be helpful though, given the number of times those aforementioned social media posts appear, posted by people who really seem to have no idea where to start looking. All of these composers are "googleable", so researching their music is not difficult.

Allan, Kathleen	Canada
Andrew, Kerry	UK
Ari Randall, Bethany	USA
Barnett, Carol	USA
Beamish, Sally	UK
Bebbington, Amy	UK
Bettinis, Abbie	USA
Bingham, Judith	UK
Briggs, Kerensa	UK
Burk, Katherine	USA
Burk, Margaret	USA
Burrell, Diana	UK
Campbell, Hilary	UK
Cattley, Sarah	UK
Coxhead, Elizabeth	UK
Daley, Eleanor	Canada
Dunphy, Melissa	Australia/USA
Forbes L'Strange, Joanna	UK
Frances-Hoad, Cheryl	UK
Grigorjeva, Galina	Estonia
Johnson, Emma	UK
Jones, Tamsin	UK
Kendall, Hannah	UK/USA
Kimble, Elizabeth	USA
Larsen, Libby	USA
Laurin, Rachel	Canada
LeFanu, Nicola	UK
MacDonald, Sarah	Canada/UK

Martin, Stephanie	Canada
McGlade, Becky	UK
McGregor, Gemma	UK
McDowall, Cecilia	UK
Musgrave, Thea	UK/USA
Nixon, June	Australia
Panufnik, Roxanna	UK
Parker, Alice	USA
Pritchard, Deborah	UK
Portman, Rachel	UK
Quartel, Sarah	Canada
Randall, Gail	UK
Rimkus, Sarah	USA/UK
Rooney, Annabel	UK
Rose, Kathryn	Canada/UK
Samuel, Rhian	UK
Shaw, Caroline	USA
Sparkhall, Olivia	UK
Stratford, Elizabeth	UK
Tabakova, Dobrinka	Bulgaria/UK
Ward, Joanna	UK
Watson Henderson, Ruth	Canada
Weir, Judith	UK
Wheeler, Janet	UK
Willis, Alison	UK

February 2020
"The Sarah MacDonald Choral Series"

Many readers will be aware of the spotlight that the Anglican Association of Musicians has shone on the under-representation of female composers in liturgical music programming.[53] In the UK, this issue has also been in the public consciousness, as you will recall from my April 2019 UK Report (which can be found earlier in this chapter). Recent activity on this side of the pond has included the ground-breaking Multitude of Voyces publication of a wonderful new anthology, containing twenty-two anthems for mixed voices composed by women, both historical and living, ranging from a 16th-century Italian nun to a 21-year-old recent graduate from Cambridge.[54] Two further volumes are currently in preparation,[55] and more may follow. The first volume of the anthology was launched by my choir at Selwyn College, Cambridge in November 2019, and is already in use in cathedrals, colleges, and parish churches across the UK.

In a parallel development, I am delighted to announce a new series of octavo publications of liturgical choral music by female composers for

---

53. See the September 2019 and October 2019 issues of the AAM Journal for excellent articles on this subject.

54. *Sacred Music by Women Composers – SATB anthems.* Multitude of Voyces. Salisbury 2019. Distributed by Stainer and Bell. https://www.multitudeofvoyces.co.uk/

55. Volume 2, for upper voices and women's voices, and Volume 3, Advent to Candlemas for mixed voices, were both published in 2020..

which I will be the series editor. This idea was the brainchild of David Schaap, founder of Selah Publishing Co. Inc., the highly respected music press based in Pittsburgh. Selah was established in 1987, and is run by David and a dedicated staff. It boasts over 150 composers and thousands of titles, choral, instrumental, and congregational. The choral catalogue contains works of all levels of difficulty, different voicings, with various accompaniments, for children and adults, and in many contrasting styles. Their choral subscription programme allows registered choir directors to receive perusal copies of all of their new publications. In this exciting new series, we expect to release about eight to ten titles twice each year, in January and in June. The first batch of pieces should be rolling off the press at just about the time that this issue of TAO drops through your letterbox.

Initially I am using personal contacts to source repertoire. Perhaps not surprisingly, I have a number of musician friends and colleagues who are women, and who compose (that's not necessarily the same thing as being a Female Composer, of course). I have invited friends whose music I enjoy performing myself, and I have aimed for a mixture of established names, working church musicians, and recent students who are just beginning their careers. The featured composers in the first release include Cecilia McDowall, Eleanor Daley, and Stephanie Martin, as well as Elizabeth Kimble, Annabel McLauchlan Rooney, and Elizabeth Coxhead. Every release will also include some of my own music, and one of the January 2020 highlights is a new hymn-anthem which I composed for Richard Nelson in Cleveland last year, and which seems to have been rather popular on social media. I gather that a full set has already been pre-ordered, so I hope that David at Selah will be at least partially recompensed for his investment in me!

We are already planning the June release, which will contain music for Advent and Christmas, so if you aren't on Selah Publishing's mailing list, do please contact them. Alongside living composers, eventually I hope to provide editions of historical works as well, particularly by those who are only just being rediscovered—the likes of Raphaella Aleotti, Leonora d'Este, Caterina Assandra and other such composers of wonderful Renaissance and Baroque polyphony which has hitherto languished in conventical archives, or was published anonymously, or (even worse) under a male pseudonym.

As I have been communicating with composers and conductors about this new project, I have been trying to ascertain the reasons why female composers continue to be under-represented, despite the fact that there has been near parity of post-secondary music education enrolment at least at the undergraduate level for many decades. Anecdotal evidence suggests that women are far less likely to submit unsolicited scores to publishers, and that many seem to prefer self-publishing arrangements, even if (or because?) they aren't especially good at self-publicity and marketing. In addition, although many musicians compose out of liturgical necessity, the women who do this seem less inclined to consider the last-minute-descant or the unexpectedly-successful-introit as potentially permanent additions to the repertoire. It also appears that the percentage of women carrying on to study composition at postgraduate level is still significantly lower than men. Our hope is that with a female series editor, we may be able to overcome some of the apparent reticence, and thereby help directors of music out there to represent us more equally.

Despite this drive in positive discrimination, I am keen that we are not ghettoised. We intend to promote as wide a range of styles and voicings as possible, in the hopes that music by female composers is not always relegated to the children's choir, or to the family service, or to university women's choirs. I would like to see this repertoire be given equal weight in the Solemn High Masses, sung by professional mixed ensembles, choirs of men and boys, and anyone else who wants to promote this crucial cause. So, If you are—or know—a female musician who has composed liturgical choral music, please do contact Selah Publishing at http://www.selahpub.com/ to enquire about submitting your music to be considered for this new series.

Chapter 8

Girls and Boys Come Out to Play/Sing

One of the most controversial and talked-about issues in UK church music since the early 1990s is the inclusion of girls and women in cathedral choirs. This chapter features columns that have dealt with this matter specifically, and with related concerns such as the under-representation of women in high-profile roles of musical leadership.

Working with Teenage Girls' Voices

The University of Cambridge recently introduced a new master's degree, the one-year MMus in Choral Studies. Students work with the university's many choirs and conductors, participate in masterclasses, receive conducting coaching, and attend seminars and lectures on a wide variety of choral topics, both academic and practical. The course is in its infancy but is proving successful and popular, and provides a comprehensive immersion in the English Choral Tradition as manifest in Cambridge.

Most English church musicians are trained as apprentices. Their formative years at school, university, initial professional posts are usually occupied in watching, observing, and assisting a director of music, thus learning "on the job". The concept of academic study, reading in advance, writing papers, undertaking research, let alone having proper conducting lessons, is extremely new for potential church musicians here, as evidenced by the creation of such courses as the Cambridge MMus, which seeks to combine the traditional apprenticeship scheme with a more rigorous academic schedule of learning.

Early in the year, I presented an MMus seminar entitled "Working with teenage girls' voices", with a particular focus on the needs of the changing adolescent female voice. Although I am Director of Ely Cathedral Girls' Choir and one of the directors of St Thomas Fifth Avenue Girl Chorister Course in New York City, and spent many years as assistant organist (i.e., an apprentice) in churches with girls' choirs, I was surprised to find myself considered to be the local expert on this specific topic, having never done any real reading or research about such matters. As I wrote the seminar, I was reminded that an awareness of current literature, and the ability to verbalise what we have always done instinctively, are just as valuable as the hands-on training that the English system provided.

In my requisite literature survey, I discovered three common things: 1. Much has been written on the negligible differences between boys' and girls' younger voices (the "Pepsi Challenge" of the choral world);[56] 2. A particular generation of male conductors continue to be endearingly patronising about girls' choirs (fortunately most of them are retired now); and 3. Predictably, the changing male voice has been studied extensively, while the changing female voice has received considerably less attention. Nonetheless, what has been written should constitute essential reading for anyone charged with the care of young female voices.

I have always been concerned that choral conductors should have a detailed knowledge of singing technique, no matter what the ages of their singers. Having prepared and delivered my seminar, I am even more convinced that those in charge of teenage girls' choirs must understand the effects of puberty on the adolescent voice in order to avoid vocal damage. As well as the expected increase in size of the larynx, vocal tract, and vocal folds, girls also experience increased breathiness, huskiness, hoarseness, voice cracking, noticeable register breaks, and decreased and inconsistent ranges. Most importantly (and this is documented in several of the papers, as well as anecdotally), singing often feels more effortful and difficult through a girl's teenage years.[57]

As teenage girls attempt to retain the ease of their prepubescent singing voice, tension can develop in many places, and it is the conductor's

---

56. A summary can be found in Howard, Barlow, and Welch "Vocal production and listener perception of trained girls and boys in the English Cathedral Choir" in *Proceedings of the International Society of Music Education*. Salt Lake City 2000.

57. An excellent summary can be found here: *British Journal of Music Education* "Adolescence, Singing Development and National Curricula Design". John M. Cooksey and Graham F. Welch, especially the section entitled "The changing female voice". http://journals.cambridge.org/action/displayAbstract?fromPage=online&aid=2913256

duty to diagnose it and help the singer to release it. Potentially dangerous singing technique manifests itself in tension in the tongue root, the jaw, and the neck and shoulders. In addition, the larynx often rises (especially approaching the *passaggi*). It is crucial to engage a trustworthy singing teacher, with whom the conductor should communicate frequently. It should be stressed that the main focus of lessons during voice change should be on developing a healthy and relaxed technique, and not on superficial issues (no matter how essential in the long-run) such as polishing German pronunciation.

Some solutions which can be used in choir practices include singing with the tongue hanging out of the mouth. This prevents retraction of the tongue root, though it does look a little silly, and can cause tension in other places, so shouldn't be used for extended periods of time. Similarly, it can be helpful to hold the lower jaw with the hand to ensure release of muscles and/or to sing while standing against a wall to ensure that the neck remains in line with the body, and the jaw isn't pressed forward. Singing while yawning, which automatically lowers the larynx, is also extremely useful, and a favourite of the Ely girls, who rehearse at 0755 every morning. It is also critical that the conductor demonstrates healthily because children learn by imitation, even as they grow older.

Choral warm-ups need to be sensible as well as stretching, encouraging relaxed and healthy sound production (sing down first, rather than up; "bubble" the lips, hum, and buzz before vocalising on vowels). Girls need to be taught to be cautious but not precious, with their own (changing) ranges; they need to have the courage to stretch their voices, with no fear of high (or low) notes, but also to develop the sense to stop on days when it isn't working. They also need to be encouraged to speak with good technique, avoiding pressing on the voice in an attempt to sound more authoritative (this is a distinctly female problem).

Although the bulk of my seminar was about the effects of voice change on teenage girls, I also discussed behaviour, discipline, gaining and maintaining respect (*never* patronise them), the unavoidable issue of Child Protection and Safeguarding, group atmosphere in rehearsal, which mechanisms of cathedral boys' choirs translate to girls' choirs and which do not, my own methods for teaching sight-reading, the importance of consistency and rigour in musical decision-making, vowel formation, regional pronunciation, the International Phonetic Alphabet, and liturgical choral repertoire, including what to avoid when dealing with changing voices—the soprano part of the Kyrie from Darke's *Communion Setting in E* is easy for unchanged voices; it is virtually unsingable for teenage girls, especially on a Sunday morning.

Of course I hope the seminar was useful for the MMus students, but it was particularly fascinating for me to back up my extensive practical experience with some well-documented research. The English apprenticeship system certainly provides a superb training ground, but background reading and methodical study are also important. I trust that all students on our new MMus course will see both sides of this educational coin. I will close this column with one of a few gems discovered during my research: in a 1960s book about girls' choirs in UK schools I was intrigued to read that "Most girls' choirs have a rule that membership automatically ceases upon marriage."[58] Well, that's good news for all spinsters who are fond of singing!

---

58. Coleman, Henry, and West, Hilda. *Girls' Choirs*. Oxford 1962.

December 2011

If I Were a Man,
I Would Be a Lay Clerk

I recently delivered an after-dinner speech to the annual gathering of the Society of Ely Choristers, on the potentially controversial topic of women in cathedral music in the UK. My audience consisted of present and former choristers (male and female) ranging in age from 12 to 85, as well as organists, lay clerks, and clergy. While preparing the talk, I discovered a humorously poignant Facebook page entitled "If I were a man, I would be a lay clerk", which seemed to encapsulate a current anxiety. Girls' choirs in UK cathedrals have nurtured a generation of women who are skilled and committed liturgical singers. While former boy choristers are able to go on to sing in UK cathedral choirs as countertenors, tenors, and basses, no such opportunity exists for former girl choristers. Although they can sing services in mixed parish church choirs, this must be the upper limit of their ambition.

A little history can perhaps help to illuminate aspects of this contentious topic. At Chichester Cathedral, during the Second World War, two women sang alto with the men and boys' choir, but they were hidden behind a curtain to avoid causing dire offence. In 1978, eight-year-old Susan Hamilton made history when she was admitted to the boys' treble section of St Mary's Cathedral, Edinburgh, and the top line there has remained mixed ever since. The gauntlet was truly thrown down in 1991, however, when Salisbury Cathedral introduced its girls' choir. Between 1991 and 2010, a further 27 UK cathedrals set up girls' choirs, with Durham being the most recent. Nearly all operate two separate top lines (the exceptions are Edinburgh and Manchester, and a handful of provincial 'parish church' cathedrals, where the treble lines are mixed). [59] The opportunities available in girls' choirs are varied: some take choristers at the same ages (about 8 to 12); others, like that at Ely (which I direct), admit girls from age 13, (not possible with boys, for obvious reasons). Some girl choristers sing the same number of services as their male counterparts; others sing fewer. Boarding requirements and financial bursaries differ (or do not) according to the means of the cathedral and/or the school.

It is something of an understatement to claim that the development of girls' choirs has been controversial. Salisbury's decision sparked the setting up of the charmingly conservative Campaign for the Defence of the Traditional Cathedral Choir. The perhaps well-intentioned patriarchs associated with this group are convinced that girls' choirs will necessarily "sound the death-knell" of the boys' tradition. Concern that the girls will "scare the boys away" is coupled with flowery rhetoric about the "butterfly-like transience" of the boy treble voice. Verbose arguments against this assault on the establishment conclude that girls' choirs are set up "merely for the sake of political correctness". There has also been a good deal of so-called academic research into the differences between girls' and boys' voices (the choral version of the Pepsi Challenge). [60] In general, the debates and discussions have generated more heat than light.

After a cathedral choristership, liturgically-aware young singers (male and female) often aim for a university choral scholarship. Cambridge, Oxford, Durham, Royal Holloway, and King's London, among others have developed outstanding undergraduate liturgical choirs over the

---

59. A number of master's and doctoral theses have been written about this topic in the early 21st century, though it is changing regularly as more cathedrals form top lines of girl choristers, so even some very recent ones, such as the seminal 2015 study by Amanda Mackey are already out of date (https://research.bangor.ac.uk/portal/en/theses/new-voice-(4008cb60-df90-44a3-88d9-f557e89180e7).html) .

60. Several articles have been published by David Howard and Graham Welch.

past thirty years. After graduation, many of the men go on to cathedral lay clerkships—but where do the women go? Apart from London parish churches, where small professional ensembles sing Sunday services only, only one cathedral has offered women the opportunity to sing daily services, namely the adult professional choir of Christchurch Cathedral, Dublin (not in the UK, of course, but close enough for a discussion of this kind). Sadly, their budget was drastically reduced in the financial crisis of 2008, and the music programme has not recovered. At present, therefore, options for daily liturgical singing involving women are effectively non-existent.

In spite of this, one year ago a recently-graduated Law student and Choral Scholar from my choir at Selwyn College, Cambridge, was appointed as the first full-time female lay clerk of a major English Cathedral. For two years, despite several costly recruitment drives, Peterborough Cathedral had been without a permanent countertenor, and finally the director of music made the brave decision to advertise for "an alto"— i.e., of unspecified gender. The appointee is an outstanding musician who is wholly committed to liturgical singing, even to the extent of abandoning the lucrative career towards which her academic degree more obviously pointed. Although this appointment prompted much wailing and gnashing of teeth by the Campaign members, there have also been some more constructive reactions, notably in the January 2011 issue of *Cathedral Music*,[61] which features two excellent articles on the subject.

Concerns about repertoire and sound quality feature regularly in arguments against the use of contraltos in cathedral choirs. While it is true that much of the standard repertoire was written with countertenors in mind, it is also the case that plenty of commonly programmed music (e.g., Brahms, Bruckner, Parry) was written for contraltos, and the boys (or girls) often have to assist countertenors in higher sections. The versatile range and colourful sound created when countertenors and contraltos sing together is extremely successful, and it is the norm to find both men and women in university choirs' alto sections. Indeed, some objections

---

61. *Cathedral Music* magazine is the official journal of the charity Friends of Cathedral Music.

to these arrangements tend towards the practical rather than the musical. When asked about appointing female undergraduate contraltos to the
choir of St John's College, Cambridge, the late George Guest is reputed to
have said "that's all very well, but what would we do about showers when
we are on tour!"[62]

Nonetheless, it may be that times they are a-changing, even in the
good old UK. In recent years, various women have managed to break
through the glass fan-vaulting in other liturgical musical roles. Over the
past three years, women have been appointed to the posts of director of
music at three cathedrals: Chichester, Guildford, and Lichfield. Talented
and ambitious young women currently hold number two and three positions at Durham, Lincoln, and Southwell, and there are several others
pursuing university organ scholarships at the moment. Ironically (though
fortunately for me), despite its horror over girls and women singing in
cathedrals, the Campaign "has no view on the matter" of women playing
the organ or conducting. Presumably, when a woman in the organ loft,
she can't be seen, so there is no need to hide her behind a curtain.

The best conclusions to my reflections thus far consist of further
unanswered (unanswerable?) questions. If a male alto is not available, is a
woman better than silence? What should we do with adult sopranos, who
surely must not usurp the place of boys and girls in the front rows, given
the crucial need to train future generations? Why is there such resistance
(in certain quarters) to girls singing liturgically, but not to women in other
roles of musical leadership? In my own case, I have been fortunate: I have
a vocation to liturgical music, and I have been given a rare opportunity to
exercise this calling both at Cambridge and at Ely. Had I been a singer,
however, I would probably have fallen silent by now.

---

62. *A Guest at Cambridge: the autobiography of George Guest.* Paraclete Press. 1994.

July 2016

Gender Politics in the
House of Commons

"**B**ecause it's 2015 . . ." This is how Prime Minister Justin Trudeau responded when asked why 50% of his new cabinet were women. It was the first time in Canadian history—indeed, possibly the first time in any western democracy—that the percentage of women holding senior positions in the government had been so high. In the UK, only 30% of the current cabinet are women; at the time of writing, in the States the percentage was even lower, though Barack Obama appointed more women to the cabinet than any previous president.[63]

Perhaps unexpectedly, these statistics were actually discussed at a recent meeting of the Royal College of Organists' Academic Board, of which I am a member. As its name suggests, this committee normally considers such things as the appropriate wording for ARCO counterpoint examination rubrics, or the number of staves and configuration of clefs for FRCO score-reading tests. Gender politics in the House of Commons is not a standing item on the agenda. Nonetheless, the gender imbalances in the UK government were directly related to something that the RCO has been grappling with of late, namely the conspicuously low percentage of women (only about 15%) who are members of the organisation, coupled

---

63. https://en.wikipedia.org/wiki/List_of_female_United_States_Cabinet_Secretaries

with the low numbers of women working as professional organists in the country as a whole.

If I'm honest, gender is not something I normally pontificate about. Personally, I have always been opposed to co-called "positive discrimination" in recruitment for any field. I find it patronising—and, yes, given its etymology, I am fully conscious of the irony in choosing that particular adjectival participle. Having said that, I am of course aware that when successful applicants are men, the appointment panels that have selected them tend, correspondingly, to have consisted primarily of men. The discussion at the RCO meeting prompted me to reflect upon the gender ratios in the organist sector across the UK.

It is undeniable that the pool of professional concert organists in the UK is predominantly male. A quick calculation of the ratios of British organists represented by one well-respected agency shows that only 33% of them are women. Nonetheless, some of the most eminent and internationally respected performers happen to be women. The most prominent of these is perhaps Dame Gillian Weir (now retired, so I am willing to mention her by name), but other renowned female British organists will also be familiar to many TAO readers. In addition, there are those with diverse careers that involve various combinations of performing, directing, scholarship, composition, parish music, and teaching. This list includes many well-known women, including a past-president of the RCO, the world's leading authority on the harmonium, and someone with an incredibly lengthy and influential catalogue of organ-related publications.

The cathedral world provides the most obvious manifestation of the presence (or lack thereof) of women organists in the UK, and there is a public forum dedicated to this topic on the ABRSM website. Since girls' choirs were introduced in cathedrals just over 20 years ago, more girls are learning the organ, but nonetheless, at the time of writing, there are only seven women in permanent musical positions in Church of England cathedrals (number one posts are held by women at Guildford and Lichfield; number two (or equivalent) posts at Rochester, Durham, Gloucester, Lincoln, and Ely (i.e., me)). Most of the 44 Anglican cathedrals have three or four tenured musicians on their staff. Even at a conservative estimate of 130 organists permanently employed by C of E cathedrals across the country, the percentage of women organists in such posts is less than 5%. In addition, there are two cathedrals which currently employ women in the one- or two-year temporary positions of Organ Scholar (London and Chichester), with another beginning in September 2016 (Truro). One surprising quirk about these statistics is that of the ten women in total who will be employed on a permanent or temporary basis as organists at UK Anglican Cathedrals by September 2016, half are foreigners (three Canadians, one New Zealander, and one American). Change, it seems, is sometimes instigated from the outside, rather than from the inside.

As readers know, Oxbridge colleges are the historical musical training ground for cathedrals in the UK. Over the past 25 years, an average of around seven of the approximately 40 Organ Scholars in Cambridge at any one time have been women, and there have never been fewer than two. The statistics for Oxford are roughly the same. Oxbridge chapels' Directors of Music are also predominantly male. I was appointed to Selwyn College in 1999, and was the first woman in the history of either university to hold a Director of Music post. There are now two other women in similar posts in Cambridge (though one of those is not an organist), and also one at Oxford. With about 35 Directors of Music across the two universities, these gender ratios are self-evidently striking.

Given all of this, it is not surprising that the RCO has been concerned about this issue recently, and is working to identify the reasons and any potential solutions. In the meantime, I will continue vigorously to encourage members of Ely Cathedral Girls' Choir to take up the organ as soon as they achieve grade 5 piano or can reach the pedals (whichever happens sooner). And although female organists are certainly underrepresented, the patron saint of music herself, St Cecilia, provides at least one worthy precedent.

Ely Cathedral Girls' Choir:
New Directions

*This article, an extended version of my UK Report from
August 2018, was published in Cathedral Music magazine, a
publication of the Friends of Cathedral Music. It was published
in November 2019, and is reprinted here with permission.*

The UK's choir school system is internationally known and respected. Pupils who sing the top (treble) line in their cathedral choir receive a financial reward in order to attend the school associated with their cathedral. The reward usually takes the form of free music lessons, and a scholarship or bursary towards the cost of school fees, since the vast majority of the country's choir schools are independent fee-paying (often boarding) schools. There are choir schools at most of the 42 Anglican cathedrals in England, as well as at various other churches and colleges, both Anglican and Roman Catholic. The education that choristers receive is second-to-none, with the obvious musical skills acquired through daily professional performances complemented by the transferable skills of discipline, self-confidence, and reliability. The tradition is an ancient one, dating back to the Middle Ages, and historically, choir schools educated only boys. Over the twentieth century, most of the schools have become co-educational, although there remain a couple of high-profile exceptions.

In 1991, Salisbury Cathedral School was the first to admit girls to the front row of the cathedral choir, in a not uncontroversial development. In fact, some trail-blazing choir directors had been experimenting well before then: St Davids Cathedral in Wales has had an all-girl top line since 1966. Harrison Oxley added girls to the boys' top line at St Edmundsbury in the early 1970s, but subsequent opposition from a new Provost ultimately prompted Oxley's resignation in 1984. In 1978, the first girl was admitted to the top line of St Mary's Episcopal Cathedral in in Edinburgh, and that front row has remained mixed ever since. Since 1991, all but a small handful of English cathedrals and 'Royal Peculiars', have formed a separate girls' choir, or admitted girls to their pre-existing top line of boys. For some (Salisbury, York, Exeter, Durham), there has been a laudable ambition to achieve parity, regardless of gender. Their girls and boys are the same age (7 to 12) and sing the same number of weekly services for the same financial reward. In other places, the girls range in age up to 18 (the end of secondary schooling in the UK), and are drawn from various local schools—i.e., not the cathedral choir school—and have schedules ranging from one or two services per term (Canterbury), to one or two services per week (Winchester and Guildford).

When Ely Cathedral introduced girl choristers in 2006, they were recruited from the older age range, i.e. 13 to 18. The intention was to provide secondary-school-age girls with a comparable experience to that enjoyed by younger boys. Notwithstanding this, complete parity was deemed inappropriate, since academic commitments and the social/emotional needs of teenagers had to be considered. Two or three services per week, rather than the boys' five or six, has been the norm since the girls' choir's inception. Recently, however, it became apparent that change was required.

A brief diversion into the UK's education system is now needed. In 2006, when Ely Cathedral Girls' Choir (ECGC) was set up, compulsory public examinations (GCSEs taken at age 16, AS-levels at 17, and A-levels at 18) comprised a combination of modular assessment, course-work submissions, and end-of-year examinations. In addition, university tuition fees were amongst the lowest in Europe. Two significant developments have occurred in the past few years: university tuition fees[64] were tripled in 2012, and in 2015 the then Education Secretary, Michael Gove, began a systematic revision of the school examination system. In an attempt to remedy a perceived lack of rigour, Gove eliminated all modular/continuous assessment, and abolished AS exams, with the result that both GCSEs and A-levels are now entirely based on final written examinations taken after two full years of study.[65]

Those who have any experience in the education sector will be well aware that modular assessment has for decades been known to improve girls' results.[66] The UK's new 'Govine' system will inevitably adversely affect the performance of girls in particular. Since university offers are based upon school-leavers' grades, the dramatic rise in tuition fees placed even further weight upon school examinations. Combining an intensive cathedral choristership with this academic pressure became untenable.

In addition, over my ten years directing ECGC, I have developed serious vocal concerns about running a choir of girls from age 13 to 18. Until 2018, I auditioned girls at age 12 and they began in the choir at 13. Usually, a substantial growth spurt occurred in the months between voice trial and arrival in the choir. Over ten years at Ely, I have noticed that height change occurs first, and voice change usually about two years later. This anecdotal observation is conveniently backed up by medical research.[67] Of course, specific physiology and vocal training play an important role in vocal development and voice change, but I am convinced that the change from girl-treble to soprano/mezzo, or (very occasionally) contralto, occurs during about age 14/15. I recently used two members of ECGC to illustrate this to a group of Cambridge MMus students. The two girls, one in

---

64. UK university fees are set centrally by the government (those in England, Wales, and Northern Ireland by the government at Westminster, and those in Scotland by the devolved government at Holyrood), and are the same at all universities.

65. As a related aside, Gove's English Baccalaureate prescribing compulsory GCSEs does not include Music as a core subject. Consequently, the number of pupils taking GCSE and A-level Music has dropped dramatically over the past two years. (https://www.classicfm.com/music-news/decline-music-gcse-ebacc/).

66. http://ciea.org.uk/linear-vs-modular-exams/

67. http://www.leedberg.com/voice/pages/female.html

Year 10 and the other in Year 12, had had identical chorister training, first as Durham Cathedral choristers (age 7 to 12), then at Ely (from 13). In addition, both had had the same singing teacher throughout. Both sang short passages, one after the other; the former was audibly still a treble, but the latter very definitely a young soprano.

The combination of unchanged, changing, and changed voices is an easily surmountable obstacle in a large choir that rehearses once or twice a week after school. In a group of just 18 girls who sing together every morning at 0755, a time of day well documented as being totally unnatural for teenagers,[68] it results in potential vocal damage both in older girls (who under-sing, in order to blend) and younger (who over-sing, in order to be heard). In addition, the sixth-formers who mature into mezzo-sopranos often struggle to continue singing soprano. Even those mezzos who have access to their falsetto after voice change can develop uncentred technique and vocal fatigue. Since the top two years of a cathedral choir's front row are by definition the most experienced singers, it is not convenient to lose them early due to voice change, as any conductor of a boys' top line will attest. That ECGC was structured in such a way as to make that loss inevitable seemed to me unwise: it would be akin to setting up a choir in the 21st century which had boy trebles from ages 10 to 16[69]. In summary, ideally the top two years in the choir should be those at which the child is strongest and most confident musically, and also at the peak of the maturity of his/her treble voice. For girl choristers, I am persuaded that the ideal age range is therefore age 10 to 15, or school years 7 to 11.

Readers will know that mixed university and adult choirs' alto sections comprise a combination of voice types. There are often a few countertenors and contraltos of course, but by far the most common voice type in a mixed choir's alto section is that of mezzo-soprano. It is also

---

68.   https://www.birmingham.ac.uk/news/latest/2018/02/later-start-times-for-teenage -pupils.aspx

69. For further information on the current average age of the onset of puberty in boys (and subsequent voice-change), notably the effects of increased protein in the western diet after World War II, as well as the raising of concert pitch over the past two centuries, see https://www.telegraph.co.uk/news/religion/8052873/Choirs-in-deep-trouble -over-voices-breaking-early.html and https://en.wikipedia.org/wiki/Boy_soprano

the case that if any girl wishes to carry on singing in a cathedral choir while at university, either as a choral scholar or lay clerk, she will have no choice but to sing alto, since the back row is the only place where adults can be accommodated. The sixth form (Years 12 and 13) provides an ideal opportunity for girls to learn to sing alto, just as in those two years the boys whose voices have begun to settle are learning to sing tenor and bass (or, less commonly at that age, countertenor). It goes without saying that boys will need to learn a completely new voice part when they move from the front to the back row of the choir—indeed, the baritones and basses also need to learn to read in a different clef. Girls who do the same (whether they are sopranos, mezzos, or that great rarity, the true contralto) also need to learn to learn a new part. Singing alto requires a different way of thinking, of listening, and of reading: the inner voice part does not just require a change of range or tessitura, but necessitates a new way of hearing one's place in an ensemble. A few years ago I had to train two of my Year 13 girls, both of whom had developed into mezzo-sopranos, to audition as altos for Cambridge choral scholarships. Amusingly, they both applied to sing in Selwyn College Choir, which I also direct, and it was in teaching them the skills that they needed in order to audition successfully for me—though I had trained them both since they were 13 years old, and knew perfectly well what they were capable of—that I realised just how much they had to learn.

Along with the important educational and vocal considerations out-lined above comes the issue of young adulthood. Although there is of course a difference in expectations and behaviour between an 11-year-old and a 15-year-old, it is significantly less marked than the difference between a 13-year-old and an 18-year-old. Girls in particular are young adults by the time they reach 16, and forcing them to adhere to a time-table that was set up in the 19th century to cater for ten-year-old boys actually doesn't bring the best out of them. Schools have known this for a long time: sixth-formers often have a special separate common room, they wear a less-prescribed uniform, have fewer lessons (classes), and are expected to work independently in their free time. Society allows them to learn to drive, to drink alcohol, to vote, and to be independent. They are transitioning from school pupils to university students: walking them in a crocodile from the boarding house to breakfast every morning at 0725 in order to be on time for chorister practice is much more likely to produce resentment and rebellion than good singing.

I hope that readers have understood the reasoning behind the need for change in the structure of the girl chorister routine at Ely Cathedral. I am of course grateful to those who set it up: I was not allowed to sing in a cathedral choir as a child or as a teenager, even in the enlightened country I call home, and I would have given my eye-teeth to have been allowed this opportunity when I was younger. Nonetheless, the educational changes imposed upon us, combined with the vocal, emotional, and social needs of teenage girls, has made these developments crucial.

Fortunately, a substantial intake to King's Ely from local preparatory schools occurs at Year 7, and from September 2018 we admitted girl choristers from the age of 11. Once the transition period is over (we have 'grandmothered' in all existing choristers and will allow them to sing until the end of Year 13 if they wish), girls will finish their time as choristers at the end of Year 11, after a substantial break in choral duties for the summer GCSE examination period. Those who wish to stay on as sixth-form choral scholars will join our lay clerks and former boy choristers in the back row, singing as young adults on a reduced choral timetable, learning how to prepare music on their own.

This first year has been challenging, with nine new girls in Years 7, 8, and 9, comprising nearly half the choir. Teaching so many of them at once how to sing, listen, read, process, learn, perform, etc., has caused me more than the occasional sleepless night. But I am persuaded that we are moving in the right direction. Hopefully this will result in a thriving—slightly younger—cathedral girls' choir, with vocally healthy former choristers achieving magnificent school examination results.

August 2019

#PlayLikeAGirl

C ambridge was hot and humid; thousands of camera-wielding sight-seers clogged the narrow streets; impatient residents pushed through the throngs trying to run their errands; undergraduates sped past on bicycles in myriad directions. Meanwhile a group of 35 young people were bravely negotiating the crowds, chatting nervously, and admiring the ancient architecture.

It is not uncommon for visitors to tour this very small city (population 125,000) in very large groups, especially in the summer. There are guided sight-seeing excursions, school-groups on educational outings, potential students on reconnaissance trips, visiting academics in various disciplines, international summer school pupils, Anglican-choral-music lovers on pil-grimages, and, not infrequently, groups of (usually elderly) Pipe Organ Enthusiasts exploring the extraordinary variety of instruments (about 45 different organs, ranging from I/3 to IV/80) in the space of the city cen-tre's four square miles.

The aforementioned nervously-chatting, architecture-admiring young people fell into the latter category. They carried assorted back-packs con-taining books ranging from "Piano Exam Pieces Grade 1" to battered Breitkopf editions of Bach's organ works. Most tellingly of all, several of them clutched a pair of shoes in their hands. Leading their adven-ture were Anna Lapwood (Director of Music at Pembroke College), and

Yours Truly. However, this was a group of Pipe Organ Enthusiasts with a difference—and their two leaders were unusual as well (and not just because we inadvertently dressed the same as each other). Not only was every participant under the age of 18, but they were also all female.

In the UK, arguably the most senior liturgical musical roles are those of Cathedral or Oxbridge Director of Music (DoM). Historically, the typical route to such a post has been as follows: cathedral chorister-ship → senior school music scholarship → Oxbridge organ scholarship → cathedral organ scholarship → cathedral assistantship → cathedral/Oxbridge DoM post. The vast majority of holders of these posts have fol-lowed exactly this route; and since that education was available only to boys until relatively recently, the vast majority of them are male. Indeed, at the time of writing, just 9% of Cathedral organists and 8% of Oxbridge DoMs are female.

The establishment of cathedral girls' choirs over the past 25 years has, of course, begun to make a difference. It is already the case that the percentage of female Oxbridge organ scholars has risen from 5% in my undergraduate days, to about 25% now. Nonetheless, in the meantime, some active positive encouragement is required, and thus "The Cam-bridge Organ Experience for Girls" was set up to encourage young women to explore the Queen of Instruments.

The annual one-day event is free to attend, and the standard in play-ing ranges from the 11-year-old beginner pianist who has never seen an organ console, to ambitious teenagers already preparing for organ scholar-ship auditions. The itinerary included an introduction to the organ, small-group visits to play a selection of contrasting instruments, lunch, and a short recital. The day was topped off by a demonstration of the organ at King's College, given by Stephen Cleobury, who was particularly touched to be asked for his autograph by one of the youngest participants. Three of the most accomplished players performed a piece each on the King's organ. They will no doubt one day enjoy recounting the tale to their grandchildren about the day that Dr Cleobury acted as their registrant and page-turner!

There are, of course, many administrative and logistical hurdles to overcome when organising an event such as this. Written parental/

guardian permission was acquired for photographs and video to be taken and posted online[70]. Special dietary requirements and allergies were logged with college dining halls. Appropriate numbers of background-checked adults were present throughout the day. Senior Tutors had to be persuaded to allow us into the colleges, all of which are currently closed to visitors due to university examinations. Girls were divided into small groups according to their age and their experience, and Anna spent an enjoyable evening researching obscure organ stop names for the groups (the Gravissimas, the Clarabellas). I was particularly proud of our specially-produced lanyard name-badges which the girls wore, to ensure that we didn't lose them in the crowded streets.

There are many taster days and residential courses available across the UK for young organists, and with one important exception[71], inevitably, there are three times as many boys on those courses as there are girls. What Anna and I noted about our taster-day in Cambridge was that even the shyest of girls was willing to "have a go", since they were only surrounded by their peers. We have both seen those girls refuse to go anywhere near the console when in the company of teenage boys, no matter how encouraging the tutor may be.

When I arrived home, the first thing that popped up on my Twitter feed was a lovely photo of a dozen or so professional organists, many of whom are my friends. The photo consisted of one cathedral's assistant organists and organ scholars, past and present, who were gathered to mark the retirement of an eminent DoM. When I juxtaposed those 12 smiling men with the assembly of inspired young girls in the iconic chapel at King's College, I was reminded again why our event was so very important.

---

70. You can see photos and videos of the day by following "Organ at Cambridge" on Facebook or Twitter.

71. The Jennifer Bate Organ Academy (http://www.stcatherines.info/jboa), now in its 15th year, was the first single-sex residential course for young female organists. Anna is an alumna of the course, and I am a former tutor.

February 2020

Since Singing is So Good a Thing, I Wish All [Boys & Girls] Would Learn to Sing!⁷²

*This article was written for Cathedral Voice, a publication
of the Friends of Cathedral Music. It was published in
February 2020, and is reprinted here with permission.*

Some months ago, I was invited to respond to the story of the girl
whose mother sued Berlin Cathedral for not accepting her daughter into their boys' choir,[73] and to Lesley Garrett's berating King's College Choir for not admitting girls.[74] More recently, Rochester Cathedral announced the introduction of a mixed top line of boys and girls who will sing every service together—a first for a medieval UK choral foundation.[75] The armchair-experts' online grumbling was bad enough a few

---

72. attributed to William Byrd
73.   https://www.telegraph.co.uk/news/2019/08/15/nine-year-old-girl-sues-german-all-male-choir-discrimination/
74.   https://www.theguardian.com/music/2018/dec/06/lesley-garrett-says-kings-college-choir-must-accept-girls
75.   https://www.rochestercathedral.org/articles/2019/11/12/rochester-cathedral-announces-introduction-of-mixed-treble-line

months ago; Rochester Cathedral's decision caused social-media mayhem. In response, instead of another polemic, I offer a more dispassionate "logicising" of this issue.[76]

One of the frequently-raised assertions is that boys and girls "sound different". It is well known that in blind tests, even professional choir-trainers can rarely differentiate between individual unchanged boys' and girls' treble voices.[77] Conversely, if a 9-year-old treble and a 17-year-old soprano sound the same, then something is wrong. It is every conductor's responsibility to ensure that each singer develops healthy, age-appropriate vocal resonance. In addition, a choir's sound is moulded by its director: cathedral treble lines whose equivalent-age girls and boys are trained by the same person are often indistinguishable. Finally, the acoustic in which they sing must be considered: in Cambridge, the contrasting architecture of the chapels of King's and St John's is manifest in their choirs' distinct sounds, even though both choirs are identical in size, age, and gender.

Concern is often expressed that if girls join an all-male front row, boys will leave. Unfortunately, the decline in the number of boys in parish choirs since the 1970s supports this argument. Martin Ashley's insightful book *How high should boys sing?* attributes this in part to differences in performance motivation: whereas girls tend perform to impress adults, boys generally need to impress each other.[78] The idea that society now considers the arts "girly" pastimes does not help—consider the recent media reaction to young Prince George's ballet lessons.[79] Moreover, since girls mature earlier (although their singing voices change later),[80] even a mixed group of similar-age children will include those who are at different stages, both educationally and psychologically. Anna Lapwood's excellent

76. I am grateful to colleagues who contributed to this article: Edmund Aldhouse (Ely), Katherine Dienes-Williams (Guildford), Francesca Massey (Rochester), Timothy Parsons (Exeter), Oliver Hancock (St Mary's, Warwick), and David Price (Portsmouth).

77.   https://www.independent.co.uk/news/uk/this-britain/girls-singing-voices-are-just-as-pure-as-boys-86112.html

78. Ashley, M. (2009). *How High Should Boys Sing?: Gender, Authenticity and Credibility in the Young Male Voice*. Aldershot: Ashgate.

79. https://www.youtube.com/watch?v=yDx4gIWUIbo

80. MacDonald, S. E. A. (2019), 'Ely Cathedral Girls' Choir: New Directions', in *Cathedral Music*, November 2019

piece about this issue celebrates the shared experiences of trebles who are in gender-specific teams of their own.[81]

Another recurring question is whether singing less frequently must necessarily dilute excellence. Only a handful of UK cathedral/collegiate choirs remain where a single top line sings eight services every week. Inevitably, with two front rows, there are repertoire gaps—I know myself what it's like to realise mid-rehearsal that the boys and not the girls sang every last Fifteenth Evening[82] in recent memory. However, with increasing academic pressure causing mental health issues even at primary school level,[83] as well as changing parental priorities,[84] isn't more flexibility simply a requirement of modern life?

Lest you fear I have forgotten, of course I acknowledge that girl choristers do not become the tenors and basses of the future. This is countered by the fact that not all boy trebles sing as adults, and not all adult male singers are former choristers. Indeed, the majority of the tenors and basses in all but the most elite Cambridge choirs are young men who discovered their love of singing after their voices changed. In addition, the lauded though relatively recent flowering of the UK's professional choirs over the past few decades is surely due in part to the availability of more chorally-experienced women.[85]

One indisputable fact is that fewer children at Rochester will benefit from a chorister education. Whereas there is currently provision for 40 choristers, in future this will halve. That the leftover resources will be redirected towards outreach activities for other children and young people in the diocese is very welcome, since it addresses the significant problem that in too many places, this training is only open to those who can afford

81. https://jessicamusic.blogspot.com/2018/12/smash-all-male-choirs-choral-expert.html
82. The whole of Psalm 78 is prescribed by the Book of Common Prayer for the fifteenth evening of the month—73 verses of Anglican chant. That is a lot of Cranmerian English for the average 10-year-old to sing before supper.
83. https://reclaimingschools.org/2019/06/07/primary-school-tests-and-childrens-mental-health/
84. https://www.openaccessgovernment.org/childhood-extracurricular-activities/64921/
85. Choirs such as the Monteverdi Choir, the Tallis Scholars, the Sixteen, Polyphony, as well as countless other smaller mixed professional ensembles were all founded in the past 50 years.

to pay independent school fees. In my view, this is a far greater concern than whether boys and girls sing together or separately.

When all else fails, opponents of innovation often resort to the age-old notion of "tradition". As a child in Canada, I was baffled that tradition dictated that I was not allowed to sing in our cathedral choir, but my brothers were, despite the fact that I was more musically accomplished. We must recognise that the "priceless heritage"[86] we so cherish is alive and breathing: it must be susceptible to change in order to grow and flourish, and indeed to survive. I hope that future contributors to this important discussion will be more circumspect than was evidenced on Facebook earlier this month. The views expressed, unlike the future front row at Rochester, were hardly balanced, and featured rather more invective than encouragement. Surely sharing our love of this life-changing music as widely as possible must be our objective, and indeed our joy?[87]

---

86. The motto of the Friends of Cathedral Music is "safeguarding a priceless heritage".

87. In May 2022, the final Anglican Cathedral in the UK to announced admission of girls to their choral foundation, namely St Paul's London, where a second, equal top line of girls will be introduced in 2025. Chichester and Hereford Cathedral had already announced that they would admit girls to form a mixed top line in earlier in 2022.

#PlayLikeYourself

I was a conspicuously un-sporty child during the 1970s and 80s, and I recall often being the target of age-old catchphrases like "you run like a girl" and "you throw like a girl". These insults weren't just reserved for female classmates either: sensitive, smaller, less masculine-presenting boys were also subjected to derogatory remarks from their more "manly" peers. Perhaps I'm overly optimistic, but I like to hope that school children today are a little less unreconstructed, given the amount of training they receive at school in appropriate ways to treat each other, regardless of sex or gender.

Earlier in her career, the British organist Anna Lapwood was told by a (male) adjudicator that she needed to "play more like a man". Since that remark, she has used the hashtag #PlayLikeAGirl on social media posts, in a subtle but pointed attempt to turn "[insert verb] like a girl" into a more positive and desirable attribute. Despite the notable popularity that this campaign has had amongst musicians, I recently heard from a former female organ student of mine, who had been instructed by her current (male) teacher that her playing needed to be "more masculine".

I presume (hope!) that most of you, both male and female, are raising your eyebrows in a combination of bemusement, horror, and righteous indignation. Nonetheless, there must be something concrete lurking behind this instruction, since it continues to be used frequently enough to warrant notice. And so I will use this column to muse upon this out-moded gendered vocabulary, in order to try to understand exactly what it is that is perceived as lacking in the playing (substitute throwing or running, as you wish) of those of us of "the fairer sex".[88]

A few years ago, a Cambridge undergraduate English Literature student was told by a male professor that her essay needed to be written "in a more masculine style". She asked her Director of Studies (the academic responsible for organising supervisions and booking supervisors) exactly what this criticism meant. Conveniently, that academic was a Theoretical Linguist, and knew of statistically significant stylistic traits that revealed differences between men's writing and women's writing.[89] For example, statistically, women use epistemic hedges (phrases such as "it seems", "I think that", "possibly", and the like) more frequently than men.[90] Thus, the following sentence is more likely to have been written by a female student: "It seems apparent, therefore, that Shakespeare was a good playwright", whereas her male counterpart would more likely simply state "Shakespeare was a good playwright." Said Director of Studies suggested that the undergraduate in question remove all such hedges, insert a few more polysyllabic abstract nouns, and bingo, the masculine version of her essay was complimented highly by the aforementioned professor.

This example works well for literature, but how does it relate to organ playing? Before we start, it's important to note that statistically, the organ is more likely to be played by men,[91] although there are, of course, many outstanding and successful female organists. The instruction to "play more like a man" could mean any number of things depending on who utters it, but unfortunately I know of no pre-existing studies of this topic, as there are for writing-styles. The thoughts below are therefore entirely conjectural.

Both Anna Lapwood and my aforementioned student were teenagers when this directive was issued to them. If I were being entirely honest

---

88. A 16th-century phrased used to describe women. And yes, dear reader, I am using it ironically.

89. He also happens to be my husband, which is why I know this anecdote.

90. Much has been written on this topic; here is one example: https://www.degruyter.com/document/doi/10.1515/glot-2017-0002/html

91. https://www.societyofwomenorganists.co.uk/statistics

(though perhaps a little uncharitable), I would suggest that what characterises the playing of a not insignificant number of teenaged *male* organists is a combination of sloppiness, bluster, inadequate attention to detail, and an assumption that pulling out lots of stops will fool their listeners. Were I to ask a young female organist to play more like her male peers, it might not result in a better performance.

More seriously, though, what could actually be behind the instruction? Is it to do with precision (of rhythm?), or accuracy (of notes?), or registration (do women play more quietly than men?), or touch (is a man's legato better than a woman's?—men do tend to have larger hands), or confidence and authority (is there a perceived lack of these rather nebulous qualities in a woman's playing?). I'm speculating, of course, but crucially, these issues and more could be addressed if specific directions were given, rather than what appears to be merely a lazy, inappropriately-gendered shortcut. As an aside, I cannot help but wonder whether the instruction would have been phrased differently had the player been hidden behind a conveniently-placed Positif-de-dos.[92]

In the end, as teachers our goal must be to help our students find their *own* voice, and express their *own* musicianship. They need to play neither "like a man" nor "like a girl", nor indeed like anything other than *themselves*, whatever form that individual may take. Enabling that honesty of expression, regardless of their sex or gender, or indeed of our own, is our duty and our responsibility, and it should not require a column such as this to remind ourselves that the use of unbiased language to accomplish this is simply non-negotiable.

---

92. For a fascinating discussion of sexism in the organ world, including the need for blind auditions for Classical musicians, see https://www.societyofwomenorganists.co .uk/post/spotlight-on-equality-and-diversity-in-the-organ-world

Chapter 9

Callings, Careers, and CPD

This chapter looks at organist/conductor employment norms, working conditions, salaries, and other such professional concerns, including the opportunities and expectations for Continuing Professional Development on both sides of the Atlantic.

February 2010

A Musician's Long Hours

The other day, a friend of mine updated her Facebook status with a complaint about working 14-hour days. She is an academic musicologist in an obscure university slightly southwest of Milton Keynes.[93] I was somewhat amused by her complaint, and made a flippant comment along the lines of "What, only 14?" This prompted an unexpected and lengthy exchange, involving several mutual friends and colleagues, about the exploitation of overworked and underpaid academics and musicians in the UK. It was obviously a topic ripe for discussion, and much heated argument ensued.

This got me thinking about the nature of vocation: why is it that some of us are willing to work ridiculous hours for next to no pay? Are those of us who have a vocation (rather than a job) really working to our fullest potential, or are we actually just being exploited? None of us gets paid to work a 14-hour day, and in the UK, where the salaries of academics and musicians are (in general) insultingly low already, why do we tolerate this kind of treatment? This was the essence of the Facebook discussion, with a few amusing references to ineffectual European Union work directives thrown in for good measure.

---

93. i.e., Oxford.

The topic is a serious one though. Two weeks before this event, in the middle of an already very busy term, I had concerts in Cambridge, London, and Edinburgh in the space of just four days, as well as the regular round of services, rehearsals, teaching, meetings, and administration, not to mention desperate attempts to find time for my own personal practice (the concert in Edinburgh was a solo organ recital). I am certainly not trying to outdo my Oxford friend, but I think I was pushing 17- or 18-hour days when I made my light-hearted comment, and I hadn't had a day off for about four weeks. My usual term-time day begins with email on the train to Ely at 6:15am, and ends (on a good day) by about 10:30pm. Like my colleagues, I tend to work a seven-day week during term, though a slightly later start on a Saturday is something to look forward to.

There is constant worry here in the UK about the "brain drain" from Britain to the States, with many excellent academics and musicians searching for work on the other side of the Atlantic. When I consider that many of the posts advertised on the AGO website are full-time jobs, with just one or two Sunday services per week, this trend is not surprising. By contrast, at Selwyn, as at most Cambridge colleges, the post of director of music is only part-time, despite having three or four choral services during the week, as well as on Sundays. Most college-based directors of music are not actually paid for music preparation and solo practice time: these must be squeezed into what are traditionally overtime hours, since academic teaching (also not part of the contract for many of us, but classed as informal self-employment) has to take place during normal working hours. My post at Ely, as Director of the Cathedral Girls' Choir, is also part-time, despite the fact that the girls rehearse four mornings a week before school, and sing two or three services every week. Many readers have wondered how I manage to combine these two posts, but since Selwyn and Ely are both 50% time, adding up to a total of just 100%, that leaves the other 50% of my time for my freelance career (!)—and I only actually conduct six services in a normal week. I won't discuss the worrying issue of salary scale—suffice it to say that organists in large American churches are paid significantly more than those in UK cathedrals and colleges, and that academic salaries are simply not comparable, even at the highest levels.

At any rate, notwithstanding my friends' and colleagues' Facebook concerns, there are certainly some advantages to this lifestyle. Since everything that I do is part-time, and a good deal of it is freelance, I piece together a bespoke and musically satisfying existence that includes a combination of playing, conducting, recording, teaching, examining, writing, composing, arranging, and so on. This gives me considerable control over my time, despite the fact that it can be exhausting and feel unfocussed, particularly in the middle of term. So, a couple of weeks after this legendary Facebook rant, when I was given tickets to the last round-robin day of the ATP world final tennis tournament at London's O2 Arena, I was pleased indeed not to have one, predictably-timetabled, full-time job. Instead of needing to ask anyone's permission, I simply rearranged my schedule for the day, set up and email vacation message, and got on the train. I spent an amazing few hours watching Nadal, Davydenko, Djokovic, and Soderling trying to outmanoeuvre each other with power and guile.

Ultimately, I don't know whether we should be more concerned about exploitation and overwork, or whether we should actually be grateful for the freedom we have to make music (and watch tennis) in so many and varied ways. I would love to reflect at greater length upon such complex and profound matters, but, if you'll excuse me, I have to dash to the chapel to conduct Evensong.

August 2011

You Want to Be a Musician
When You Grow Up?

A few weeks ago I travelled to the Royal College of Music (RCM) in London to participate in a talk entitled "Careers in Music" (I do realise that this concept may sound like an oxymoron). The audience numbered about 200, and consisted primarily of student instrumentalists and singers from the four main London music conservatoires (the RCM, the Royal Academy of Music, the Guildhall, and Trinity Schools of Music), all about aged 15 to 17, along with a handful of parents and teachers. The Expert Panel, of which I was a member, was made up of five established musicians, representing a variety of professional perspectives: freelance performers, specialist conservatoire teachers, cathedral and university musicians (whom I represented), arts administrators, and the like. We began the session by recounting what it was that had called us to a career in music ourselves, and how we had gone about following that call.

I started by reminiscing about my days studying the piano at the Royal Conservatory of Music in Toronto, at the end of the 1980s, when my fellow students and I all planned (or at least hoped) to launch our careers with the winning of a major international competition. I think we all felt that represented a pure and undiluted route to musical success. (The other even less realistic option was to find a long-lost member of the Court of

Esterházy to act as patron.) We did our time waiting tables, teaching six-year-olds where middle C was, and playing in the pit orchestra of second-rate musicals, in order to pay the rent, but we all were secretly dreaming of the day when we would be "discovered" and get on with our proper Career in Music. Sadly, in my youth I didn't win anything much more glamorous than second place in my Provincial Music Festival, and so my solo career was not launched with an exclusive record deal or a concerto performance with the Berlin Phil. (Incidentally, neither were those of very many of the other brilliant young musicians who were my colleagues.) Since those student days, I have pieced together a varied and fascinating career as a liturgical musician, an organist, a conductor, a teacher of traditional harmony and counterpoint, a composer, a recording artist and producer, an examiner, a répétiteur, a lecturer, and, of course, a writer of columns for prestigious organists' publications, not to mention numerous other musical activities that I never imagined when I was practising virtuoso pianistic fireworks in preparation for those alluring competitions. I only very occasionally think back on those dreams of glory and wonder if my career so far has been merely second-rate.

Back in London, as the other four eminent members of the panel reminisced, I was delighted and relieved to hear that they too had followed unconventional routes into their current careers. One of them, a distinguished singer whose name appears as soloist on most of the CDs I own, couldn't decide as a student whether to become a professional rower, an orchestral oboist, or a piano teacher. After an injury to his hand during an outing on the river, he had no choice but to learn to sing! Another was a serious solo pianist whose Oxford undergraduate room was too small for a piano, so he had the college harpsichord instead. Now, he is well known in the UK as a continuo player and most of us had no idea that his heart was actually in Chopin and Liszt. The other panel members also had their own stories to tell, and we were all left wondering whether the single-minded musician whose high-profile solo career is launched after winning a competition actually even exists at all. I hope that the varied and realistic life stories that the audience heard that day will widen the views of those students whose visions of competition victory are as skewed as mine were at their age.

The talk continued with a lengthy question-and-answer session, and one of the key topics of discussion was that of tertiary education. In the UK, there has traditionally been a choice of paths: university music departments tend to provide an academic/musicological education whereas conservatoires offer more practical performance training. Indeed, many universities, including Cambridge, do not require an audition to study for a degree in Music: admission is based on school academic criteria alone (achieving an 'A*' in Biology is more important than the results of a recent violin exam). Conservatoire entry, on the other hand, is by competitive audition, and school exam results are less important. The panel encouraged the students to research the curricula they might follow—was the balance between theory, history, analysis, and their practical studies, right for them at their chosen institution? In addition, the choice of principal teacher was stressed—many of the panel recalled travelling significant distances in order to work with a particular mentor. We also discussed the options for those who wanted to study another subject at university (Chemistry or History for example), while still keeping their playing and/or singing up to a high standard. And of course there were many questions about fees (mostly from the parents), practicalities, application procedures, deadlines, requirements, and so on.

Despite the panel's obvious enthusiasm, optimism, and utter commitment to the study of music, we also made it clear throughout the session that a Career in Music is a financially risky venture (unless you find that Esterházy prince, of course). Members of the panel recounted amusing and familiar stories of parental horror when university courses in Medicine or Law were abandoned in favour of Music. None of us had managed to purchase a house until at least twenty years into our working lives, and all had had the equivalent of more than one soul-destroying table-waiting job. To add insult to injury, a musician's working hours are both long and unsociable (16-hour days are standard), weekends and public holidays are usually ignored, and a hand-to-mouth existence is the norm, particularly in those precarious years immediately after leaving the comparative safety of full-time education.

However, for those of us who have continued to dedicate our existence to music despite all its insecurities and inconveniences, there was some significant common ground: certainly we all had a musical vocation or calling (in some cases it verged on an addiction). Communal hilarity was caused by the thought of putting on a suit and going to "work" from 9 to 5. I admitted to being a musician partly because I am constitutionally incapable of doing anything else, and the vigorous nodding from the rest of the panel members attested to the fact that I am not alone. And I think it is true to say that those who are called to a Career in Music will not have any choice in the matter. As the great Ray Charles is purported to have said: "I was born with music inside me. Music was one of my parts. Like my ribs, my kidneys, my liver, my heart. Like my blood. It was a force already within me when I arrived on the scene. It was a necessity for me—like food or water."[94]

---

94. Widely attributed to Ray Charles (1930-2004), American singer-songwriter, pianist, and composer.

A Lucky Break

Here in England, church musicians are trained in a curiously illogical way. Usually, after putting musical foundations in place during a university organ scholarship and a year or two in a church or cathedral organ scholarship (the number three post), an organist will spend perhaps 10 or 15 years as an assistant organist or sub-organist (the number two post), playing for all choral services, accompanying choir and congregation, amassing a repertoire of liturgically appropriate solo works, honing improvisation skills, polishing psalm and hymn playing, and developing the many and diverse skills which are required of a liturgical organist. So far, so reasonable.

However, following these years of intense organ-focussed preparation for promotion, upon appointment to a number one post (director of music), most organists promptly drastically reduce their time at the console, and become primarily conductors. This is rather like a person spending years training hard to become a nurse in a neurology department, and, when this complex task has been accomplished, the individual concerned is expected to be a proficient brain surgeon. Not all skills can be acquired simply by observing other people making use of them. Of course a reasonable amount of conducting experience will have been gained at university and beyond, but the development of and concentration on organ playing during the first twenty years or so does not prepare anyone specifically for a conducting career. Ironically, in many cathedrals the number one post retains its historical title of "Organist and Master of the Choristers", but the post-holder actually rarely plays the organ since assistant organists and organ scholars do that instead. Indeed, occasionally, directors of music have been known to relinquish the limelight, and to return to the number two post, in order to play the organ more regularly.

In my own case, I took up the organ specifically because I wanted to be a choral conductor. I knew that in order to achieve one goal, I would need to develop tenuously related skills. I did my three-year university organ scholarship, and began my requisite apprenticeship in a number three post, with a view to spending long years as an assistant organist, in order eventually to gain a number one post, and so achieve my goal of becoming a full-time conductor. Unfortunately (or not, as the case may be) a mechanical fault in my bicycle resulted in a badly broken collar bone just a few weeks into that number three post, and my liturgical organ playing (along with much of the rest of my life) had to be put on hold indefinitely. As it happened, just about the time that I regained the use of my left arm, the number one post at Selwyn College, Cambridge was advertised. Because this is a university position, and therefore slightly outside the normal route for organists and conductors, I didn't need to have spent those years playing the organ in order to be considered for it, and I was duly appointed to the position of full-time conductor some time before most of my university contemporaries had even finished their time in number three jobs. It was, you may say, a lucky break!

Perhaps because I had not had those aforementioned 10 to 15 years, I did arrange to carry on playing the organ liturgically, though not at Selwyn, where I have had a string of very able undergraduate organ scholars, several now pursuing the very career path that I unexpectedly by-passed. Instead I spent many years playing at Little St Mary's Church (LSM) in Cambridge, the local Anglo-Catholic establishment. Here I built up all of those skills listed above, with particular focus on liturgical improvisation, for which there is considerable demand at LSM, where they are always finding something else to cense during hymns. LSM is a congregation full of musicians, students, academics, and retired clergy, and they sing "lustily and with a good courage".[95] playing hymns and accompanying congregational plainsong is a joy, especially on the very lovely new Kenneth Tickell organ that was installed a few years into my time there.

As some of you will know, a couple of years ago I took on the additional post of Director of Ely Cathedral Girls' Choir, where I also have a dedicated assistant organist. One of the things that had to be sacrificed in order to fit in these new duties was my position at LSM. At first, I thought that I really had achieved what I had set out to do—I was conducting Choral Evensong five or six times a week, in two stunning ecclesiastical buildings, and was, as it were, beyond the need for playing the organ. It surprised me therefore earlier this year to realise how much I was missing liturgical organ playing. I have kept playing recitals, of course, but what I really wanted to do was play hymns, improvise, accompany, and play solo repertoire not for its own sake, but for the sake of the liturgy.

Consequently, I contacted LSM and asked whether they might be willing to have me back from time to time. On the first Sunday I played, I realised how quickly those skills can become rusty: simultaneously leading and accompanying the ebb and flow of the Merbecke Creed; having to cadence earlier (or later) than planned during a hymn extension; modulating from the key and style of the organ prelude to those of the choir's introit; accompanying plainsong psalms in modally peculiar tonalities; improvising a gospel fanfare on a less-than-inspiring gradual hymn; timing the beginning of the (liturgically appropriate) closing voluntary to allow just the right amount space for quiet prayer after the blessing and dismissal. All of these demand very different ways of playing, listening, and responding from those required in a recital situation.

I have been very fortunate in realising my ambition to be a choral conductor much earlier than expected thanks to that fortuitous (though painful) collar bone incident in 1998. I have come to realise however that although I may originally have taken up playing the organ as a means to a choral conducting end, I don't wish to do the latter at the expense of the former. Indeed, since most directors of music spend much of their time

---

95. Wesley, John. Directions for hymn singing in *Select Hymns with Tunes Annext*. Bristol. 1761.

giving musical and technical instructions to assistant organists and organ scholars, it is crucial that their organ-playing skills remain sharp and well-honed. So, I would encourage all of my colleagues who think that they have moved beyond the basics of nursing, and into the exalted world of neurosurgery, not to neglect the skills they worked so hard to perfect earlier in their careers.

November 2012

Keyboard Skills (Honoris Causa)

Once a year, in an elaborate and formal ritual which includes lengthy processions through the Cambridge city streets, dignitaries and academics bedecked in full scarlet academical dress led by mace-carrying Esquire-Bedells and velvet-bonnet-wearing Proctors enter the University Senate House for the 500-year-old Honorary Degree Ceremony. The ceremony is conducted entirely in Latin, and is one of the highlights of the university's year—and it provides plenty of photo opportunities for camera-clutching tourists. Honorary graduands wear gowns of scarlet cloth with coloured silk linings and facings, except for the Honorary Doctor of Music (Mus.D.) degree, which has cream damask and cherry-silk robes. It is certainly one of the most exotically beautiful academic gowns I have ever seen, perhaps befitting Cambridge's history, since it offered the world's first ever firmly-authenticated Bachelor of Music degree in the year 1464.

A Doctorate *Honoris Causa* constitutes the highest accolade that the University can offer. The degrees are conferred on a total of about six to eight internationally-acclaimed recipients per year, in five categories: Divinity, Law, Letters, Science, and Music. In recent years, recipients have included the likes of Nelson Mandela, Stephen Hawking, Archbishop Desmond Tutu, Mother Teresa of Calcutta, Sir Alec Guinness, Dame Kiri Te Kanawa, Sir Peter Maxwell Davies, Chancellor Helmut Kohl, and Noam Chomsky. This year's honorary degree recipients included the Lord Chief Justice of England, three renowned bio-medical researchers, a theoretical physicist, a Nobel prize-winning chemist, and one of my childhood heroes: the pianist Alfred Brendel.

This event presented me with an unexpected nostalgia-tinged juxtaposition: the Czech-born pianist whom I had idolised from afar as a young pianist in Canada was being recognised by what is for both us an adopted homeland, in a city which I am a conductor and organist, The awarding of an honorary Cambridge degree to Brendel caused me to reflect upon my own progression from aspiring concert pianist to FRCO-certified organist. I found myself brooding upon the differences between the early training regimes offered to pianists and organists, and how the two paths can lead to the same place—or not—in later life.

When I arrived in Cambridge as an undergraduate organ scholar, in the early 1990s, I was fresh out of the Royal Conservatory of Music in Toronto, where I had been a very serious first-study pianist. I had spent many, many hours of my childhood and teenaged years practising scales, arpeggios, and other technical exercises, to hone my finger dexterity, so that I could perform Chopin Etudes and Scherzos, Brahms Piano Concertos, and Schubert and Beethoven Piano Sonatas. I owned Brendel recordings of many of these works, of course, and somewhere I still have a fading dark green boxed set of cassette tapes of the Beethoven Piano Sonatas. When I came to Cambridge, I was surprised to find that many of my organ scholar colleagues who had been first-study organists since the age of 12 or 13, had only a nodding acquaintance with Czerny and Hanon, and had instead devoted their practice time to those special mystical organ-specific skills such as transposition, score reading, and improvisation.

As a late-starter at the organ (I took it up when I was 19) I spent a great deal of time feeling rather inadequate when faced with other organ scholars who could play a hymn in a variety of keys, or accurately read a six-part vocal score in rehearsal. I definitely had some catching up to do, since I had apparently spent too many of my formative years working on chromatic double-third scales and four-octave arpeggios in tenths. It didn't help my confidence that one of my closest friends and undergraduate colleagues was a very brilliant and precocious young organist who is now director of music at a major English cathedral. At the age of 18, he was an accomplished and imaginative improviser, could realise figured bass in his sleep, and was able to transpose anything in to any key, at sight. His score reading skills didn't stop at a mere six parts either: he was perfectly happy with orchestral scores with or without transposing instruments, and ancient double-choir scores in antiquated clefs.

I was vindicated a little, however, when part of the way through our time working together, he was required to learn Sweelinck's *Chromatic Fantasia* for an exam: he was completely stumped by the 32nd-note scales in the left hand, and *I* actually gave *him* a few lessons on how to master such runs—practising in odd rhythms and with different articulations, using the metronome to build up speed, making sure that he used the same fingering every time. These were things that I had learned at such an early age that I couldn't believe no-one had taught them to him. Conversely, when he was helping me with my rudimentary transposition, he too was amazed that no-one had ever suggested to me that playing something in a key other than that in which it was written was actually a useful skill.

In the end, both he and I are now successful professional musicians, with similar musical and academic qualifications. I have learned how to transpose, and obsolete clefs in multi-part score-reading exercises no longer terrify me, and I have no doubt that my old friend is happier with left-hand passage work now than he used to be. Nonetheless, I am sure that it is the case that the skills one learns first, and spends formative years developing, are those which will always feel most natural. I know only one or two people who have equal facility with traditional organist keyboard skills as well as a serious pianist's technical dexterity—undoubtedly they had an even more stilted teenaged social life than I did!

Reminiscing over the past few days since the Honorary Degree Ceremony here has been cathartic. I think I will go and dust off my old cassette tapes of Alfred Brendel's early Beethoven Sonata cycle, and listen to the clarity of his impeccable technique and his unparalleled musicianship. I'll remember his magnificent playing while I think of him parading through the Cambridge streets in his cream damask and cherry silk robes.

And then I will go and practise some transposition.

November 2013

The Observational Visit

E arlier this year, I found myself organising practice sessions on the Létourneau at Selwyn College, and being observed in rehearsals at Ely Cathedral by a statistically improbable number of visiting North Americans. Some were on holiday, others on Sabbatical, a number on specific programmes of Continuing Professional Development. I enjoyed getting to know these visitors while they were here, although throughout many interesting discussions, I found myself concerned by some of the questions that were put to me. It became apparent that despite the fact that we are living in a global village interconnected via mobile phone and the internet, seemingly it is still difficult to set up this sort of itinerary from afar. So I have decided to devote a column to answering questions in advance for those of you who might be considering a trip to the UK to observe the English Choral Tradition in action, or to sample a couple of particularly intriguing church, chapel, or cathedral organs while on holiday.

I shall begin with some very practical advice regarding transportation. The easiest way to get around in the UK is by train. With the exception of a few supposedly out-of-the-way places (like Wells and Ripon) which lost their branch lines in the cuts inflicted on British Rail in the 1960s (a Google search for "Beeching Report" will reveal the whole sad story), the vast majority of the UK can be reached easily by the now-privatised rail system. There are just a few things you need to know to survive. The network functions mainly in a north-south direction, centred on London, thus rendering east-west journeys (e.g., Cambridge to Oxford) impossible without bouncing in and out of London. For North Americans (and Europeans, to be fair) it will seem expensive: although tickets purchased in advance are reduced in price, the need to book a specific train means that this only works well for long journeys (e.g., Peterborough to Edinburgh). If you are travelling on a frequent commuter route (e.g., Ely to London) it is not worth buying a ticket in advance, since nearly the same advance discount applies to tickets purchased on the day of travel, except during the weekday rush hour, and there are three or four trains per hour on those common routes. If you know that you will to do a lot of travelling, and you plan your trip at least six months in advance, you can purchase a BritRail Pass (though British Rail ceased to exist when the network was privatised in the mid-1990s). These are only available for purchase by non-UK residents, and they are not cheap, so it is worth ensuring that the price you pay for one pass is actually less than the total cost of your various individual journeys. You can access a detailed journey planner at www.nationalrail.co.uk/.

I was surprised that a couple of these visitors were spending exorbitant amounts on accommodation. Of course accommodation will be relatively expensive in major tourist centres (which includes most cities with cathedrals and ancient universities), however access to more economical accommodation is easily arranged. The University Rooms Group, a recent international initiative, rents student accommodation in university cities across the world. A visit to www.universityrooms.co.uk will enable you to stay in an historic Oxford undergraduate room for as little as £40 (about $60) per night. This compares more than favourably with Oxford hotel prices which can average around £100 (about $155) per night, and is also available in other university towns including Salisbury, Bath, London, and Cambridge (four of the top ten most expensive UK cities).[96] Of course, if you want a real deal, you can always find a Travelodge, but since

---

96. These are 2013 prices.

they are usually located on city outskirts, what you save on accommodation will likely be made up on taxi fares.

The timing of your trip is important if you want to experience the English Choral Tradition in full. Most cathedral choirs sing regularly throughout the school year, which lasts roughly from early September to the end of June, with a one- or two-week Half Term break in the middle of each of three terms. You will need to look carefully on cathedral websites to determine specific term dates, since most cathedral schools are independent (private) schools, and can set their own dates. If you are hoping to hear choirs with senior school members (this includes a number of cathedral girls' choirs, for example) you should avoid May and June, since the girls will be taking school examinations (GCSEs and A-levels). Observing choral activity in Oxford and Cambridge can be particularly awkward, since our three terms are so short (only eight weeks each) and the third term is almost entirely taken up with examinations.[97]

Mundane practicalities aside, the question of whom to observe, and/or which organs to play remains paramount, of course. Personally, I would recommend arranging to hear a wide variety of choirs (cathedrals, parish churches, college chapels, secular ensembles both large and small) which include a broad range of diverse personnel (young boys and girls, teenagers, university students, young professionals, seasoned lay clerks), attending both rehearsals and services, and organising practice sessions on an assortment of organs (foreign, domestic, tracker, electro-pneumatic) in a selection of different buildings. This variety will provide for deeper and more realistic insights into the scene here in the UK than you would obtain if you were simply to hear the choirs and organs most frequently represented in your own CD collection. Most importantly, feel free to contact directors of music directly by email (every website has a "contact us" page), explaining the purpose of your visit. You may not receive a prompt response in every case, but I know that I speak for the vast majority of my colleagues when I say that if the time is available, we

---

97. For a discussion of the effects of examinations on extra-curricular endeavours like choral singing, see October 2011 on page 46.

will go out of our way to assist visitors in setting up enriching and engaging itineraries.

Finally, the only other visitors' enquiries which struck me particularly were posed by those who were not members of the AGO, and who therefore quizzed me on a variety of subjects which have already been addressed in past issues of this column. Manifestly, if you are reading this, you needn't worry about those details.

September 2014

SCF: My Shadow

Earlier this year, I received an unsolicited email from an undergradu-ate choral musician at a rural American liberal arts college (which I will admit I'd never heard of). The young man in question was enquiring (well, "inquiring" actually) about observing the English Choral Tradition in action—and, amusingly and flatteringly, he was eager to shadow *me* in particular, at both Selwyn College and Ely Cathedral. He wrote the most charmingly polite email (it was positively Edwardian in both style and syntax), so I replied readily, suggesting various options. As this visit is coming to an end, I thought I would give you a sense of the things he's done, how it was organised, and, most importantly, the many things that I have learned from him, turning what seemed at first like a one-sided adventure into a cultural exchange.

In our ensuing emails, we worked out logistics. College term dates in the States do not coordinate well with ours here: just as things finish over the Atlantic, and you are blessed with a lengthy period to devote to interesting research projects, on this side of the Pond we launch into six weeks of university and national school examinations, which take their toll on choral performances in universities and cathedrals.[98] Unfortu-

---

98. For a discussion of the effects of examinations on extra-curricular endeavours like choral singing, see October 2011 on page 46.

nately, my new shadow's dates coincided with our examination period, but he was very gracious about the resultant complications. Our Bursar had kindly agreed to offer him a reduced "research rate" on room rental for four weeks, meals would be available in the college dining hall at student prices, and he even managed to convince his own university to support the venture financially, so everything was set.

The morning after his arrival in the UK, we met for breakfast to discuss his plans, and the past four weeks here have indeed turned out to be as hectic as we anticipated. His time in Cambridge and Ely has included what I hope has been a good range of activities: he has sung several services with Selwyn Choir; he has observed and taken copious notes on any number of rehearsals and services at Selwyn, and also at Ely Cathedral with the girls and lay clerks; he has attended Formal Hall (a Harry-Potter-esque meal with a Latin Grace, where jackets, ties, and academic gowns are compulsory, although owls are optional); he has sung for the ceremonial installation of an Honorary Canon in Winchester Cathedral; he has studied new repertoire and read several articles; he has sung on the recording of an iPhone App for the Tour de France, which (despite its title) starts in the UK, and will be cycling through Cambridge this summer; and he has demonstrated extraordinarily imaginative transferable artistic skills by designing a large poster board for Ely Cathedral Girls' Choir on the occasion of the National Gathering of the Friends of Cathedral Music.

Lest any readers worry that I have selfishly kept him entirely to myself, he has also had the opportunity to observe rehearsals and services at a variety of other Cambridge Colleges, including King's, St John's, and Trinity. He spent a hugely valuable week at St Paul's Cathedral in London, he worked once or twice with the Cambridge Masters of Music in Choral Studies (MMus) students, and he also seems to have spent very large amount of money in the main music shops in Oxford and London. So I hope we've all managed to give him a rounded experience of the choral scene here.

As I mentioned above, however, what has perhaps been the most interesting side of this whole adventure is what *I* have learned from *him* over our many cups of coffee and lengthy conversations. In particular, I have been introduced to the choral tradition which is practised at his college in the States, and I have been fascinated to learn about the impressive quality of singing, the repertoire, the routine, the training, the audition process, and the rivalries with other similar college choirs. The latter of these is particularly intriguing, since we have such rivalries here too, of course—geographically the colleges are closer together (a few hundred feet rather than a few hundred miles) but the characteristics of the inter-collegiate rivalry are exactly the same, including intense debate on how much money is spent on glamorous publicity, and how much vibrato the sopranos do or do not use!

Amongst the various differences between his university choral train-ing, and that which he has been observing here, we have discussed in particular the distinction between choirs which must sight-read and learn music very quickly for frequent (often daily) performances, such as UK cathedral and collegiate chapel choirs, and those which prepare in great depth for perhaps just one two performances per month (or even fewer), singing entire concert programmes from memory, and polishing reper-toire at a level of detail that I rarely (if ever) manage, such as is the norm in the choir to which he belongs. Although the latter approach is represented in the UK, notably in the National Youth Choirs of Great Britain, in the liturgical world here, where we often have just 15 minutes to rehearse for a weekday Choral Evensong, the speed at which we have to get through repertoire is certainly not conducive to memorisation, and more often than not has to compensate in panache for what it lacks in polish.

Spending four weeks in the UK liturgical environment obviously had an effect on my shadow, however: although he could still recite every detail of his university choir's concert tour programme from several months earlier, at one point I asked him what he had heard at Evensong the day before, and it amused us both greatly that he could not remember. It is a mark of someone accustomed to the daily "heat and serve" method that if they are asked what is on the music list for Evensong a few hours before the rehearsal on the day, they will probably not be able to tell you!

His month here with us was extremely enjoyable, and I hope that he also found it diversified and edifying. From my point of view, I hope that he will be the first of many shadows, since I have so enjoyed learning from him. I also hope that I will get to hear his university choir in person one day—answers on a postcard if you've guessed which one it is!

Waterfalls and Wind Pressure

The anticipatory nature of publishing deadlines mean that although I am writing this column on a sunny morning in late August, you will be reading it in November, as the winter closes in and the busy Advent season looms ominously. This should explain why this month's column draws upon the long and venerable tradition of a "what I did on my summer holidays" essay. At this time of year, it is impossible to avoid other people's vacations. Facebook is bombarded with photos from exotic locations, adorned with envy-inducing descriptions such as 'it is 30 degrees C (or 85 F) in the shade!'. The most common summer destination for my musical colleagues in Britain is the European mainland. Throughout July and August I am inundated electronically with photos of my friends drinking fine wine in the South of France or exploring medieval monasteries in Italy, as well as countless images of Baroque organ cases in Northern Germany and the Netherlands, and (occasionally) some proper vacation snaps involving beaches in Spain or Portugal. This year, when people asked me about my summer plans, I surprised them by revealing that my European holiday destination was not a conventional corner of the Continent, but rather the Gothic-cathedral- and Rococo-organ-case-free zone of Iceland.

Any of you who have been to Iceland will know just how extraordinary the place is. Over a wonderful ten days my husband and I drove nearly 2000km (c.1200 miles), and our daily activities included hiking up mountains, gazing at glaciers, walking over, under, and through waterfalls, swimming in hot-springs pools in remote hills, surveying desolate lava fields and black volcanic beaches, marvelling at spouting geysers, and exploring the huge inter-continental rift valley which bisects the site of the country's ancient parliament. In addition, we paid homage at several sites from the Icelandic Sagas, we saw many cute Icelandic horses, plenty of sheep, an Arctic fox or two, and, of course, puffins. Thankfully, we arrived back in the UK a week before the Bárðarbunga volcano began its current rumblings.

This may all sound rather like an advert for the Icelandic Tourist Board, but my trip was not (of course) entirely devoid of musical encounters. A particular cultural highlight was a visit to Reykjavik's magnificent, if controversial, new concert hall, Harpa, home of the Icelandic Symphony Orchestra and the Icelandic Opera. Built at a cost of $150 million USD during the aftermath of the 2008 banking crisis, there were repeated pleas within Iceland for the project to be abandoned. However, the hall was constructed as planned, and it opened in 2011. Its design is inspired by the characteristic ice and rock formations of the surrounding landscape. It is a stunning structure of steel and glass, both clear and coloured, which catch the 21 hours daily of summer sunlight in startling ways. Although we didn't attend a concert (on our one free night in the capital, the main performer was Bryan Adams, and notwithstanding my latent Canadian nationalism, I felt I could manage without him), the imaginative building itself was more than sufficient.

Also, in between the waterfalls and the puffins, I actually heard, saw, and played a fascinating selection of pipe organs. At the east end of Reykjavik's imposing Lutheran church, Hallgrímskirkja, whose 73-metre tower (an imaginative architectural portrayal of volcanic basalt columns) affords fabulous 360-degree views over the city, can be found a 1985 II-9 Frobenius (Denmark). As an undergraduate, I was organ scholar at Robinson College, Cambridge, whose chapel houses a 1982 II-26 Frobenius. It was poignant to see my Frobenius' little brother thriving in Hallgrímskirkja. The west end instrument is a magnificent 1992 IV-72 Klais (Germany). On the day I visited, I was fortunate to hear the Klais being played, as an organist was preparing Franck's *Chorale nr. 3 in A minor* for a recital the following day. After every one of the (frequent and gratuitously loud) cadences, the numerous tourists in the building clapped effusively. For me however, the playing was sadly lacking accuracy, skill, and precision. I suppose this is a salutary lesson about practising in public places, something that we organists are often obliged to do: it is dangerous to assume that all the people listening are musically-ignorant tourists.

A few days later, I discovered another Frobenius (1963 III-17) in Skálholt Cathedral, about 90km east of Reykjavik. Skálholt had been an important episcopal centre throughout the Middle Ages, and these days the cathedral hosts an active concert series. Nostalgia for my undergraduate days prompted me to enquire whether I might be permitted to play, having explained that I was a visiting organist and was familiar with Frobenius' instruments. The answer was categorically negative. Perhaps there should be some form of official, internationally-recognised organist ID that can be used to prove credentials when travelling abroad? Admiring the case of a fine instrument is one thing, but being able to play it is quite another.

My most significant encounter with Icelandic organs occurred about 65km east of Reykjavik, in the tiny seaside hamlet of Stokkseyri (population 445). Here we found the workshop of Iceland's only organ builder, Björgvin Tómasson, who trained in Germany, but who has lived and worked in Iceland for many years. He tunes and maintains 110 of the country's 115 instruments, and he has also built several organs (including a chamber organ for the eccentric Icelandic singer-songwriter Björk), one of which is located in the parish church beside his workshop. He was kind enough to let me play this beautifully crafted II/18 tracker, which has a superb action and some truly lovely colours. He shares his warehouse with a fish-processing plant, and part of it is ingeniously set up as a comprehensive display of the history and mechanics of organ building. When we arrived, he was in the midst of enthusiastically teaching a seemingly musically-uneducated teenage Polish boy how to tune reeds! I very much enjoyed playing the instruments in his display room, although I will admit that I struggled with the 18th-century Austrian chamber organ (which Mozart might have played, of course) the bellows of which I had to pump by pedal as I played.

Although the scenery—the waterfalls, the glaciers, the hot-springs, the mountains—was undoubtedly the real highlight of my trip to Iceland, it was truly fascinating to learn a little about the country's organ culture as well. I would strongly recommend such a holiday if you want something slightly less conventional. However, if you decide to go, remember to pack your organ shoes as well as your hiking boots. And of course, make sure you check the volcano alerts before you set out. Sjámust!

A Whistle Stop Tour

I was 21 years old when I first visited the UK, and had been longing to come to England for over a decade by then. I'd never experienced the delights of a red-eye transatlantic flight (something I am all too familiar with now), but fortunately, upon arrival, excitement and adrenaline overcame my exhaustion. I got the Tube from Heathrow directly to Westminster Abbey, where I spent several wonderful hours marvelling bleary-eyed at the architecture. Over two weeks, I visited as many cathedrals as possible on my Brit-Rail pass, and the only non-ecclesiastical tourist activity I partook in was a steam-train journey near Chester. Anyone looking at my travel itinerary that summer would have known immediately that I was an organist.

I assume that, like me, many of you also forego the allures of castles, theme parks, and stately homes and instead head straight for the cathedral in any new city (with or without steam-trains). The UK is particularly rich with ecclesiastical architecture, and one can see a lot of it in one visit. This is largely because the UK is only about 94,000 square miles, compared to North America's nearly 9.5 million square miles. Ironically, because my first visit was in August, I heard no English choirs. My main musical memory of that trip is of hearing Herbert Howells' *Dallas Canticles* sung in York Minster by a men and boys' choir from Texas, who spoke with the broadest of southern American drawls, but sang with the cut-glass accents of the British aristocracy.

That trip began my life-long relationship with the UK, which I have been sharing with you in this column for nearly eight years. Since you must by now have a pretty good sense of cathedral and collegiate music in East Anglia, I have decided to take you on a regional ecclesiastical tour of the UK. To this end, I have enlisted the assistance of my colleagues around the country, and from next month, every second column will come from a different cathedral or major parish church, whose directors of music have generously offered to give you a taste of life in their places of worship.[99] I hope that this will be of interest, especially to those of you who have heard enough from me after all this time!

By way of introduction, I thought you should have some statistical and historical background to put things into context. Firstly, it is important to remember that not all of the UK's iconic ecclesiastical buildings are actually cathedrals: Westminster Abbey is not the seat of a bishop, and therefore is not a cathedral. Despite the regular protestations of tourists, Cambridge does not have its own cathedral: King's College Chapel is merely a (rather large) private chapel, and Cambridge city and university are actually part of the diocese of Ely.

As well as many great churches and chapels, there are a total of 44 Anglican (Episcopal), and 19 Roman Catholic, cathedrals in England, Wales, and the Channel Islands, whose years of foundation range from the 4th to the 20th centuries. Scotland and Northern Ireland also have a number of cathedrals of both denominations, all but three of which are 19th- or 20th-century foundations. In addition, there is a large variety of Orthodox cathedrals across the British Isles, but for the purposes of TAO's UK Report Rough Guide, we will stick to Anglican and Roman Catholic cathedrals and greater churches in England for now.

Every cathedral and church has its own unique history, liturgical flavour, musical personality, and overall character. Broadly, the Anglican cathedrals can be divided into three main groups: the ancient medieval cathedrals, the 'parish church' cathedrals, and the newer foundations. In the first category are those buildings whose origins date back many

---

99. A select few of these guest columns are published, with the permission of their authors, as Chapter 14 in this volume.

centuries. Ely Cathedral, for example, was first founded as a double monastery for men and women in 672AD, and has been the seat of the diocesan bishop for over a thousand years. On the other hand, although Bradford Cathedral in West Yorkshire has been a place of worship since the ninth century, it was a parish church variously in the dioceses of York and Ripon until 1919, when it became a cathedral in its own right. Finally, there are the likes of Liverpool, Truro, and Guildford cathedrals, which were built in the 19th and 20th centuries, entirely from scratch, for brand new dioceses.

Since the reign of Henry VIII (king from 1509–1547), England's relationship with the Catholic church has not been without its complications. The most important of the various acts of Parliament in relieving post-Reformation restrictions was arguably the Roman Catholic Relief Act of 1829. The building of new Roman Catholic cathedrals and churches began in earnest in the 1850s, and despite being rather younger than their Anglican counterparts, their importance is enormous. Arundel (1873) and Westminster Cathedrals (1910) are two particularly beautiful examples of neo-French-Gothic and neo-Byzantine architecture respectively; Clifton (1973) and Liverpool Metropolitan (1924) are striking in their mysticism and modernity.

I hope you enjoy the contributions of my colleagues over the coming months, and perhaps find interesting places to visit when you next brave a transatlantic red-eye. Those of you with geeky hobbies like me might also be interested to know about the Cathedrals Express, a steam-train which takes visitors between cathedral cities. I have often wondered how many patrons on those journeys are actually organists. Perhaps I will take a trip on it soon, entirely for TAO 'research' purposes, of course. . . .

Keeping Body and Soul Together

As I write this, Advent and Christmas are looming. As you read it, Lent will be upon us, with Holy Week fast on its heels. Needless to say, these are two of our busiest seasons. During the first three weeks of Advent this year, I have no fewer than nineteen services and concerts in five different cities. By the time Christmas arrives I am unlikely to be in the mood to celebrate the arrival of our Saviour with genuine enthusiasm, and I daresay I am not alone in feeling similarly subdued about the Resurrection after the frenzy of Holy Week.

Unlike people with "normal jobs", clergy and musicians work long hours, evenings, and weekends as a matter of course. In the UK, the luxuries of personal practice and score preparation are unpaid extras, usually undertaken outside of salaried time. I admire in particular those of you with children, who manage to clothe and feed them, carry out school runs, and help with homework, despite having to take choir practices before and after school. It adds further weight to the word "vocation".

Unrealistic weekly hours aside, we are also on show and expected to perform impressively, even at Evensong on Easter Sunday, after having suffered sleep deprivation for over a week, and having not wanted to (or not been allowed to!) disturb the meditative silence of the building by practising the organ after Palm Sunday. Clergy are expected to deliver their finest sermon on Christmas morning, despite having led four carol services, three children's crib services, morning and evening prayer, and midnight mass in the preceding 36-hours—quite apart from having found time to pen a few wise words in the first place.

Of course, many of us thrive on this pressure, since we love performing. We grew up working longer days than our peers—hours of instrumental practice as teenagers, long after our friends were outside playing in the park (or, nowadays, inside playing on computers). Evenings and weekends were the time we most looked forward to; choir practices and Sunday services were anything but a chore. Presumably for many of you, this description is not unfamiliar, and that this was why you chose this career—or rather, why it chose you. A "vocation" is, etymologically at least, a calling.

Here in Cambridge, everyone overworks, all year round. And it's not just musicians and clergy, but also academics and students—writing essays, lectures, conference papers, monographs. It is essential to find about 28 hours in each day, and a large chunk of that involves managing email and other tedious-but-necessary administrative tasks. Cambridge is full of people who thrive on this intensity: high-flying intellectuals, many of whom are trying to climb up the greasiest of greasy poles as rapidly as possible.

It should perhaps be obvious that this lifestyle is not entirely advantageous. Many people who love intensity and thrive on pressure, eventually find that their mental health is rather perilously balanced. The fact that liturgical musicians are usually vocational workers makes things even more precarious, since the relationship between who we are and what we do is mutually interdependent. Social media allows us easily to compare against others how much we are doing, how many complete-works-of-Bach organ series we have played, or indeed, how many carol services we have conducted over a short period—and that has made things worse. The pressure to perform better than—or at least as well as—one's peers can become overwhelming, and taking one day off per month (let alone two days off per week, as people with "normal jobs" do) can prompt feelings of guilt.

This tacit expectation to work all the time has triggered a significant problem with mental health in Cambridge's student population, but its academics, musicians, and clergy are also at risk. In my own recent experience, when three senior choir members resigned their Choral Scholarships at Selwyn in quick succession for unrelated but equally legitimate reasons, I found myself unexpectedly with an incomplete and inexperienced soprano section. Consequently I suffered several bouts of acute insomnia as I worried about forthcoming high-profile engagements.

To remedy the insomnia, I surprised myself. When I have a headache, I need ibuprofen or acetaminophen, not herbal tea. However, rather than asking my doctor for sleeping tablets (the analgesic equivalent), I booked a session with a Cognitive Behavioural Therapist (the counselling equivalent of the herbal tea remedy). Contrary to my preconceived prejudices, she was absolutely brilliant, and helped me with numerous underlying anxieties—and not just those caused by sopranos. Those of you who have emailed me recently will have seen one of her brilliant solutions, an autoreply which allows me to respond when I actually have time (i.e., *not* immediately after evensong). My Facebook friends have seen another of her suggestions, in that I now have a real hobby. I bought an excellent new camera, and am making time to take photos, something I've loved doing since I was a teenager. Indeed, I'm occasionally inclined to go on a photo shoot rather than practise—hopefully that won't end up increasing rather than decreasing my stress levels!

Anyway, the moral of this column is as platitudinous as it is elusive. Look after yourselves, and make sure you don't work too hard, especially at Christmas and Easter. Take time to care for yourself, as well as caring for everyone else. It's not easy to do (especially for Type A Personalities) but if we don't, everything can unravel pretty rapidly.

Chapter 10

In Memoriam

I nevitably, over 12 years of writing these columns, there have been some notable people "who now rejoice with us, but upon another shore and in a greater light."[100] Some of these have been major international figures whose influence on our field is immeasurable. Others were more locally or personally important. May their memories be a blessing.[101]

---

100. From the Bidding Prayer for the service of Nine Lessons and Carols.
101. Traditional Jewish honorific for the dead.

March 2011

BJ's

A s 2010 drew to a close, the musical landscape here in Cambridge changed irrevocably. Many of you who have visited this city over the past 30 years will no doubt have made a pilgrimage to number 10 Green Street, to spend some time in the legendary shop "Brian Jordan Music, Books, and Facsimiles" (or simply "BJ's" as it is affectionately known to generations of Cambridge music students). On 1 December 2010, Brian Jordan, the proprietor, died suddenly of a heart attack, aged 76. Within a few hours, the Facebook page hastily set up in his memory had over 1000 members from all around the world. His funeral Mass, for which I played the organ, took place at Little St Mary's Church, where he had been a faithful member of the congregation for many years. The church was packed, and the mourners constituted a roll call of famous musicians and musicologists, the likes of which gather together so rarely that there is no official collective noun that can be used to refer to them.

Brian's shop could easily feature in *Harry Potter's* Diagon Alley— walking through the door is like stepping back in time. On entry, one is greeted by a Victorian leather-topped desk in the middle of the front room, on which stands no till, no computer, no digital bar-code-reading machines, just a few papers and scores. When Brian did succumb to the need for a chip-and-pin card reader a few years ago, he hid the hand-set in the desk drawer, as if its very presence required an apology. In the back room, music, books, and facsimiles are stacked from floor to ceiling in shelves on every wall. All instruments, from all musical periods, are amply catered for. Choral music can be found in ancient and bulging filing boxes, arranged in a charmingly muddled "alphabetical order" by composer. The viol and recorder shelves include the latest editions of all manner of neglected gems, as well as proper facsimiles for early musicians with good eyesight. Surely this is the only music shop on earth where one can literally *browse* the lute section, or leaf through facsimile part-books of any of the Byrd and Tallis *Cantiones Sacrae* publications? There are collected editions of various composers, the complete *Musica Britannica*, hundreds of books on music and musicology, every opera and oratorio score you've ever heard of (and plenty that you haven't heard of), countless Eulenberg miniature scores, academic journals, catalogues, an inconceivable selection of different sizes of manuscript paper—and so on, and so on, and so on. And that is only half of the full experience: the rickety stairs lead up to the second-hand department, where unnumbered mysteries await discovery.

In recent years, to be fair, the upstairs room has also housed a computer, because Brian did eventually acknowledge that the advance of technology was unavoidable. Their website is extraordinarily impressive and detailed (www.brianjordanmusic.co.uk/) and the shop now benefits from a booming internet trade. The name of the software package that is used to maintain the practical side of the company is, amusingly, "Mind Your Own Business". In spite of these technological advances however, Brian continued to personify the bygone allure of his shop. From behind the desk in the front room, he would greet every one of his customers personally, by name whenever possible. The price of every item in the shop is written in pencil in the inside front cover in his meticulous handwriting. However, he rarely charged his regulars the official price, and discounts were an act of courtesy. Often shy and awkward, he would fumble for the correct change in the pocket of his fading tweed jacket. The telephone was usually buried beneath an Urtext edition somewhere, so he could rarely find it swiftly when it rang. Every Friday he rode his bicycle round the colleges delivering orders of music neatly wrapped in brown paper. He was unfailingly polite, charming, and gracious, and always endearingly eccentric.

Brian was also a genius in an emergency. I have known him to arrive at a chapel in person within minutes of a phone call, carrying a set of

Evening Canticles when an error in the music list had left a panicked director of music without the right copies for the service that day. My favourite anecdote on the Facebook *In Memoriam* page was recalled by an old student friend of mine: "Earlier this month he delivered—overnight— a piece by George Malcolm (which had been out of print for eighteen years) in a special edition by Faber. Of course, Faber had sworn blind that this had never existed." Once, long before the invention of email and the internet, I made the mistake of trying to purchase music from somewhere other than BJ's: in a North American music shop, in a city which shall remain nameless, I attempted to order 30 copies of a particular edition of a Palestrina Mass for my church choir. I knew I was in trouble when I had to spell out the name "P-a-l-e-s-t-r-i-n-a". I gave up (of course) and phoned Brian, who ensured that the copies arrived via airmail within the week.

Most importantly though, Brian's encyclopaedic knowledge of the repertoire and the available published (and often unpublished) editions was staggering. Although he had an impressive array of catalogues behind his desk, he rarely had to consult them in order to locate the precise work his customer was looking for, whether it was a piece of contemporary Russian piano music, or an obscure bit of Portuguese polyphony. In particular, his specialist knowledge of early music was second to none, and displays from his shop were a routine fixture at early music festivals throughout the UK and mainland Europe. In these days of websites, electronic databases, and online catalogues we often know where knowledge can be located—but this is not the same as actually possessing that knowledge. Brian was one of the last of those rare old-fashioned booksellers who could still advise his customers even in the event of a power-cut.

Fortunately for all of us, Brian's legacy will continue, at least for the time being, as his widow, Anne, and his two sons will carry on running the shop. Generations of musicians think of Brian Jordan as a Cambridge Institution, and his loss will be felt keenly throughout the musical world, as well, of course, by his family and his friends. Rest in peace, dear Brian, and thank you for the music.[102]

---

102. Sadly, the shop closed eventually in 2013. The website is still live at the time of writing (June 2020).

D∣S

A few weeks ago, I was involved in organising a memorial celebration for my late organ teacher. Most readers will be familiar with the name David Sanger, and probably also with the tragic circumstances of his death last year. His funeral was a private family event, but since David had been a musical mentor and friend to generations of organists, many of us wanted to find a way to say a proper farewell to him. The format of the event was slightly ambiguous: officially, and in accordance with David's wishes, it was not a memorial service, but rather a concert in celebration of his life. Nonetheless, it certainly gave the hundreds of people there the opportunity to mourn, and also to celebrate the life of an extraordinary player and an influential teacher. The congregation or audience (whichever you prefer), had travelled from all over the world—Australia, the States, Canada, mainland Europe, and of course from across the UK.

Since David taught for more than 30 years in Cambridge, the city provided an appropriate place for the celebration. The event was held in Great St Mary's, the University Church, which has two organs: the historic University Organ at the west end, a 1698 Father Smith III/33, rebuilt and restored at various times, most recently by N. P. Mander in 1995; and at the east end, the parish organ, a 1991 Kenneth Jones (also III/33). For the whole of the preceding week, those of us involved with organising the event took over the church's organ practice rota completely. Music-loving tourists would have been fortunate indeed to be taking photographs and browsing the souvenir stand to the accompaniment of the eminent organists who were taking part, though the long-suffering verger more than earned his overtime pay that week.

On the day itself, the BBC dropped by for some interviews while last-minute practising and registration checking were in progress, and this was followed by a rehearsal of about 50 singers who gathered to sing two of David's choral pieces as part of the celebration. The choir included David's nieces, nephews, friends, men who had been boy trebles in David's church choir in the 1970s but hadn't sung since their voices had changed, a substantial handful of cathedral directors of music, and many of David's organ students from numerous generations, including current Cambridge and Oxford organ and choral scholars.

People began to arrive well over an hour before the recital began. The roll call of esteemed organists was extraordinary—Francis Jackson, Andrew Nethsingha, James O'Donnell, Stephen Cleobury, Christopher Herrick, Philip Moore, to name but a few. Rubbing shoulders with such musical elite were David's friends from his home in the UK's Lake District, with whom he had played tennis, hiked in the hills, and spent many happy hours in his village pub. He lived for some 30 years in a converted chapel in Cumbria, where he loved the outdoors and was a central figure in village life, and many of those friends had not realised the extent of David's international renown as a teacher and recitalist.

After some brief words of welcome from Stephen Farr, a student of David's for many years, we launched into a rousing rendition of David's arrangement of the great Easter hymn "O filii et filiae" ("O sons and daughters, let us sing"), which is scored for the somewhat improbable, but opportunely available, combination of choir, congregation, and two organs (it was written for Westminster Cathedral). Tim Brown (Clare College, Cambridge), an old friend of David's, conducted this, and the two organs were played by Richard Beckford (South Carolina State University), and Ian Tindale (Selwyn College, Cambridge), both students of David's.

The celebration continued with nearly two hours of outstanding organ playing. We had J. S. Bach from Timothy Byram-Wigfield (St George's,

Windsor), Seth Bingham from Clive Driskill-Smith (Christ Church Cathedral, Oxford), a piece of David's from Hans Fagius (Royal Danish Academy of Music), Frank Bridge from John Scott (St Thomas' Fifth Avenue, New York City), Jehan Alain from Stephen Farr (Worcester College, Oxford and St Paul's, Knightsbridge), J. C. Oley and more David from Philip Rushforth (Chester Cathedral), Max Reger from David Goode (Eton College), Johannes Brahms from Jon Laukvik (Norwegian Academy of Music, Oslo), and Louis Vierne from Kevin Bowyer (University of Glasgow). The programme also featured Stephen Farr and Hans Fagius playing a Samuel Wesley duet for organ—David's two duet partners here partnering each other in his absence and to cherish his memory. The playing throughout was impressive, sophisticated, compelling, and stylish. David would have been justifiably proud of his protégés.

Finally, I conducted the choir in David's very lovely setting of the words "Go forth into the world in peace". It offers a fitting description of the manner in which he lived his own life: "be of good courage, hold fast that which is good, render to no man evil for evil, strengthen the faint-hearted, support the weak, help the afflicted, honour all men, love and serve the Lord . . ."

Congregation and performers gathered in Selwyn College afterwards for a reception. Copious amounts of tea, coffee, wine, cake, and other delights were consumed; David's latest CD, music of J. S. Bach recorded in Norway shortly before he died, was officially released; and there was much cathartic and entertaining reminiscing. The printed programme is also filled with stories and anecdotes, vividly bringing to life the kind-hearted, generous, mischievous, and inspirational teacher, who had such limitless dedication and commitment, both musical and personal, to his art, his students, and his friends.

David Sanger's legacy as a teacher is unparalleled in the UK: generations of organists were influenced by his extraordinary musicianship, his attention to detail, his scholarship, and his staggeringly comprehensive knowledge of the repertoire. Those of us who are teachers ourselves would do well to follow his example—it is both a privilege and also a responsibility to advise and guide the next generation, and the task must not be undertaken lightly. This celebration of David's life provided the opportunity to say farewell with dignity and respect, and, significantly, it allowed us, his many students, the chance to express our indebtedness and our gratitude.

David Sanger was someone whose life and work entirely refuted George Bernard Shaw's well-known and provocative epigram about *doing* versus *teaching*.[103] He *could*, and he *did*, and, in addition, he *taught*, selflessly encouraging others to attain the same levels of skill and interpretative brilliance that he himself possessed. Few musicians are able to accomplish this. David was a rare talent, and those us who were fortunate enough to study with him will never forget his self-deprecating and inspirational teaching.

---

103. George Bernard Shaw (1856-1950). Irish playwright and critic.

November 2015

JGS

In early August, I spent a week in New York City at St Thomas Choir School, running the annual Girl Chorister Course. It ended just days before John Scott died. I am sure that, like me, many of you experienced a profound sense of shock and grief at the loss of someone so young, so brilliant, so influential, and so obviously adored. One of the Facebook posts which stood out for me was from a singer friend who did not know John at all, but whose circle of friends overlapped significantly: "Today I find myself mourning the loss of a man I never met. [. . .] His loss is palpable through your many postings of reminiscences and obituaries, and I send you all love as I share in your grief." It was a poignant expression of how profoundly this sad event affected the international musical community.

Inevitably, this awful news has coloured my memory of this year's girls' course. Although it was a successful week of rehearsals, services, and Manhattan sight-seeing, a retrospective ache now accompanies my recollections. Ironically, I had always intended this issue of UK Report to focus on the course, partly in a subtle attempt to accomplish some surreptitious recruitment for 2016. However, it seems even more significant and appropriate now, since John was a conspicuous embodiment of how the UK and the USA could combine to produce church music of the highest order. Some of you may recall that I wrote about the St Thomas Girl Chorister Course in November 2011, when I discussed musical training, vowel production, liturgically appropriate footwear, touristy activities, and the honour of being a part of the worshipping life of that beautiful and historic Fifth Avenue church.[104] This time, I will focus on two highlights: the spectacular singing and the therapeutic laughter.

This year was the tenth anniversary of the founding of the girls' course at the choir school. Not surprisingly, John Scott was instrumental in setting it up and nurturing it. Consequently, he was keen to mark the anniversary in a suitable way, and so we organised an international composition competition. This was open to composers of all ages, and it required them to submit newly-composed settings the Magnificat and Nunc dimittis for two-part upper voices and organ. Some divisi was permitted, and the task was to write something practical for a weekday Evensong (a Stanford-in-B-flat-esque setting, rather than a Finzi-for-Double-Choir epic). The judging panel consisted of John Scott, Sarah Baldock (the other Girl Chorister Course director), composer Judith Bingham, and me. We whittled down over sixty submissions to two winning works, one by the American Randall Svane, and the other by the Brit Philip Moore. It was (I can assure you) entirely coincidental that, yet again, the UK and the USA were equally represented. Both works are entitled 'The St Thomas Service', and they are published by Encore Publications (thanks to John's initiative).[105]

Not surprisingly, performing two world premières in the space of three days with 35 girls from about 15 different states was not entirely straight-forward. The singers had to learn the hard way that Spotify and iTunes are not helpful tools when the task is to master entirely new works. However, in both cases, the girls triumphed over awkward dissonances, complex rhythms, and unfamiliar musical idioms, to produce impressive and assured performances with which both composers were delighted. It was wonderful to see this project come to fruition, though it will always be sad for us that John himself never heard either service.

The girls were full of energy and good humour, and a fair share of the laughter this summer was occasioned by "Mrs Steele", an early benefactor of the choir school, whose rather forbidding portrait hangs in the dining

---

104. See September 2011 on page 159.
105. To order copies visit www.encorepublications.com.

room, overlooking the pupils as they eat. Since it was the tenth anniversary, both Sarah Baldock and I were present for the course (the so-called 'Odd' and 'Even' Sarahs as explained in my 2011 column on page 126). Sarah Baldock, it seems, is able to channel the spirit of Mrs Steele, so at meals, she provided commentary and advice on dining table etiquette for young ladies, in a Downton-Abbey-esque English accent. Some particular gems included lessons on the proper handling of the knife and fork ("your food is already dead, so there is no need to skewer and lacerate it further"), chewing with the mouth shut ("your neighbours have no desire to observe your victuals on their final journey"), and correct usage of the napkin (never called a "serviette" in polite company, of course). Plenty of hilarity ensued, and I think many of the girls learned valuable lessons about which fork to use when, quite apart from how to fit the words of the Magnificat into various combinations of 5/8, 7/8, and 12/8 time.

Despite the fact that our memories of the 2015 St Thomas Girl Chorister Course will always be tinged with sadness, we did have a wonderful time, and the tenth anniversary celebrations were fitting indeed. I am sure that John would have been proud. I hope you'll allow me to encourage you to send your girl choristers to St Thomas choir school in future summers. The opportunities for learning professional musical skills, not to mention formal dining etiquette, are second to none. In the meantime, we will continue to pray for the St Thomas community, for John's family, and for his many friends and students as we mourn his untimely passing.

DVW

I am sitting down to write this column shortly after hearing the momentous, though not unexpected, announcement of the death of Sir David Willcocks at the age of 95. By the time you come to read this, the mystical, but also manic, festive season will be about to begin. Sir David's name is, of course, inextricably linked with Christmas: the carol books, the recordings, the broadcasts, the arrangements, and, of course, those descants.

I actually cannot remember first learning the Willcocks descant to *O come all ye faithful*. I feel as if I must have been born already knowing it. Quite apart from its sentimental place in my seasonal reminiscences, it is unquestionably a musical and technical tour-de-force, motivically coherent and tightly controlled. It opens in melodically and intellectually satisfying counterpoint with the tune, featuring contrary motion, sequences, and a 7-6 suspension at the cadence. It continues with the soaring 'Glory' phrase leading sequentially from the top G, through two secondary dominants, into the dominant itself; at about the Golden Section, the trebles increase the intensity by doubling the organ's dominant pedal, with the iconic "O come" octave Ds. It ends with a triumphant recalling of the first 7-6 suspension, this time a fourth higher, over the final cadential 6/4. For me, it is only beaten by the third quarter-note-beat of the sixth bar of page 41 in the green carol book.

My parents' record collection was a major contributor to my knowledge of Willcocks' descants. In particular, the 1964 "Festival of Lessons and Carols" (ZRG 5450, Argo label) recording was a favourite of mine from a very young age. As a child, I always awoke much earlier than the rest of the world on Christmas morning, and I would sit in the dark and wintry eastern Canadian dawn, with the Christmas tree lights on for illumination, and listen to this recording over and over again. Particular highlights include the chorister who read the first lesson (never has the phrase "who told thee that thou wast naked" been declaimed so expressively), and the wonderful *Alleluya! A newe work is come on hand* by Peter Wishart (1921–1984), which remains one of my favourite anthems. There was also the memorable record cover, on the front of which is a photograph of the choir demonstrating some of the most peculiar facial contortions imaginable. On the back of the sleeve the tracks are listed in Germanic Gothic script, which I recall struggling to read as a child.

In the 1980s, Sir David came to my (then) home town—Victoria, British Columbia—every summer to lead a week-long workshop with an ad hoc choir. When I was twelve, I was considered old enough to join in, despite being the youngest member by at least two decades. That year the repertoire was Handel's four *Coronation Anthems* (my friends on Facebook will have seen that I still treasure my autographed copy of 'Zadok'), and Aaron Copland's masterpiece *In the beginning*. My mother, a professional singer, was to be the mezzo soloist. Perhaps not surprisingly, the Copland proved rather difficult for the assembled volunteer members of southern Vancouver Island's community choirs, and in the end, Sir David decided that we weren't up to performing it, and suggested that my mother should sing something else instead. One of the great highlights of my musical career to date remains my experience as a twelve-year-old, turning pages for Sir David Willcocks, at the organ of the Anglican cathedral in Victoria, while he accompanied my mother singing the 'Qui sedes' from the *B Minor Mass*.

Nearly 20 years later, I met him again in Cambridge, when he was in the audience (!) for a performance of Vaughan Williams' *Hodie* which I conducted in the University Concert Hall. The photograph of me with Sir David at the post-concert reception is also carefully preserved. Over the next decade, I often bumped into Lady Willcocks walking their dogs (their home is just down the road from Selwyn College, and indeed, they were married in Selwyn Chapel in 1947, as Lady Willcocks' father was then Senior Tutor at Selwyn), and one time I mentioned to her that my mother-in-law, an artist, had painted Sir David's portrait from the image on the front cover of his book *A Life in Music* (2008). The afternoon that we had tea with them, and gave Sir David the painting, remains a highlight of my mother-in-law's career to date, even though she suspected that Sir David would have preferred her to have painted him as a younger man.

He was a great musician and an influential teacher; he was a gracious and gentle man; he was a mentor and an inspiration to millions; his descants and reharmonisations are legendary. One of the most shared images on social media this past week has been a photo of the "Word" chord—you know the one I mean. It is surely the most powerful and well-placed half-diminished-seventh chord in the repertoire. That chord will sound different this year, as will the "O come" octave Ds, and the glorious F natural on that setting of 'herald'.

Sir David Willcocks lived a long, rich, and fulfilling life, and he exerted a profound influence on everyone in our profession. Given his great age, the news was so much less traumatic than that of John Scott's untimely death last month, and yet it has touched many of the same people as deeply. May they both rest in peace, and rise in glory.

Chapter 11

Politics and Religion

In polite company, one is not meant to discuss either of these topics. In this chapter, both are explored, from passport woes, to musical expressions of faith and liturgical spirituality.

On Being a Migrant Worker

For many months now, the news has been dominated by the Syrian refugee crisis. In Europe, the difference between refugees and economic migrants (or migrant workers) can be especially difficult to unpick. The open border policy of the European Union, which allows citizens of EU member states to roam, live, and work freely throughout the union, has meant that it is sometimes tricky to distinguish those fleeing war and persecution from those simply seeking a more prosperous way of life.

I have always considered myself a migrant worker. For 25 years I have lived and worked in the UK on my Canadian passport, having been granted "Indefinite Leave to Remain" as the spouse of a British citizen. Unlike in the States, where a number of senior musical and clerical roles in the church are held by foreigners (particularly Brits), there are very few of us here in the UK. Cathedral musicians in the migrant worker category include a New Zealander, an American, and three Canadians, while the tiny handful of non-British bishops and deans includes the Archbishop of York, a Ugandan refugee.

Because the UK cannot limit the movement of EU citizens, in order to control statistics it has taken instead to curbing the privileges of non-EU migrants, including (ironically) members of the Commonwealth. Consequently, it has become increasingly difficult to open a newspaper, or to return to the UK after a holiday, without feeling unwelcome. Like many professionals, I did not change my name when I got married, and I travel on my own a great deal—immigration officers frequently appear disturbed by such subversive actions. More than once, when asked to explain the surname anomaly, I have had to restrain myself from asking what century they were living in. And so, earlier this year, I gave in, and applied for British citizenship. I now hold two passports, Canadian and British.

The process of becoming a UK citizen is complicated and expensive. Fortunately, I was spared the indignity of the first step, the English language proficiency examination, because I come from an English-speaking country (I didn't remind them that 25% of Canadians speak French as a first language). The second step is the "Life in the UK" test, in which applicants are expected to demonstrate a knowledge of this country far beyond that of anyone who was actually born here. In preparing for this test, I learned such things crucial to survival in Britain as when women were granted the vote in Wales, the role that Boadicea played during the first-century Roman occupation, how to distinguish between a Magistrates' Court, a Sheriff's Court, a Civil Court, and a County Court, what is meant by the "Grand National", when the feast day of the patron saint of Scotland falls, what the queen's official relationship is with the various Channel Islands, and the correct recipe for making a traditional Christmas pudding (yes, really). I did not require any knowledge of musical history before the Beatles. But by far my favourite task was memorising the Horrible Histories' monarchs' song (Google it—you won't be disappointed).

After the test came the 35-page application form, in which I was required to list my parents', grandparents', spouse's, spouse's parents', and spouse's grandparents' names, as well as my income, my spouse's income, mortgage details, phone and internet contracts, education, work, and so on. A further section required details of every time I had left the UK over the previous three years, including dates, destination, and reason for the trip. The form and various official documents were sent off with a large cheque—nearly £2500 GBP ($3750 USD)—and tightly crossed fingers. Anyone for whom English is a second language, or who lacks a substantial income, must find the whole thing utterly discouraging.

The next stage in the process was a rather invasive private interview at the passport office with an immigration officer who knew more about me than I knew myself, including who insures my car, and what the last major purchase was on my credit card. In the end, I actually had quite a good conversation with him about ecclesiastical Gothic architecture, as it turns out that he is a big fan of Ely Cathedral, and had actually heard the girls' choir in a concert once—or maybe that was just one of his subtle interrogation techniques?

Finally, I had to undergo the Citizenship Ceremony. A large group of new citizens was ushered into the courtroom to swear allegiance to Her Majesty Queen Elizabeth II (this was part of the ritual at the beginning of every day at elementary school for me), and then to sing the national anthem ("God save the Queen"). Presumably for a nice local touch, it being Cambridge, the CD we sang along to was that of King's College Choir singing Benjamin Britten's arrangement, in B flat major. When we got to the top Fs in "Send her victorious", all eyes turned in my direction. I considered recouping some of my money by charging them a performance fee—I am a soprano, after all.

My new passport arrived safely ten days later. If I'm honest, little has changed, although I am grateful that airport passport control is a rather faster process for me now. I am fortunate to be a citizen of two relatively peaceful and wealthy countries. I pray that both of them, and all others who are able, will ensure that the millions who really need our hospitality are made to feel welcome and safe.

Canadian Music in the UK

This article first appeared in Organ Canada, the official publication of the RCCO, in the issue published to mark 150 year since <u>Organ Canada</u> Confederation in 1867. It is reprinted here with permission.

In 2017, Canada celebrates 150 years since confederation. This is a commemoration not without controversy. The profoundly damaging consequences of European colonisation on Canada's First Nations are still being endured, both on the national stage, and in the personal lives of many Canadians. Nonetheless, despite its complications, colonialism has played an enormous role in the shaping the current identity of the country. Certainly, the inherited cultural influences of western Europe, and specifically of British Anglicanism, have defined my own development and subsequent career.

Throughout the first three quarters of the twentieth century, thousands of Europeans emigrated to Canada to set up what are now its flagship cultural institutions. Most of the country's symphony orchestras, ballet schools, theatre and music festivals, music conservatories, and liturgical choral traditions were established by European artists, teachers, directors, dancers, and musicians, who came to Canada where opportunities were plentiful. The Royal Winnipeg Ballet, the Stratford Shakespeare Festival, the Victoria Conservatory of Music, and the choral traditions in most of our churches and cathedrals, were created in this way. In addition,

Canadian-born artists and performers expected to spend time studying in Europe or Britain, learning the roots of their discipline, before returning home to establish institutions or build influential careers. St Michael's Choir School in Toronto and the Montréal Symphony Orchestra were founded by Canadian-born visionaries who studied in Europe. Eminent Canadians such as artist Emily Carr and writer Robertson Davies both studied in England before spending their extraordinary careers in Canada.

These institutions and individuals are prized as among the most influential and important musical and artistic traditions in Canada, and they continue to sustain significant and respected international reputations. The Royal Winnipeg Ballet was the first institution in the Commonwealth upon which Queen Elizabeth II bestowed the title "Royal" in 1953. The men and boys' choir of St George's Cathedral, Kingston, was the first overseas choir to sing at Westminster Abbey in 1954. Michael Tippett came to Ottawa himself in 1972 to conduct the Canadian première of *A Child of our Time* at the National Arts Centre (a performance in which my parents sang). Many great European conductors have held posts with Canadian orchestras (including Andrew Davis, Simon Streatfeild, Otto Klemperer, and Günther Herbig).

In the 1970s, immigration laws were tightened, limiting the influx of Europeans and requiring that jobs be given to Canadians first. In addition, Canadian Content (affectionately known as "CanCon") was introduced, demanding that all cultural output contain a certain percentage of material that was written, composed, produced, performed, or presented by Canadians. The quality of said output was not referred to in the legislation, merely the nationality of its creator. My musical training took place under this new legislation, and every competition or exam programme had to contain at least one piece of music by a Canadian composer. If one applied for a grant, played in a public recital or competition, broadcast on radio or television, CanCon was compulsory. It could be argued that this protectionist policy went too far: by seeking to defend our television networks from the overwhelming influence of our neighbours to the south, we risked marginalising our great European cultural heritage. I was particularly irked as a teenager, when in a piano exam I had to forego a work by Brahms in favour of something pleasant but merely competent by Oskar Morawetz (who, like Brahms, was not born in Canada).

My personal grumblings aside (Canadian *dis*Content?), one positive implication of the imposition of CanCon obligations was that Canada had come of age, and now had its own post-colonial cultural identity which needed to be nurtured and shared, as well as protected. We no longer required the patronage of our European forebears, but could contribute on an equal footing with the rest of the world. So, has this actually happened? Have we contributed *bona fide* Canadians (whatever they are!) to the international cultural stage? Manifestly, the answer is yes. Perhaps they did not all spend the entirety of their careers north of the 49th parallel, or on the western side of the Atlantic, but they are world-leading names in their fields: singers Ben Heppner, Gerald Finley, Nancy Argenta, Daniel Taylor; pianists Glenn Gould, Oscar Peterson, Angela Hewitt; writers Margaret Atwood, Lucy Maud Montgomery, Pierre Burton, Timothy Findley; musicians Leonard Cohen, Joni Mitchell, Celine Dion; artists including members of the Group of Seven and Emily Carr, quite apart from the magnificent First Nations (i.e., non-European) work by the likes of Bill Reid, Roy Henry Vickers, and Robert Davidson. In addition, there are legions of Hollywood actors, film directors, and numerous pop musicians, many of whom have bigger names in the business than their American colleagues (though we don't all have to be 'Beliebers').[106]

In light of the 150th celebrations, I was charged by the RCCO to investigate one small corner of the cultural community, namely the UK's organ and choral world, to ascertain whether there is any CanCon present here. I contacted my colleagues in British cathedrals, major parish churches, and Oxbridge Colleges about this matter, and the rest of this column will outline the results of my survey. From a personnel point of view, there are a few Canadian organists living and working in the UK. Apart from yours truly, there are the current Assistant Organists at Lincoln, Chester, and Edinburgh cathedrals (though by the time you read this, the latter will have returned to Canada to take up the post of

---

106. The name by which fans of the popular singer Justin Bieber are known.

Director of Music at Christ Church Cathedral, Victoria).[107] In addition, Orgues Létourneau have five instruments in this sceptred isle: opus 43 (25/II) can be found in Pembroke College, Oxford; opus 70 (35/II) is in the Tower of London; opus 71 and opus 72 are 4-stop continue organs, both in London; and opus 95 (30/III) can be found in Selwyn College, Cambridge (entirely coincidentally, of course).

Of particular interest were the results of the repertoire request. I wrote to about 100 organists and conductors, and had an encouraging response rate of about 40% (that's more than normally turn up to vote in national elections here), so I hope that these results are plausibly representative. Perhaps not surprisingly, the name which appeared in nearly every answer was that of Healey Willan (who emigrated to Toronto from the UK in 1913 at the age of 33). *Rise up, my love* is in regular (i.e., at least annual) use in about 15 UK cathedrals (nearly 40% of the Anglican cathedrals in the country) as well as in a number of college chapels. Willan's *The three kings* and *O Lord, our Governour* also feature frequently, as do his numerous Missae Brevae and Evening Canticle fauxbourdon sets. His *Introduction, Passacaglia, and Fugue* for organ, as well as some of his smaller works, are in the repertoire of a number of organists. Other Canadian composers whose names appeared were Matthew Larkin (*Adam lay ybounden* for upper voices is a particular favourite); Denis Bédard (one cathedral Assistant Organist plays nearly all of his published works); Eleanor Daley (*Upon your heart* is popular with Oxbridge choirs). Stephen Chatman, David Creese, Derek Holman, Ruth Watson Henderson, Ernest MacMillan, and Doreen Rao were names which also came up, in addition to my own. Of course, whether or not I count as CanCon anymore is perhaps a moot point—though according to the Wikipedia site for Canadian Content (yes, there really is one) being a Canadian citizen is sufficient, even if I am not currently resident.[108]

From these results, it seems that we are indeed contributing to the international Anglican choral scene (or at least that in the UK) in our

---

107. In 2020, the then no. 2 at Chester Cathedral was appointed to the no. 1 post at Coventry Cathedral, a building with significant Canadian connections (see the RCCO's Winter 2020 issue of *Organ Canada*).

108. https://en.wikipedia.org/wiki/Canadian_content

admittedly niche discipline. Crucially, on this side of the Pond, this music is being performed because it is good, and it is consciously chosen, and not because fulfils a nationality box-ticking exercise. Healey Willan's *Rise up my love* is a masterpiece that stands proudly alongside Brahms (which, *pace* Oskar, your *Scherzino* does not). I did not know Eleanor Daley's *Upon your heart* until the results from this survey came in. Enough people said how much their choirs loved it that I have now ordered at set for Selwyn Choir—again, not because it is Canadian, but because it is beautiful.

Perhaps the original protectionist agenda was important in the 1970s, even though for many of us who grew up under its edicts, the word "CanCon" has always been rather pejorative. Notwithstanding the aforementioned colonial complications, which by necessity must provide thought-provoking context for any anniversary celebrations, we should be proud of the European cultural heritage that we have inherited and made our own, and we should also be proud of the country that we have become. The wounds that were inflicted over past centuries will take many more years to heal, but we are slowly moving in the right direction.

In Quires and Places Where They Sing

By the time you read this, the nights will be closing in, there will be a late-autumnal chill in the air, and the comforting smell of wood-burning stoves will infuse the sombre evenings on the way home from work. The short days of winter (and they are very short in the UK—by December we will have only about seven hours of light each day) can be difficult to endure. One of the great privileges of my life is that nearly every day of the week before I go home, I conduct Choral Evensong. Those 30–40 minutes at the end of the day, with candlelight and music, help greatly to mitigate the effects of winter.

The much-loved service of Evensong was first introduced during the Reformation, in the 1549 Book of Common Prayer (BCP), the first English (i.e., as opposed to Latin) prayer book. The then Archbishop of Canterbury, Thomas Cranmer, reduced the total number of daily Roman monastic Offices from nine to two, and the two new English services, Morning Prayer (Matins) and Evening Prayer (Evensong) have been said or sung daily, nearly unchanged, in Anglican houses of worship ever since. They consist of lessons from the Old and New Testaments, psalms, prayers, responses, and canticles (literally "little songs"). In the 1662 edition of the BCP, there is a rubric at the end of the liturgy itself, which allows for an additional and voluntary musical offering: "In quires and places where they sing, here followeth the anthem." In nearly all UK Anglican cathedrals, most college chapels, and many larger parish churches, Choral Evensong is still sung at the end of every working day at about 5:30pm. The service is much less frequent in the States, even on Sundays, and only a handful of major choral foundations sing it during the week.

I recently took the Chapel Choir of Selwyn College, Cambridge on tour to the States. As well as a number of concerts, we sang Choral Evensong in the Cathedral Church of St John the Divine in New York City, and in Washington National Cathedral. Although the choir enjoys the glamour of an evening performance with applause and standing ovations (thank you Pittsburgh and Philadelphia!), as a liturgical choir, they are most comfortable donning cassocks and surplices and singing Anglican Chant and a set of canticles to a quiet gathering of the faithful, even when the choir themselves outnumber the congregation. It was the height of the summer tourist season, so this was not actually the case in New York or Washington, but it does often happen in our college chapel, and in many cathedrals.

Having said that, evensong congregations in the UK are seeing something of a resurgence. Although numbers on Sundays mornings are declining every year, weekday evensong attendance has increased significantly over the past few years[109]. Intriguingly, the congregational participation in Choral Evensong amounts to nearly nothing—the choir and clergy sing the majority of the service, and the congregation is allowed a short moment of quiet reflection where emails, phone calls, and distractions are removed, however briefly. By contrast, on Sunday mornings, committees of greeters pounce on visitors and newcomers, the passing of the peace causes untold discomfort in many, and everyone is expected to join in lustily with numerous (sometimes unfamiliar) hymns. At Choral Evensong, visitors and regulars alike can hide behind a pillar and listen, experience, and perhaps pray, without interruption—the ancient words,

---

109. For more information on the resurgence of this beautiful evening office, see the following reports: https://www.churchtimes.co.uk/articles/2018/26-october/news/uk /cathedral-attendance-rose-by-three-per-cent-last-christmas; https://www.telegraph.co .uk/news/religion/12176998/Looking-for-Britains-future-leaders-Try-evensong.html; https://www.thetimes.co.uk/article/holier-than-thou-students-most-likely-to-attend -church-pm83b6q5r

the music, the ritual, and the lack of participation provide the space that allows for those all-too-infrequent glimpses of holiness.

Over the years, I have noticed a number of differences between the UK and American services of Choral Evensong. It may come as a surprise to you to know that the *Phos Hilaron* (the ancient Greek hymn 'O gladsome light' sung in most services in the States) is rarely used here, except occasionally as an introit or an anthem. No-one sings the Creed on a monotone. And we only sing a hymn (and then just one) on occasional major feast days. The service only lasts about 30–40 minutes, and there is a notable lack of pomp and ceremony on the proverbial "wet Tuesday in November".

Lots of you in the States run chorister programmes with children coming two or three days a week to rehearse for an hour or two after school. Why not devote 30 minutes of that rehearsal time to singing Choral Evensong for the neighbourhood around your church? You don't need the *Phos Hilaron*; you don't need four hymns; you don't need the opening confessional rite; you don't need an anthem; you can use the same printed service sheet every time; you don't need a sermon; as it's a non-sacramental service, you don't even need clergy. Once a week, not on a Sunday, why not try a straightforward, mostly plainsong/Anglican Chant upper-voices Evensong at about 5:30pm. Two of your older choristers could read the lessons; you could sing the cantor's part; the prayers can be short and simple, led by a parent. Not only will your choristers' confidence improve by "performing" more frequently, but perhaps an exhausted lawyer, secretary, paramedic, teacher, or PhD student might catch a brief glimpse of holiness after a long and stressful day at work. And sure, the congregation might only consist of four chorister parents who arrived early to collect their children—but they might need it too.

Chapter 12

Pandemic

No-one in the world has escaped the impact of COVID-19. The Performing Arts sector has been devastated by the restrictions on large gatherings, and the narrative on singing in particular was extremely damaging. At the time of publication, we are still emerging from the crisis, and this chapter brings together the columns which dealt with the pandemic.

September 2020

A Letter from Lockdown

For months now, I have successfully put off writing about the only topic on anyone's mind, but I think it is time to address it. I am not a scientist, though I hope by the time you read this, the Public Health England-sponsored studies of the Lay Clerks at Salisbury Cathedral will have proven that singing is not as dangerous as sky-diving, despite what you might read on Facebook. I am also trying to overcome the bleakness looming over me by resisting sarcasm, despite the fact that it is currently okay to gather in large crowds to shout/scream/cheer/"sing" about the winning of a soccer game,[110] but singing is banned in the Church of England. Irony is the only reaction that preserves sanity, surely?

In mid-March, we were all washing our hands more often, but nothing much else had changed. At Selwyn, we were looking forward to concerts in various UK cities, a live BBC Radio broadcast, and recording two new CDs. In Ely, the choristers were preparing for Holy Week and Easter and a concert tour to Amsterdam. There were also the post-exam balls, dinners, leavers' services, graduations, and year-end rituals to enjoy. But suddenly, everything was cancelled and everyone went home. Schools, universities, shops, restaurants, pubs, businesses, places of worship, and

---

110. https://www.itv.com/news/2020-06-25/thousands-of-fans-celebrate-in-the-streets
-as-liverpool-win-premier-league/

gyms, all closed overnight, and the Church of England closed its buildings completely for the first time in 800 years—even the clergy were refused entry.

Over the next few weeks, it became apparent that this was an Opera rather than an Introit. Working from my kitchen table, like many of you, I diversified. Selwyn was unique in Cambridge in holding a bespoke YouTube service every week during the Easter Term, using no pre-recorded material, and with services open to anyone to "attend". Readers and preachers came from the extended college community, and the choir recorded themselves singing at home on their phones for me to knit together (making a "virtue" of necessity quite literally).

The only minor complication was that I had never used video or audio editing software in my life. Let's just say that in the first week of term, my learning curve was slightly steeper than that of COVID-19. Most of you will have made at least one virtual choir video by now (it is probably a necessary rite-of-passage for all conductors who experienced this pandemic), but just in case you haven't, here's a brief précis of how it works (or at least how I did it).

1. film myself conducting an audio 'guide track' (usually a recording of the choir singing a piece from a previous performance); send to choir with PDFs of scores
2. choir record themselves individually singing their own part with guide track, wearing headphones so they only record their own voice; they send MP4 file to me
3. I download and sort videos into SATB folders and extract audio to import into Audacity (free audio software)
4. audio files are lined up; individual singers balanced and mixed; overall parts balanced and mixed; various corrections made (muting occasional wrong notes, adjusting tempo/tuning/ensemble, etc.)
5. graphic equaliser is employed, reverb added to blend overall sound and compensate for limited acoustic of singers' living rooms
6. final audio file and all individual videos imported into VideoPad (basic commercial software) and lined up

7. each individual video edited for details like exposure, cropping, size, etc.

8. a variety of split-screen options are chosen so all singers (and me as conductor/organist) appear on screen simultaneously

9. rest of service downloaded and imported (readings, psalm, sermon, prayers, etc.) and everything put into order

10. text overlays added and spell-checked (names, words for the hymns, copyright details, titles)

11. scene transition cross-fades added, various speakers' volumes normalised

12. file exported from VideoPad into an MP4 (can take up to two hours)

13. MP4 sent to chaplain for checking, corrections, re-exporting if needed

14. final version uploaded to YouTube, made public, and links shared on social media/via email

15. a strong G&T is poured, and I collapse in a heap

For the first few weeks, it was an all-consuming task, taking over 80 hours to produce a 25-minute service. By the end of term, I could finish a whole service in about 30 hours, including time for editing, exporting, downloading, uploading, converting, etc. It was intense and frustrating work, resulting in several sleepless nights, but I am grateful to have done it, and to have learned these new skills.[111]

The choir also learned new skills. Singing alone in front of one's phone requires a confidence, a discipline, and a perfection that the safety of the choir stalls does not. I am sure that they would agree with me that it is a poor relation to being able to breathe, resonate, enunciate, communicate, and make real live music together as one instrument, but it is better than nothing at all. Any of you who have done this will understand. With the raising of a conductor's eyebrow, ensemble is fixed in live performance in a split second. Editing individual video submissions requires

---

111. The services are viewable on the Selwyn Chapel YouTube channel: https://www
.youtube.com/selwyncollegechapel

painstaking and time-consuming use of the mute/amplify/adjust tempo/ tuning features—which takes *hours* to achieve the same effect that the aforementioned raised eyebrow can achieve in milliseconds.

We must all keep faith—singing is a life-giving communal human activity which has developed and thrived over many millennia. We will be able to sing together again safely one day, and in the meantime, even if we are only able to do so once rather than twice, we must nonetheless continue to pray.[112]

---

112. St Augustine: "He who sings, prays twice."

November 2020

A Light at the End of the Tunnel?

In mid-August, the results of two major studies into aerosol and drop-let emission during singing and wind-playing informed a significant change in UK government guidance.[113] As I write, both papers are in the peer-review stage; by the time you read this, they should have been published. The pre-publication results demonstrated (entirely unsur-prisingly) that singing is no more dangerous than speaking or breath-ing. England has therefore been planning for the resumption of choral activities with the new academic year. Social-distancing continues to be important, though the distance needed between singers is no greater than that required between people in shops and restaurants.[114] It is crucial that rehearsal and performance spaces have adequate ventilation—fortu-nately for the Anglican Choral Tradition, ancient draughty churches are fine on that front. The stories about a handful of choirs which experienced

---

113. Research conducted by Dr Declan Costello, ENT surgeon and professional tenor (PERFORM), and a study involving lay clerks from Salisbury Cathedral as well as ama-teur singers and wind players (SOBADRA), sponsored by Public Health England and Her Majesty's Government Department for Culture, Media, and Sport are summarised here: https://assets.publishing.service.gov.uk/government/uploads/system/uploads/attachment _data/file/914628/S0695_Aerosol_and_Droplet_Generation_from_Singing__Wind _Instruments__SWI__and_Performance_Activities.pdf.
114. Two metres without mitigations, less if other mitigations are in place (e.g., a screen, or a mask, or that singers are standing side-by-side rather than facing each other).

outbreaks of COVID-19 in March were tragic, but given how little we knew of the disease at that point, to lay blame at the door of singing itself, rather than considering poor ventilation, hugging, close proximity, meal-sharing, and all of the other non-socially-distanced things which choir members are wont to do, was unfortunate. The entirety of a world-wide activity well-known to be beneficial to people's health[115] was devastated by one webinar in early May,[116] and many people are still suffering the repercussions.

It was a relief for all of us when scientific evidence began to supersede anecdote and anxiety, and consequently, in the UK tentative steps towards recovery are taking place. In-person planning meetings have resumed (Zoom has been useful, but we need human contact), though with a few differences: hands are washed and sanitised on entry and exit, everyone wears face-masks, we sit further apart than usual, and the windows are wide open despite the early autumn chill. In addition, every meeting features a prop unusual for anything other than the annual gathering of the International Society of Haberdashers: a measuring tape.

The most important change here is that individual venues are now permitted to make their own risk assessments. Until recently, the same restrictions were in place for vast cathedrals which seat 2000 people, as for tiny chapels which accommodate only forty. Sensibly, we are now able to put in place our own procedures to allow for a safe resumption of in-person choral worship. Such risk mitigations include ensuring that singers are spaced an appropriate distance apart (hence the need for a measuring tape), that they are not facing each other, or are singing behind Perspex screens. Face-coverings are required by law in all places of worship in the UK, though those leading worship may remove them when praying, preaching, reading, or singing.

Many cathedrals with a professional back row (i.e., adult altos, tenors, and basses), have begun services with lay clerks in the first instance. This usually comprises only six or eight singers (easily socially-distanced), and

---

115. https://www.ox.ac.uk/research/choir-singing-improves-health-happiness-%E2%80%93 -and-perfect-icebreaker

116. Webinar given by the ACDA and NATS on 5 May 2020 which erroneously implicated singers as "super-spreaders" of the coronavirus.

there is a significant body of music (Byrd, Victoria, Tallis, et al) for lower voices. Along with more traditional repertoire, the Director of Music at York Minster commissioned three contemporary composers (Philip Moore, Becky McGlade, and myself) to write new pieces for the lay clerks' first services of Choral Evensong, as a forward-looking contribution to a renewed and living tradition. Most cathedrals' boy and girl choristers will return to singing services over the first few weeks of September. Particularly helpful guidance for choir schools allows for choristers to be "bubbled up"—since they are a small, consistent group of children in a regular before- and after-school activity, they do not need to be socially distanced.

University term begins in early October, and since most chapels are much smaller than cathedrals, other options must be considered. Some Cambridge colleges are intending choral services to be covered by half the choir at a time; the smallest of the chapels are looking at groups of just four or six singers for each service. At Selwyn, where we are blessed with a large chapel, we will be able to field the entire choir for each service, but we will sit on socially-distanced chairs in front of the altar, rather than in the choir stalls, since that allows for a bigger (also socially-distanced) congregation. Many chapels are installing webcasting equipment with a view to livestreaming service, allowing elderly, vulnerable, or self-isolating members of our congregations to participate from home, as well as keeping geographically-distanced congregations engaged.

Of course, by the time you read this, circumstances might have changed, and we might be back in lockdown, local or national. Until there is a viable vaccine, this possibility continues to be real. But if lockdown recurs, at least we know that it will be temporary, and we can be confident that an existential threat to our raison d'être will not overshadow the hope of recovery.

January 2021

Between the Lockdowns

As I sit down to write (All Saints' Day), England has woken up to four weeks of renewed COVID-19 restrictions. Restaurants, pubs, shops, gyms, hairdressers, leisure centres, and anything else that can be deemed "non-essential", will close. Places of worship are allowed to remain open for private prayer and livestreamed services with no congregation. This is an improvement on March's lockdown, when church buildings were closed completely, and services were relegated to the kitchens and studies of clerics across the country. By far the most significant difference this time is that schools and universities will remain open, and in-person teaching is expected to continue.

It remains to be seen what effect this has on the many liturgical choirs which have restarted since September, including my own choirs, one a collegiate university chapel choir, and the other a cathedral choir in a choir school that uses the cathedral building as its school chapel. The educational institutions which provide the infrastructure for these choirs remain open, and "broadcasting services" is specifically listed as acceptable in the government guidance, but it is currently unclear whether we will be allowed to continue singing? Undoubtedly, much will have changed between my writing of this column, and your reading of it, so I will discuss instead what we have already done.

Enormous time, effort, and money was expended by churches when they reopened after the spring lockdown in order to ensure that they were COVID-secure. Safe and socially-distanced choral singing returned at the beginning of the academic year, and there has not been a single outbreak of the coronavirus that has been linked to live music-making——rehearsals, services, or concerts——including singing or wind-playing, those two much-maligned artforms which have suffered from such a negative and unhelpful narrative since last March.

It won't surprise you to know that August was spent buried in official Risk Assessments. In these lengthy written documents, every possible danger was described in detail, mitigations were considered and implemented, equipment purchased, signage posted, personnel informed, and Health and Safety Officers persuaded. It was revealing to work through all of the things that a choir does in order to function which are not normally considered risky, but procedures for which needed to be completely rethought in order to ensure the safety of members of the choir and of the congregation.

In Selwyn College, thanks to the Victorians, we have one of the largest college chapels in Cambridge, so social-distancing is easily achieved. Whereas many of my colleagues have only been able to field half of their choir at a time, singing services with just Decani or Cantoris, or just the upper or lower voices, in Selwyn, the entire choir has been present from the beginning of term. Our much-loved Choir Vestry (see December 2014 on page 343 for context), on the other hand, is too small to allow for social-distancing with more than about six people at a time, so the majority of the choir are now keeping their cassocks and surplices in their college rooms. The Risk Assessment had to include the likely added cost of replacing vestments which do not survive a year on an undergraduate's dorm-room floor.

Socially-distanced singing with a brand new choir has been challenging. My choir at Selwyn this year has a very large proportion of first year undergraduates (about 70%) so there was always going to be a steep learning curve. Interestingly, as a result of having to stand two metres away from the next person in their section, the new members are singing with impressive independence, and are responding to me as conductor much earlier in the year than usual, rather than hiding (both physically and musically) behind a section leader a year or two above them. (An added bonus is that they haven't even caught each other's start-of-term colds.) By contrast, in Ely, the girl and boy trebles are classified as a consistent school activity "bubble" which means that they do not need to socially-distance from each other. Since new choristers at Ely are between the ages of seven and nine years old, this has been a relief. On the other hand, if one of them were to have contracted the virus (fortunately they have not), we would have to have self-isolated the entire treble section, and every publicity post which includes a photograph of the choristers has to feature the word "bubble" prominently, in order to avoid social media backlash and internet trolling.

The unpredictable British weather has played its part too. By far the most important risk mitigation in any indoor setting is ventilation. Windows and doors are left open during rehearsals and services, leading to loud bangs thanks to unexpected gusts of wind, and near arctic temperatures in the choir stalls. Regular ventilation breaks are built into the schedule, when all members of the choir must go outside, regardless of the meteorological conditions. There are definitely services where I have felt more likely to have contracted hypothermia than COVID.

The impending lockdown could result in silence at Remembrance, Advent, and on the feast day of St Cecilia, patron saint of music and musicians (and my birthday). But it shall pass. Until then, risks must be mitigated, precautions taken, hands washed, masks worn, distance preserved. And then, we will return, and will build again the tabernacle of the Lord. Our song will be renewed, and will be brought again unto the temple.[117]

---

117. Acts 15:16, Ezra 6:5

March 2021

O' Mice and Men[118]

As I write, we are awaiting another government U-turn. Last-minute changes of policy have been characteristic in the UK over the past 10 months or so. Some political analysts say that the Prime Minister, Boris Johnson ("BoJo" for short) makes indecision his official strategy—if he waits long enough before making a decision, he actually doesn't have to in the end, since only one viable option remains. So, for example, much of the rest of mainland Europe closed its pubs, restaurants, and non-essential shops several weeks before we did in March 2020. We were (apparently) allowing for "herd immunity" to settle in, which would mean that we would be impervious to the virus (!). In the end, *quelle surprise*, the government had to shut down absolutely everything: not just shops and restaurants, but also places of worship, universities, schools, gyms, and leisure centres, as well as making it illegal to meet with friends and family outside of those with whom we live. So much for herd immunity.

Other recent U-turns include public exam results for teenagers: the annual summer examinations for 16- and 18-year olds (GCSEs and A-levels respectively) were cancelled when schools were closed last year. Instead, a mechanism was put into place by which teachers estimated

---

118. 'To a Mouse' by Robert Burns (1759-1756).
"The best laid schemes o' mice an' men
Gang aft a-gley." (*Go not awry.*)

their pupils' grades based on performance during the previous months. These estimated grades were then sent to the Department of Education to be moderated by way of an algorithm which was intended to ensure that the final results were broadly in line with previous years' performance. A rough generalisation of how this actually played out in practice was that pupils in private (i.e., independent, fee-paying) schools ended up achieving the same or higher marks than had been estimated by their teachers, whereas pupils in state-maintained (i.e., public, non-fee-paying) schools in deprived areas were downgraded by the algorithm. Not surprisingly, this caused much angst amongst anyone who would like to believe that success is available to anyone who works hard—and not just those who are able to pay for it. A massive social media campaign resulted in a last-minute U-turn by BoJo, such that all pupils were given their teacher-assessed grades in the end, but this didn't happen until after thousands of school-leavers had already missed out on their preferred university places due to having received lower grades than predicted.

Over the past eight months, there have also been last-minute U-turns on the provision of free school-meals to lower-income families during the holidays, a campaign which was spearheaded by the professional foot-baller (i.e., soccer player) Marcus Rashford; a last-minute U-turn on charging a fee to foreign-born employees of the National Health Service to allow them to use (you guessed it) the National Health Service; a last-minute U-turn on the reopening of primary (i.e., elementary) schools in June; and a particularly egregious, and well-past-the-last-minute U-turn on the imposition of quarantine requirements on travellers to the UK. While most other countries in the world had effectively closed their borders in March, the UK government's indecision finally put those quarantine requirements into effect in June—months after the proverbial horse had bolted.

The latest U-turn we are anticipating is about the reopening of schools after the Christmas break. In theory, all schools were to reopen on 4 January (the day after I sat down to write this piece). Already, just 48 hours ago, this was changed so that secondary schools (pupils in Years 7-13, which corresponds to grades 6-12) would start back later, with GCSE and A-level pupils returning on 11 January, and the others returning on

18th. Then, 12 hours later, the government decided not to reopen primary schools in London and some other areas where virus numbers are particularly high at the moment. Staff at King's Ely, the school which educates the cathedral choristers, received no fewer than twelve lengthy emails from the schools' dedicated but undoubtedly exhausted Senior Management Team on New Year's Eve—so much for a holiday. I now find myself jesting with my colleagues on the nutritional value of our headwear, as we places wagers on the likelihood that primary schools will not in fact open tomorrow anywhere in England after all. "If BoJo hasn't changed his mind by 2pm tomorrow, I'll eat my hat."

I don't know about you, but I am an inveterate planner. I have everything worked our long in advance—dates, times, rehearsal schedules, music lists, and all other related administrative documents are sent out to chorister parents and choral scholars long before any of them have actually started to wonder what time rehearsal will begin on Ash Wednesday. The past eight months have been difficult from that point of view—even without government indecision and dallying, we have all had to undo so many of our "best laid schemes". Ash Wednesday aside, even the time of the rehearsal on Epiphany is currently in doubt. The only thing that is comforting is that I know that I am not the only person in this unplanned pickle, and at the moment, I can even blame the government for it. Perhaps living like this is what it feels like to be one of those supposedly typical musicians who is a bit rubbish at administration. It's interesting, but I'll be glad when we are all vaccinated, the pandemic is over, and I can once again send out my carefully planned spreadsheets, tables, and PDFs, and enjoy the fact that they will no longer "gang aft a-gley".

April 2021

Please [Un]Mute Yourself

As predicted in last month's column, there was a last-minute government U-turn here on the reopening of schools after Christmas: most children in England went back to school for *one whole day* before being sent home again indefinitely. Although places of worship were permitted to remain open, many chose to close; some continued to livestream with professional adult singers. Since schools are closed, choristers (i.e., the children who sing treble) are not singing. As a result, this term I am experimenting with something that I had miraculously managed to avoid for the whole of 2020, namely Zoom chorister rehearsals.

During the first wave of the COVID-19 pandemic, I spent a disproportionate number of hours creating virtual choir videos of the Choir of Selwyn College, Cambridge (see September 2020 earlier in this chapter for more on that thankless task). On the other hand, I wasn't allowed to interact with Ely Cathedral's girl choristers at all, due to the restrictions of the UK government's furlough system. In one of the (limited number of) things that the Conservative Party got right in its approach to the pandemic, the "Job Retention Scheme" enables employers to claim back 80% of their employees' salaries, on the condition that they do no work associated with that position. Most employers topped up the 20%, so from mid-March to mid-August, I received my full salary from Ely despite doing nothing. The furlough scheme is more flexible now, and I am permitted to work a limited number of hours each week, while the government pays for the rest of my time. And so, two weeks ago, with some trepidation, I logged into the choir school's Zoom account, and attempted to run a chorister practice.

The first thing that I noticed was the silence. Normally, as the girls arrive after breakfast the rehearsal room is full of lively laughter and cheerful chatter. Instead, I couldn't even hear them breathing. This generation of school children is well-versed in the etiquette of the virtual classroom, and they were muted as a matter of course. I am obviously accustomed to the hush of the Zoom arrival process, but somehow, where it seems natural in a business meeting, in a children's choir practice, it is completely alien. And yes, the chaos of noise and interference when they turned their microphones on to say hello properly was not conducive to effective communication, let alone to singing, but at least it felt real.

Re-muted, we proceeded to the warmup. I sat at the piano, and progressed through a selection of the various exercises we normally begin with. Of course, all I could hear was my own playing. I could see the girls' mouths moving, but I had no sense at all of whether they were singing freely, healthily, in tune, or indeed even at all! Normally, I know when they are ready for the rest of the rehearsal—it doesn't take the same length of time every day of the week, and I judge the timing of the warmup carefully according to how they sound, look, and seem each morning. Over Zoom, I have to trust them to tell me that they are warmed up, and my well-trained and experienced ears are useless.

One of the countless musical casualties of the pandemic is the generation of children who have missed major festivals of the church year. Last year's Ely choristers did not sing for most of Lent, all of Easter, Ascension, Pentecost, and much of Trinity season. The most elaborate and melismatic of the proper plainsong Office Hymns occur during those seasons. In my Zoom-rehearsal-conductor naïveté, I presumed that teaching a unison Office Hymn would be possible, even if I had to do so by rote (an educational method I normally avoid). How wrong I was. One girl's microphone was set to cut out all frequencies above g', resulting in clear speech, but inaudible singing; the Wi-Fi signal disappeared during

a complicated phrase perfectly sung for the first time by a nervous proba-
tioner (according to her older sister who was with her); my assistant organist was evicted from the meeting every time I sent him to a breakout room
to lead a sectional; and finally, my own microphone failed completely half
way through a phrase, resulting in universal hilarity as I had to type all
instructions in the chat box. At this point, with obvious sympathy for my
plight, one of my senior girls took over. She sang the hymn one phrase at a
time, and allowed everyone time to repeat it. I took on the role of a member of the choir, and suddenly realised how much worse a Zoom rehearsal
is for the conductor than it is for the choir members. As a participant, I
heard the line sung by the leader, and I heard myself repeating it, so there
was sound throughout the exchange; as a leader, one hears the line, and
then one hears nothing.

Three weeks in to this digital regime, I am a little more accustomed to
the medium, though if I'm honest, I still don't like it, and neither do the
girls. I will end with a selection of adjectives and phrases from the girls
themselves, as typed into the chat this morning. Virtual Choir Practices
are: "awkward", "difficult", "tiring", "LOL", "weird", "odd", "strange",
"funny", "not good for learning things", "important", "better than nothing, but still cr*p".

May 2021

Roadmap out of Lockdown

By the time you read this, the UK should be on its way to resuming normality, though the health, economic, and educational repercussions of this pandemic will be felt for at least a generation to come. However, the extraordinary implementation of the vaccination programme, thanks to the National Health Service (NHS), means that already at the time of writing (the end of February) over a third of the UK adult population has already received at least one injection. Early on, the government here got a lot wrong, including reacting far too late, and handing out questionable contracts for Personal Protective Equipment and the development of a Track-and-Trace app to personal business cronies rather than to transparent publicly-funded institutions. Allowing the NHS to take control of the largest vaccination programme in the Service's history was the right decision however, and we are grateful—though not surprised—for its extraordinary efficiency and success.

Nonetheless, recovery will be a lengthy process. I am not *au fait* enough with academic economics to predict how long it will be until the global economy—let alone the local high street—returns to pre-pandemic trading levels, but I am gradually starting to work on recovery planning in my own small corner of the world. My two choirs have been in a static holding pattern for over a year, something to which I am unaccustomed—constantly striving for improvement is my custom. Having said that, I am aware that a "static holding pattern" is a fortunate place to be. There are many choirs (orchestras, theatres, museums, dance companies) whose fate has been anything but static. The catastrophic decline in income and morale has been felt most keenly by those in the arts sector. Nevertheless, I thought it might be helpful to outline my preparations for recovery, in case they helped to inspire some of your own plans over the summer, with the beginning of the 2021-22 academical year providing an obvious target for a fresh start.

One of my primary concerns is that of recruitment. By the end of this year, Cambridge will have been through two cycles of disrupted Choral Scholarship Trials, one of which took place literally as the UK went into its first national lockdown, and the second of which will of necessity occur online, while the majority of the university remains closed to in-person activity and learning. Application numbers are significantly lower than usual this year, partly due to changing priorities after such a difficult twelve months, and it is very easy to become discouraged. However, it is crucial that we remain enthusiastic about encouraging singers to our ensembles, and even if we have vacancies for the next year or two, it is possible to teach and make music with those smaller numbers who are there. I want to begin rebuilding the choir even if I have only four basses, rather than my usual six, and we all need to remember to be grateful for those who *are* there, rather than moaning about those who are not.

We can also help our choirs' revivals by choosing repertoire carefully. Simpler music sung well is far more likely to remind our singers of how much they love choral singing than attempting repertoire that is beyond their reach. This is especially true given that many choral singers will be vocally and musically out of shape when they return. Far better to find music which is in fewer parts and with long legato lines, to rebuild choral sound and vocal stamina, than to try to impress with music better suited to times that have not involved major international health emergencies. We need to remember that our singers have had everything interrupted, not just their choral activities. They will need to catch up in school and university, rebuild places of employment, and in far too many cases recover after serious illness and bereavement. The resumption of choral singing must complement the entire process of healing, so choose music wisely.

I have also found that some of the changes which were forced upon us by the pandemic are actually beneficial, and will now become part of the new routine. The most obvious of these is, of course, the use of livestreaming. At Selwyn College and Ely Cathedral, we have built up a loyal congregation around the world, some of whom "attend" Evensong over breakfast from North America, others of whom are elderly UK alumni who have loved reconnecting with the college decades after graduation. I have been able to watch friends conducting, playing, and singing, whom I have never actually been able to see perform in person. One highlight for me was the opportunity to hear the newly-formed girl choristers at Christchurch Cathedral in New Zealand, sing their inaugural service (including a piece I wrote especially for them) conducted by a former student of mine. Perhaps unexpectedly, I am also considering retaining socially-distanced rehearsal formation for the first term of each new year. New singers developed musical independence much more quickly than usual, and the choir's ensemble and intonation were significantly improved as they all listened to each other, and watched and responded to me as the conductor so much more effectively.

The need to rebuild, restore, and renew our various choral traditions is paramount, and will require all of our collective energies and commitments. I wish you all encouragement as we undertake this monumental but critical task.

September 2021

O May We Soon Again Renew that Song: Musings on Choral Recovery

This extended article is reprinted from the Journal of the Association of Anglican Musicians (Vol. 30, No. 7, September 2021) with permission.

Introduction

As I sit down to write this piece (the end of July 2021), the UK government has finally permitted congregational singing to return, after nearly 18 months of closed churches, online worship, and banned communal singing, even after in-person worship resumed. Ironically, perhaps, community singing has been permitted—even encouraged—in pubs, restaurants, and sporting stadia. In places of worship, however, the guidance and legislation have been clear since March 2020, and hymn singing has been strictly forbidden. Perhaps the hospitality and sporting industries are more directly relevant to the recovery of the economy than the church, but given the noise emanating from Wembley Stadium when England won the semi-final of the EUFA European Football (i.e., soccer) Championships (the Euros for short) in June 2021, it was rather baffling that gatherings of fully-vaccinated, distanced, masked congregation members in vast, draughty, medieval cathedrals were still being told regularly that even so much as humming *All my hope on God is founded* might cause case numbers in the country to spike. Perhaps I can be forgiven for feeling rather smug at the poetic justice manifest in a recent headline "Euro 2020 [sic] crowds driving rise in COVID-19 infections, says WHO [World Health Organisation]".[119]

Choral singing in the UK, however, particularly by choirs which could officially or loosely be classed as 'professional', resumed with confidence in early September 2020, after the release of ENT surgeon Declan Costello's eagerly-awaited government-funded study PERFORM[120], which proved that singing is actually no more dangerous than speaking, despite the negative narrative surrounding the activity since the beginning of the pandemic. Cathedral choirs, Oxbridge college choirs, professional choirs, and parish choirs whose singers were paid, were able to resume singing safely, with appropriate mitigations in place (most importantly, ventilation and social distancing). In churches, face-coverings were mandatory, however when one was actually *doing* something (reading, praying, preaching, or singing), they could be removed, so we didn't even have the inconvenience of singing in masks. Since last autumn, not a single COVID-19 outbreak has been associated with any of those choirs (at least not for choral reasons—if they got ill due to socialising with each other after rehearsals that doesn't count). On the other hand, congregations, amateur choral singers, non-paid parish choirs, choral societies, barbershop groups, pop choirs, and many other singing ensembles encompassing millions of people in the country for whom singing is a much-loved hobby, crucial for friendship and wellbeing, were not permitted to sing without restrictions (limited numbers, outdoors only) until the 17th of July 2021. The frustration with our so-called government Department for Digital, Media, Culture, and Sport—scathingly shortened by most of my friends and colleagues to the Department for [. . .] Sport—has been palpable.

Meanwhile, in the States, from what I have seen from many of your social media posts, there has been an extraordinary array of different

---

119. https://www.reuters.com/world/europe/who-warns-third-coronavirus-wave-europe
-2021-07-01/ accessed 28/07/2021.

120. https://bachtrack.com/interview-declan-costello-what-next-after-the-perform-study
-september-2020 accessed 28/07/2021.

responses to the gradual easing of restrictions during the course of 2021. Some churches and cathedrals appear to have been "back to normal" for some time, with choirs and congregations singing confidently, undistanced, and (seemingly) safely, particularly where double-vaccination is a requirement for participation in music-making and worship. Others are still worshipping online, with no face-to-face interaction at all. I presume therefore that health regulations are set more locally by state and municipal governments, unlike in the UK, where the government in Westminster is responsible for all COVID legislation for the whole of England (the devolved governments of Wales, Northern Ireland, and Scotland were responsible for their regions' regulations). This more localised approach makes sense in a country as geographically large and diverse as the USA, but the variety of behaviours has been a little bewildering to outside observers.

At any rate, notwithstanding the multifarious responses to the vaccination programmes, testing regimes, easing of restrictions, and fluctuations in case numbers as we learn to live with this virus, I have been charged with writing a piece on choral recovery, focusing in particular on our niche corner of the industry, namely the liturgical choral community which is concerned with the provision of music for use in worship in Anglican and Episcopal churches in the UK and the States. I am certainly no expert on any of the material here—this is my first ever global pandemic, too, and I know as much about infectious diseases as most other organists. Even so, I hope that some of the things I suggest in the next few paragraphs may be of at least some use to at least some of you. Drawing upon my own experience over the past year, I will address vocal health, especially in out-of-shape amateur singers and children, the rebuilding of repertoire, particularly for children and junior choirs, balancing care of the cautious with challenging the confident, managing our own expectations as leaders, especially as regards musical standards, and deciding which of the many new things we have learned over the past 18 months might actually be worth keeping. Most importantly, I will consider flexibility and adaptability, for those are probably the single most valuable qualities that we have all learned. For some readers, these suggestions will be too ambitious; for others they will be six months too late. Nonetheless, I offer all of them from an entirely personal perspective, and I hope that this paper opens the door to many conversations, rather than being seen as a method for recovery passed down from me, as if I were to presume to know more than any of my readers.

Restoring Vocal Health

At all times, one of the most important aspects of our work as choir-trainers is that of ensuring the vocal health of our singers. This is even more important now, when so many choir members have gone without exercising their vocal apparatus for so many months. Here are a few ideas for addressing this, some of which I have put into practice myself this past academic year, particularly in the first term, when my choirs returned after a six-month hiatus.

Develop and implement a regime of gentle, vocally-healthy warmups in order to rebuild your singers' technique. This can address obvious concrete targets such as re-establishing range, which was a concern for me when my girl choristers (age 10-15) began to sing again. Before the pandemic, my girls' daily rehearsal warmups included various exercises which taught them from a young age not to be afraid of high notes. This is particularly important in young teenage girls, who are prone to self-doubt and inhibitions, as the disconcerting effects of puberty take hold. I regularly warm them up to g''', which means that so-called "top C" (the "Allegri C", if you like) is comfortably mid-range for most of them.[121] Of course, after a normal summer holiday break, we would always take a week or so to recondition the muscles, but after six months off, not only did the physiology need to be rebuilt, but so too did the mentality that goes with it. And so, over a month-long regime, every morning I gradu-

---

121. For a detailed discussion of warmups, range, and vocal health in young teenage girls' voices, see Poole, Lucy and MacDonald, Sarah, 'Voice Change and the Professional Girl Chorister', Association of British Choral Directors' *Choral Research Journal*, Issue 2, September 2021.

ally increased their range by a semitone at the most, taking note of where we had got to, and building on that the next day. I had the advantage of seeing them four times each week, but even if you have only one rehearsal per week, you can encourage your singers at least to do warmups in the shower every day in order to expedite the reconditioning process.

Warmups and repertoire can also be directed towards the restoration of your choir's particular sound. One of my greatest concerns was the return of my choir at Selwyn College, Cambridge (mixed voices, all university students), where over 65% of the choir was new this year. We haven't got much acoustic in Selwyn's Victorian red-brick chapel, so the choir is responsible for creating resonance and legato themselves, rather than relying on the building to do it for them. I chose particular warmups and specific repertoire (more on this below), especially carefully in the first term, in order to focus on finding that resonant legato sound with so many inexperienced singers, quite apart from the post-lockdown out-of-shape second and third years.

There are hundreds of self-employed singers and vocal coaches whose income has suffered drastically due to lack of work over the past 18 months. Why not help them and also help your choir by inviting them in to do vocal workshops, both individually and corporately, over the first few months as your choir resumes? For example, over a course of (say) six rehearsals, have a guest voice specialist come in to direct the choir's warmup, and then, while you carry on rehearsing the music for the coming services, have your visitor take singers out to a separate room on an individual basis for 15 minutes or so each, just to do a quick vocal checkup, to make sure that they are using their voices efficiently and healthily. This would be especially useful if you have adult amateur singers in your choir who are not accustomed to having individual singing lessons.

Rebuilding Repertoire

One of the more challenging aspects of the pandemic for those of us who run liturgical choirs with children has been the loss of the collective knowledge of repertoire. In cathedral choirs in the UK, one would rarely teach a standard piece to the treble choristers—something like the ubiquitous "Stanford in B flat",[122] which in most places appears on the music list once or twice a year, would be learned by the younger trebles from the more experienced ones, as if through osmosis. Even missing just one term's singing has had a detrimental effect on the repertoire. At evensong at Ely Cathedral, we sing melismatic plainsong office hymns before the Magnificat every day of the week. My girl choristers were relatively young in March 2020, due to a recent change of age range,[123] with 14 of the 18 of them in only their first or second year in the choir. When we got to the middle of Lent 2021, the gap in their collective knowledge became painfully apparent, as we had to learn those beautiful but complicated hymns from scratch for two or three services each week. During the UK's first lockdown in 2020, the girls did not sing for half of Lent, Easter, Ascension, Pentecost, Corpus Christi, and Trinity, which seasons include some of the most complicated and melismatic of the office hymns. In the mode viii hymns set for Ascension (AETERNE REX ALTISSIME) and Trinity (O LUX BEATA), the number of notes per syllable is unpredictable and counterintuitive at the best of times.[124] Without the older girls, whose time in the choir had been unceremoniously cut short by the pandemic, the learn-by-osmosis method was not available to us, and we had no choice but to undertake a painstaking and patience-trying learning session every morning. Although the girls objected on more than one occasion ("Why can't we just sing one of the ones we already know?" they moaned), in the end, I am confident that we will face next spring with the collective knowledge of the office hymns in very good order.

One of the consequences of relearning this mandatory liturgical repertoire was the need for compromise in other places in our choral offering. During the 2020-21 year, we sang a great deal of (unmelismatic)

---

122. Stanford, Charles Villiers (1852-1924) 'Evening Service in B flat' (Op. 10); publ. Novello and Co., London, 1902.

123. For information on the recent changes at Ely, see MacDonald, Sarah, 'Ely Cathedral Girls' Choir: new directions', *Cathedral Music*, Issue 2/19, November 2019, reprinted in this volume on page 212.

124. You can hear the melismatic Ascension hymn here in a 1950s broadcast from the cathedral on the Archive of Recorded Church Music YouTube channel: https://youtu .be/dNpT6ZHIlao; accessed 31/07/2021.

plainsong—canticles, psalms, responses—and a lot of anthems in unison, especially when the prescribed office hymn was a particularly awkward one. This not only made rehearsal time less pressured, but it also allowed the girls to rebuild their legato, and their confidence. There must never be any shame at all in singing in unison, especially for a children's choir.

Simplicity was also at the forefront of my thinking as I prepared for choral recovery at Selwyn College, Cambridge as well. Although the choir's professional biography makes much of our long-standing commitment to premiering complex new music by living composers, and I have always felt the need to challenge my elite university singers, this year I took quite the opposite stance. In choosing repertoire, I consciously approached the choir's return with the intention that rehearsals and services should feel like a safe, happy place, in which the singers felt good about the music and their performances, both individually and collectively. I wanted them to enjoy and be grateful for the eight hours each week that they spent together in chapel, given that it was one of few opportunities they had to interact with people in real life instead of online. There was enough discomfort built in to the risk assessment requirements anyway—standing two metres apart from each other, the windows wide open during the cold, damp UK winter—that the musical side of things needed to feel positive. And so we too sang lots of plainsong and plenty of simple anthems, and we repeated music much more frequently than we would in a normal year. So, where Peter Aston's lovely evening service for St Andrews, Fulham Fields in southwest London[125] might normally appear just once every two years, we sang it twice this year. Eleanor Daley's gorgeous "Upon your heart"[126] actually made four appearances on the music list, in different contexts, and without apology. Where I would usually have felt the need to programme a six- or eight-part polyphonic or challenging contemporary mass setting for one of the few Eucharists we sing each term, I chose instead to do the plainsong *Missa De Angelis*—twice. It is musically beautiful, despite (because of?) being in unison, and educationally it is some-

---

125. Aston, Peter (1938-2013), 'St Andrews Service'; publ. Encore Publications, Kent, 2008.
126. Daley, Eleanor (b. 1955), 'Upon your heart'; publ. Oxford University Press, 2002.

thing that the choir should know, since the whole of the western canon has its roots in plainsong. Plainsong also has the added advantage not being dependent on the number of singers present in chapel at any one time. When Cambridge University's innovative and vital weekly asymptomatic testing regime sent choir members into unexpected self-isolation two hours before a service, we could still carry on—even if we were without the entire alto section. We were also able to perform music that would normally be overlooked, including for example the beautiful Anonymous 14thC carol "There is no rose" in the green carol book[127], which we sang one-to-a-part for Candlemas.

This conservative approach to repertoire allowed members of the choir the opportunity to rebuild their confidence and their sound, since, unusually for a Cambridge choir, they were rarely sight-reading. Conversely, a number of my colleagues at other high-profile colleges chose to challenge their singers as much as possible, in order to compensate for the time they had lost in the previous year. Interestingly, Selwyn was the only Cambridge chapel to continue offering choral worship two or three times each week throughout this past academical year, including through two national lockdowns.[128] By the end of the year, I had in front of me one of the finest manifestations of the choir of my 22 years at Selwyn. Perhaps our careful methodology was justified after all?[129]

Establishing Balance and Managing Expectations

The next topics I would like to discuss are those of the balancing of our care for the cautious and vulnerable with our need to challenge the confident, as well as the requirement to manage our own expectations. Inevitably, our choirs will consist of those who continue to be worried about catching the virus, regardless of vaccination status, as well as those who

---

127. Willcocks, David, and Jacques, Reginald, ed., *Carols for Choirs I*; publ. OUP 1961.
128. Most of the choir's services through the year are available to watch again on the chapel's YouTube channel: https://www.youtube.com/selwyncollegechapel.
129. As an aside, only one of my 30 singers actually got COVID-19 during the year, and that was nothing to do with choir, since it occurred during a vacation. Fortunately, she made a full recovery.

are keen and confident to get "back to normal" as quickly as they can. Tailoring our activities to account for both of these groups (and everyone between them) is going to be crucial over the coming year. Most importantly, keep lines of communication open, and allow people to speak to you about their concerns.

One option which could address both ends of the spectrum would be to consider splitting your choir into smaller groups more frequently. Perhaps a separate rehearsal and subsequent service with only half the choir would give confidence to those who are most concerned about resuming in-person contact. The corresponding rehearsal and service with the less cautious singers might allow you to do some more ambitious repertoire. Not only is having fewer people in the room together at a time more COVID-safe, employing varying groups of singers also allows for the exploration of a wealth of new repertoire. During the UK's second and third lockdowns, when in-person worship was permitted to continue, albeit with more restrictions, we were encouraged to use fewer singers than usual. At both Selwyn and Ely, we did services with just the sopranos, or just the altos, tenors, and basses, or just the men, or just the women, or just the girls or the boys, or just the lay clerks, or just a duo or trio of singers. Finding music for these variable groups required more creativity, flexibility, and imagination than I have had to use when choosing a music list since the beginning of my career many years ago, and the process was incredibly refreshing. In addition to the repertoire suggestions in the section above, it also provides a good opportunity to hone your technical compositional/arranging skills.[130] Over the past year, I composed and arranged a great deal, often with particular combinations of specific singers in mind. As well as a number of introits, psalm chants, descants, and a couple of anthems, I think I wrote nearly as many sets of Magnificat and Nunc dimittis plainsong fauxbourdons (for varying combinations of voices) as Healey Willan.[131]

---

130. For a discussion on the benefits of keeping these skills sharp, Sarah, 'Last Minute Arrangements', UK Report, December 2019 on page 169.
131. Willan, Healey (1880-1968), Canadian composer, renowned for his large output of liturgical choral and organ music, and in particular for his copious fauxbourdon settings of the evening canticles and his many Missae Breves.

We also need to manage our own expectations. Rebuilding is going to take time, and in order for it to be done safely and permanently, we must be patient. There will be services where the standard simply isn't as good as we would like it to be, and we must not get discouraged or frustrated with our singers. They are nervous and out of shape, and those who have worked all the way through the pandemic are also weary. Remember that the vast numbers of choral performances and church services available online is a potential danger—it is much easier now than it has been to date to compare ourselves with our nearest choral rivals, and that risks creating stress and envy, neither of which is helpful.

The New Routine

It might surprise some of the "get us back to normal as soon as possible" brigade to discover that there are a number of things about our new routine which I think are worth preserving, the most obvious and presumably least controversial of which is livestreaming. The reach of every church which invested in the necessary equipment last year has increased vastly, thanks to this medium. Vulnerable and shut-in members of the congregation have been able to stay connected to their communities, even after in-person worship resumed. In Cambridge, where our chapel congregation consists primarily of college members, students' parents have been able to watch their choral scholar children singing without having to travel. Indeed, it's not just the students who have benefitted—my own parents have "attended" the many services which I've conducted in both Selwyn College and Ely Cathedral nearly every day since the pandemic began (even though they had to watch choral evensong over breakfast, since they live in British Columbia).

Non-liturgical choirs have also profited: one of the most impressive productions has been the Voces8 "Live from London" series of weekly concerts which allowed professional choirs from the UK and the USA to gather safely in person with each other, but with a virtual audience. This in-person music-making was of course one of the things which we missed most in the initial months of the pandemic. On the other hand, the re-invention of the virtual choir, while necessary at first, is something

I have gladly abandoned, and will never do again.[132] It is a thankless, music-less task, and once compiled, if it sounds even remotely good, then it is because it has been engineered within an inch of its life. The whole point about ensemble music-making, and singing in particular, is that it occurs in the same space, with people breathing, moving, and responding together to create a single body of sound.

Another choral positive to come out of the pandemic at least with adult choir members, has been the need to distance singers from each other. At Selwyn, standing two metres away from each other has helped the students (indeed, forced them) to learn confidence and independence right from the beginning of their time in the choir. New members have not been able to hide behind older singers, either physically or musically. They have had to listen to each other much more carefully, and have learned to anticipate and respond to other singers to the great benefit of the music and their own development. (Mind you, one does have to ensure that every singer has a copy of the music—last-minute sharing when a forgetful undergraduate has lost his/her copy of the introit is no longer possible.) It took some getting used to when we returned last September, particularly with ensemble in Anglican chant psalm-singing, but it soon became second-nature. There is a transparency and clarity about the choir's sound and the acoustic in chapel which is a direct result of distanced individuals singing independently but collectively, and I intend to preserve this formation as much as possible, even when it is no longer required.

Social distancing has had the significant added bonus of all of us avoiding the annual seasonal colds and bugs which do the rounds in a college community. I also abandoned my "unless you are on your deathbed you should come to rehearsal even if you are ill" policy—even just a slight sniffle was enough for me to ask singers to stay away—and this is surely a good thing. On the other hand, with my cathedral choristers (children), who were boarders in the same household so inevitably *did* share the occasional harmless cough and cold with each other, I asked them to wear a

---

132. For a detailed description of how to create these, see 'A letter from lockdown', September 2020 on page 295.

face-covering in rehearsals if they were symptomatic, and this helped to limit the spread of non-COVID-19 illness.

Like many of you, I am a Type-A[133] sort of musician, regularly working more hours than there are in a day, ambitious, organised, and often a little stressed. I set unrealistic goals for myself, and I expect more of my students than is fair at times. Although I hope I maintained as high standards as possible, the past 18 months have certainly taught me flexibility. It has been particularly liberating not to have been a slave to termly music list. When one is suddenly deprived of seven singers due to a track-and-trace call from the National Health Service, one has an external excuse for changing the anthem at evensong—but why should "this piece is no longer appropriate for this occasion, even though I thought it might be three or four months ago" also not be a legitimate excuse? Obviously planning repertoire in advance is an important aspect of our jobs, but in the end, doing music which suits the singers where they are now, rather than where you thought they might be in some hypothetical future, is even more valuable, especially when dealing with young voices. I intend to experiment with the option of writing a termly music forecast for internal use, but only actually publishing the music list to the outside world two or three weeks at a time.

Conclusions

When it comes down to it, all we can do is risk assess our way out of this mess. Everyone's solutions will be different; every church and choir will have different priorities, make different allowances, and have different restrictions. Consideration of safety, vocal health, repertoire, expectations, care for ourselves and each other, and what our new routines will look like are just the beginning. The list of tactics and approaches will be long. Above all, flexibility, patience, and generosity will be required.

In September 2020, as choirs in the UK were allowed tentatively to begin singing again, I was commissioned to write an anthem for York

133. https://en.wikipedia.org/wiki/Type_A_and_Type_B_personality_theory, accessed 03/08/2021.

Minster Choir. As a sort of *cantus firmus*, I used the wonderful American folksong "How can I keep from singing".[134] The rest of the words of the anthem were chosen from verses from the Old Testament which had to do with music, and crucially, I looked for the prefix "re-": restore, resume, rebuild, renew, return.[135] Although it may feel like we are beginning again from scratch, there is actually an age-old tradition upon which we are relying, and we must take courage from that.

> O, may we soon again renew that song,
> And keep in tune with heaven, till God ere long
> To his celestial consort us unite,
> To live with him, and sing in endless morn of light.[136]

---

134. https://en.wikipedia.org/wiki/How_Can_I_Keep_from_Singing%3F, accessed 03/08/2021.

135. The anthem 'After this, we will return' is available from Encore Publications in Kent (encorepublications.com).

136. 'Blest pair of sirens'; words by John Milton (1608-1674); set by C. H. H. Parry, who was born in 1848 and died of the Spanish Flu, another global pandemic, in 1918.

May 2022

Resuming Cathedral Residencies

At the end of February 2022, the UK Prime Minister announced the conclusion of all legally-binding Covid-19 restrictions in England. Masks are no longer required; the test-and-trace system has been discontinued; social-distancing and vaccination passports are no more. Even the legal requirement to self-isolate after returning a positive test has been abandoned (though government guidance encourages five days at home in such circumstances). Ironically, less than a week later, I tested positive for Covid myself. Having been surrounded by it at every turn for two years, I am surprised it took as long as it did. I am extremely grateful that vaccination meant that I did not suffer particularly badly.

Although it was no longer legally required, I did self-isolate. Isolation remains "strongly encouraged" (i.e., compulsory) in schools and universities, and since I work for two such institutions, I continued to abide by the very rules which were relaxed just a week before I fell ill, both in the interests of preserving my employment status, and also (of course!) for the safety of the outside world. Co-incidentally, during that same week, I received a number of enquiries from the States asking about UK Covid restrictions, and in particular whether it was likely that long-postponed plans for cathedral residencies might finally be realised. So I thought I would answer those questions here, in case you find yourself in the fortunate position of being able to look at touring opportunities for your choirs for the first time in a while.

What Is the State of Singing in the UK[137] at the Moment?

Regular choral services resumed in most cathedrals as early as September 2020, shortly after the release of ENT surgeon Declan Costello's government-funded PERFORM[138] study into the distribution of aerosol droplets, which proved that singing was actually no more dangerous than speaking, despite the negative narrative surrounding the activity since the beginning of the pandemic. Cathedral choirs, Oxbridge college choirs, and professional choirs were able to restart safely, with appropriate mitigations in place (most importantly, ventilation and social distancing). Six months later, the UK was subjected to another full lockdown (January to March 2021), so most choirs were silent again, but since the spring of 2021, services have continued uninterrupted, and are back to their regular pre-pandemic patterns in the vast majority of places.

Are Choirs Singing Unmasked?

In churches, although face-coverings were mandatory, when one was actually *doing* something (reading, praying, preaching, or singing), masks could be removed. The fact that every time one breathes, one sucks the fabric into one's mouth must be particularly unpleasant for singers, and I'm grateful we didn't have to suffer that in choirs here. In addition, children under the age of 11 were never required to wear face-coverings in any context, so most cathedral choristers were unmasked throughout the pandemic simply due to their age (though there were plenty of arguments

---

137. The regulations discussed here are specifically for England (i.e., not necessarily "the UK"). Health decisions are the responsibility of the regional devolved governments, so arrangements in Wales, Scotland, and Northern Ireland are not always the same as those in England.
138. https://bachtrack.com/interview-declan-costello-what-next-after-the-perform-study-september-2020 accessed 28/07/2021.

against that policy, since children were common carriers of the virus, despite often being asymptomatic). As I write, many churches are continuing to encourage the wearing of face-coverings by their congregations, but this is entirely discretionary.

In addition, most choirs removed all distancing, though my experience at Selwyn College has been conspicuously different. When we returned to college in January 2022, the Dean of Chapel and I insisted that the choir should continue to distance; windows were wide open during services, even in the least clement weather of the UK winter. On the other hand, all other Cambridge choirs were back in their stalls, unmasked and undistanced. A number of my singers were concerned that we were only abiding by those arrangements for the "optics" (i.e., so that no-one complained about a lack of distancing having viewed our services on You-Tube). On the contrary, we were actually doing it to keep the choir safe. And sure enough, when the Omicron variant ravaged its way through Selwyn Choir midway through term, we were absolutely confident that none of the choir had contracted it from each other in chapel—their collective trip to a local jazz club after evensong one day was the most likely culprit!

Are Congregations Singing?

Although a significant proportion of choral singing in the UK returned in September 2020, it took far too long before anything classed as 'amateur' (parish choirs, choral societies, barbershop groups, and many other ensembles encompassing millions of people across the country for whom singing was crucial for friendship and wellbeing), was permitted without restrictions (limited numbers, outdoors only). In July 2021, restrictions were finally lifted for them, and for congregations, who have been allowed to sing continuously since then.

How Are Cathedrals Feeling about Visiting Choirs?

Cathedrals are extremely keen to resume visiting choir programmes. We have already had a number of visiting choirs for occasional weekends at Ely Cathedral, and we expect to welcome choirs for week-long residencies this summer. All testing and quarantining regulations have been removed for fully-vaccinated international travellers, so I hope that you will be able to reinstate the plans that were so unceremoniously cancelled two years ago.

This has, of course, been an unprecedented time for liturgical music, and for the performing arts more generally (not to mention the travel industry). Here's hoping that we will be able to gather in large groups once again in music, fellowship, and without fear.

Chapter 13

A Musical Miscellany

This chapter includes a selection of columns discussing various topics, including organ geekery, tied eighth-notes in English choral music, choir vestries, and singing lessons for choir members.

May 2011

For the Organ Geeks

We read much in these pages (and those of other organ-related publications) about newly installed pipe organs. In spite of the recession, these continue to be built in churches, cathedrals, synagogues, and concert halls around the world, and it is a sign of approbation for a builder to have an instrument featured in the likes of TAO, *Organists' Review*, and *Choir & Organ*. Surely, most of us enjoy admiring the glossy photos of new organs, both cases and consoles. We read the specifications eagerly, agreeing or disagreeing with particular decision according to a no-doubt unbalanced combination of scholarship and personal taste, and we all know that the higher the numbers in the Roman and Arabic secret organ codes are, the more enticing: II/22 is very nice, but IV/65 is certainly superior, while V/110 is undeniably thrilling. Or is that just me?

These installations usually involve years of planning by specially constituted committees, calling for and responding to tendered proposals, travelling to play other instruments by prospective builders, ensuring that a venue's musical and spiritual needs are met, marketing and communicating decisions, meeting fund-raising targets, and the like. The final culmination of the process, usually the blessing and inaugural recital of a new instrument, is a time of great celebration and not a little relief. On such occasions, the new organ committee has the delightful task of retiring itself for (they hope) at least 75 years or so.

I went through this myself a few years ago when Orgues Létourneau of St Hyachinthe, Québec, installed their magnificent Opus 95 (III/30) in Selwyn College Chapel. The whole process, from the initial decision to replace an unsuccessful instrument to the Létourneau's inaugural recital given by Naji Hakim, took nearly five years, and I was pleased indeed to see photos of my pride and joy featured in most of the specialist press, including on the front cover of this august publication.[139]

Recently in Selwyn Chapel we had another new pipe organ installed, though on a rather smaller scale: it is just I/3. And yet I found myself nearly as excited about its arrival as if it had been a VII/245—not least because, on this occasion, I was not involved in the lengthy planning process. Indeed, by the time I heard anything about it, the excellent English organ-builder Kenneth Tickell had already been approached, had chosen an appropriate specification, had scheduled the building work, and had already processed the first payment!

This unlikely scenario took place thanks to an elderly alumnus of Selwyn College who had been in the chapel choir as an undergraduate in the 1950s, and who decided of his own accord that we needed a chamber organ. Unbeknownst to me, the alumnus in question had spoken to a friend of his, a retired cathedral organist, to ask just where one could get such a thing, and the approach to Kenneth Tickell was duly made. Obviously I was surprised and delighted to accept such a generous gift, especially when all I had to do from an administrative point of view was to proof-read the wording on the small brass plaque on the case that indicates whence the gift originated.

Our lovely new chamber organ has suspended tracker key action, mechanical stop action, a slider soundboard, and three stops (8', 4', 2'). Conveniently, the instrument divides into two sections for easy transportation in a station wagon or small van. The carving on the wooden grill is exquisite, taking its inspiration from the neo-Gothic woodwork decoration found throughout the chapel, and the casework even incorporates the college crest at its centre. Now if that doesn't get your inner organ geek going, then I don't know what will.

---

139. TAO cover, May 2005.

Wind pressure and stop-lists aside, it is, of course, the musical benefits of this new organ that make it so worthwhile. Our music lists regularly feature the likes of Thomas Tomkins, John Blow, William Byrd, Pelham Humfrey, William Childs, Thomas Weelkes, and Orlando Gibbons. We blessed and inaugurated the chamber organ during Choral Evensong, with Gibbons' *Second Service*, and his epic verse anthem *See, see the Word is incarnate*. We continue to use it frequently for early repertoire, and in particular for the Elizabethan verse music which these Gibbons pieces epitomize: sections for soloists alternate with those for full choir, and all are accompanied by a contrapuntal keyboard part (which is sometimes freestanding and sometimes a reduction of parts for a consort of viols). Although the Létourneau's Positif division has all the right sounds for this repertoire, since the console is in the west-end gallery, about 20 metres away from the choir, the organ scholar had to communicate with the singers indirectly, by way of the conductor through a CCTV screen. Now, with the chamber organ right beside the choir, the organist can accompany the singers much more easily, so that both the "chamber" (i.e., small ensemble) nature of the music and the intimacy of the early counterpoint are significantly clearer. And in the absence of a resident viol consort, our lovely new Tickell does very nicely indeed.

I count myself fortunate to have two such beautifully and stylistically distinct organs in my care, especially since the second one involved no agonising on my part. Perhaps our humble little chamber organ will not have its moment of glory on the cover of the organists' equivalent of *Vogue* magazine, but it is cherished in our chapel nonetheless, and it constitutes a very pleasing addition to the ecclesiastical furniture. It is true of most things in life, and it is particular true of organs: size isn't everything.

May 2013

Transferable Skills

By the time you read this, I will have just completed my final meeting as a Trustee of the Royal College of Organists. I have served as an elected member of the Trustee Council for two consecutive four-year terms, and the Charter and Byelaws stipulate that I may not serve again before taking at least a year off. It has been a fascinating and challenging role, and I have learned an extraordinary and unexpected number of transferable skills during my time on the Council. If I'm honest though, although I will miss my colleagues, I am ready for a break, and I will be glad to hand over the reins to the lucky newly-elected Trustee who will take my place, and who will be a Trustee for the College's 150th anniversary celebrations in 2014. As I prepare to step down, I thought it might be of interest to readers to be given a glimpse into the internal workings of the RCO before I leave its inner sanctum for the foreseeable future.

The Trustee Council consists of 15 members, some of whom are organists, and some of whom are not, but all of whom support the RCO's primary aim and objective, namely "to promote and advance the arts and practice of organ-playing and choral directing and related activities to the highest standards of competence and artistry". Council meetings are also attended by the College's small but extraordinarily dedicated staff team, the people who deliver the RCO's regular activities, publications, examinations, and programme of events. The RCO is a national registered charity, and must therefore comply with UK government regulations for the running and governance of charitable organisations. Over the past eight years, I have learned a remarkable amount about charity law, fundraising, investment policies, accounting procedures, variance analyses, management strategies, governance best practice, duties of prudence and of care, compliance, public benefit, mission statements, aims, objectives, statutes, ordinances, and any number of other things which, on the face of it, don't have a lot to do with being able to play virtuosic pedal solos in a piece of Bach. . . . As I look back on my time, I think with some horror about how naïve I was when I took on the role in the first place.

Trustees are elected by way of a national member postal ballot. Those nominated are asked to write a short manifesto, which, in the case of those of us who are organists, generally consists of a biography of our musical training, recent recital venues, and perhaps a précis of our recording and conducting experience. As you will have ascertained from the previous paragraph, none of the things which appeared on my first election manifesto were at all relevant to my time as a Trustee. Ironically though, since Trustees are elected by the membership (a group of people which by definition includes an awful lot of organists), it is often organists who are elected, despite the fact that being able to play the complete works of Duruflé from memory is not a particularly helpful skill when it comes to discussing ethical investment policies. Charity law best practice demands that a full range of necessary abilities are represented on Trustee boards, regardless of the aims of the charity itself. On the RCO's current Trustee Council, it is fair to say that we lowly organists most definitely look to the lawyer, the accountant, the medical practitioner, and the entrepreneur for guidance on a frequent basis.

The RCO Trustee Council meets in London six times per year. The College is a virtual organisation, with no specific headquarters, so we meet in various venues throughout the city. On a Trustee Council day, I take an 8am train from Cambridge to London (a 50-minute direct route), which has the additional benefit of providing a welcome escape from the pressure of term time. At particularly busy times of the year, I will blushingly admit that I use the train journey to read the papers for the meeting, which I know is frowned upon by the RCO's absolutely saintly General

Manager who is meticulous in getting the papers out at least seven days in advance. I think she understands that I live a slightly manic life, and I hope she forgives me for this minor transgression. Once I arrive in London, I spend the requisite amount of time (grudgingly) on my least favourite mode of UK transport, the London Underground, arriving at the meeting venue for a 10am start, possibly by way of a detour into the closest Starbucks or Costa if there is time. After each three-hour meeting, there is invariably a "debriefing" in a local hostelry, with as many of us as are able to stay behind for a quick drink or for lunch. These are always extremely enjoyable social occasions, and I will certainly miss them. I then descend again into the bowels of the Tube towards King's Cross for the train to Cambridge, and cycle quickly to Selwyn in time for Evensong.

I am extremely grateful to the RCO for the experience I have gained over the past eight years, and I will certainly miss the meetings (especially the "debriefings") and the chance to escape from Cambridge (despite the Tube). In many ways, the skills that I have learned as a Trustee are more useful to the world than if I actually could play the complete works of Duruflé from memory (which, I'm sad to say, I cannot). I certainly have a much greater understanding of the workings of the charity sector, of employment law, and of government economic policy than I ever thought I would need as a church musician. I have also made a number of very good friends, several of whom have learned these lessons with me. I will continue to work with the RCO as an Examiner, and as a member of the Academic Board, which is responsible for determining the content of examination syllabi, and where my practical musical skills are perhaps more relevant. I will observe the progress of the new members of the Trustee Council with interest, as they too learn to deal with the not insubstantial challenges that face every small arts charity, especially in the current economic climate. Finally, I would just like to wish the RCO a very happy 150th anniversary!

On Singing Lessons

There has long been an anecdotal mistrust between choral conductors and singing teachers. The great tenor Robert Tear tells the story in his autobiography *Tear Here*,[140] that when he auditioned at the age of 17 for Boris Ord, then Director of Music at King's College, Cambridge, the following conversation took place:

> BO: "Have you had any singing lessons, Mr Tear?"
> RT: "No, Sir."
> BO: "Good! Then you won't ruin my choir."

Of course, this exchange takes on a rather amusing twist now, given Tear's subsequent illustrious career.

On the other hand, the singing teachers' purported view is offered in vocal pedagogue Barbara Doscher's book *The Functional Unity of the Singing Voice*:[141] "Those very characteristics which make some solo voices unique must be subdued in group singing, often to the eventual detriment of that voice." Richard Miller, in *On the Art of Singing*,[142] refers to the "history of conflict [. . .] between the training of the solo voice and what

---

140. Tear, Robert. *Tear Here*. André Deutsch. London. 1990.
141. Doscher, Barbara. *The Functional Unity of the Singing Voice*. Scarecrow Press. USA. 1994.
142. Miller, Richard. *The Art of Singing*. OUP. 1996.

is expected of a singer in the choral ensemble." These concerns obviously supersede the most notorious single issue of the use of vibrato in choral singing,[143] and express a wider unease about the overall health and character of solo voices which are involved in ensemble work.

Given the date of the King's anecdote above (1956) it can be concluded that in the UK it is now considered rather old-fashioned for a choral conductor to express this sort of suspicion. Enlightened directors of all serious university and cathedral choirs have for a number of years now insisted that their choir members have regular individual tuition with a professional singing teacher. Indeed many cathedrals and colleges have their own exclusive vocal specialists who give one-on-one tuition, coach soloists, consult regularly with the conductor on matters of vocal health, and care for changing voices in children and teenagers.

As a conductor myself of two choirs consisting of young singers (middle- and high-school-age girls at Ely Cathedral, and mixed university students at Selwyn College, Cambridge), I find that there is rarely enough time in rehearsal to deal with singers' individual technical needs in a focused manner. I can and do point out a tense jaw here, a raised shoulder there, and misshapen vowel elsewhere, but it is in their individual lessons that I expect these issues to be addressed at a much more detailed level, and by a teacher with proper training in vocal pedagogy.

Pace Doscher and Miller, but it is probably true to say that in the UK there are more singing teachers who are aware of, and sympathetic to, the technical needs of choral singers (as well as the needs of soloists) than one might find in the States. This is partly due to the fact that many of the singing teachers working for colleges and cathedrals here began their careers as choral singers, before going on to study and work as soloists. It is also the case that there is a relatively high proportion of choral singers per capita in the UK, partly due to the cathedral and collegiate traditions. (Contrary to the accepted belief that England has the world's most active choral tradition, according to Dr Google, Dubai, Florida, and Finland all actually boast the highest number of choral singers per capita internationally!)[144]

---

143. For a discussion of vibrato in choral singing in the UK, see February 2013 on page 6.
144. Search done at the time of writing, June 2013.

It is possible, however, that the tension between choral conductors and singing teachers is still unresolved in some corners of the world. I recently heard a particular university choir which has benefited from considerable financial investment intended to develop it from its roots as a humble assortment of provincial volunteer student singers, into a slick, ambitious, and nationally-recognised ensemble. It consists of a (disconcertingly small) number of university undergraduates, and a (disconcertingly large) group of older experienced paid professional section leaders. The choir sings together for about 12 hours per week, and tackles difficult and substantial repertoire on a regular basis. Notwithstanding their generous annual budget, one of the things which has been consciously *cut* in recent years is funding for individual singing lessons for its student members.

I was concerned and surprised to learn this, since this university was certainly not to be found in some halcyon (though sadly fictitious) location where 19-year-olds with mature voices and secure vocal technique arrived straight out of high school. The conductor seemed to be striving for an unflinchingly loud, old-fashioned, middle-aged English lay clerk sound, and therefore the young students were obliged to prioritise sheer volume over vocal health. The resulting tension in the tongue root and/or the extrinsic muscles of the larynx frequently produced a rather strangulated tone and alarmingly approximate intonation. Needless to say, the resulting sound of the choir was, alas, not always aurally attractive. In a situation like this, it is easily understood why Barbara Doscher and her colleagues around the world have expressed concern over the vocal health of choral singers.

It seems to me to be obvious that, first and foremost, choral conductors need to understand something about singing technique. They must also understand the need for their singers to receive professional, individual tuition, in order to ensure that their techniques are sound, and that they are using their voices healthily and efficiently. This is particularly crucial with young voices (and "young" should be used to define a voice up to the age of about 30). By definition, there is also a need for patience—unless a choral conductor is dealing with a fully professional choir whose members are all over 30—and inconsistency must be allowed for, indeed encouraged, as young singer are allowed to experiment (healthily) with their developing voices. At the very least, even just on "Occupational Health and Safety" grounds, some regular individual damage limitation should be available for singers whose voices are changing. When I first arrived at Selwyn, 15 years ago, I found that the "Health and Safety" legal argument was an extremely effective way of convincing my College Bursar that we needed to increase the singing lesson budget.

Choral conductors and singing teachers should be able to work together to ensure individual healthy vocal production and sound technique, as well as the resultant vibrancy of choral colour which will be achieved if every singer in the choir is producing the most relaxed and resonant sound that they are capable of. Finally, in case any of you are in doubt, I would, of course, have accepted Robert Tear into my choir as a first year undergraduate as well, though I would most certainly have sent him straight to my college singing teacher just as soon as he arrived.

Configuring Cupboards for Cassocks

Those of you who "like" the Selwyn College Choir Facebook page will have seen that we began the new academical year here with an exciting development. For the first time in the choir's 132-year history, we actually have a dedicated Choir Vestry. The fact that we had survived so long without one came as a surprise to many, including some college alumni, who had not realised that we had hitherto dressed for Evensong in a variety of corridors, vestibules, foyers, and other neglected corners of the college. This may seem an inconsequential and insignificant (though convenient and practical) development in my choir's history, but the process of getting the room fit for purpose prompted me to consider the wider implications of such spaces for a liturgical choir such as mine.

When I became Director of Music at Selwyn 16 years ago, the choir's vestments were kept on coat-hooks in the organ loft at the west end of the chapel. A system was in place whereby before and after each service, they would proceed up one spiral staircase, robe or disrobe as applicable behind the organ case, and carry on down the other spiral staircase. This was impractical in numerous ways: it was a noisy procedure, and no matter how hard they tried to keep quiet, the stillness before Evensong was always disturbed. They were not allowed upstairs before the completion of the organ voluntary after the service, so whenever the Organ Scholar played something longish, the choir were inevitably late for dinner. Also, there was no room for them to leave coats and bags, and the thin dusty passageway between the organ case and the west wall was not conducive to keeping surplices white.

After a couple of unsatisfactory Terms, I managed to convince the powers-that-be to move us to the large outer vestibule of the main public loos below the dining hall (hardly an improvement for the choir, but significantly better for the congregation). Again, there were impracticalities. When a conference was taking place in the large room next to the choir cupboards, it was difficult not to disturb them. Indeed, on one occasion, a vociferous tenor nearly caused a major diplomatic incident when ranting loudly in the loo about the inconvenience of the conference guests, only to find that one of them was in the cubicle next to him. To be fair, after an intense two-hour-long rehearsal and service, the continued need to remain silent was understandably challenging.

When that vestibule was redeployed about 10 years later, we were moved to a lengthy and (mostly) unused corridor under the kitchens. The cupboards were nicer and bigger, and fresh paint and large mirrors helped to make the hallway look more spacious. However, the cassock cupboard doors and the access door into the hallway could not be open simultaneously; coats and bags left on the floor caused the Health and Safety Manager to have paroxysms, but coat-hooks along the wall were not permitted by the Fire Warden. Most amusingly, the hallway provided the only wheelchair access to the elevator into the dining hall, so if any of our most elderly Fellows wanted to come to dinner after chapel, they would have to be wheeled through the middle of the entire choir in various stages of un-dress. I knew that something would have to change. . . .

So, last year, when a complete refurbishment of one of our accommodation buildings was underway, I convinced the Bursar to put a student music practice room into the plans, which allowed me to take over the old music practice room near the chapel, and have it converted into our first ever Choir Vestry. College staff spent two weeks over the summer cleaning, painting, designing, re-wiring, building, and cleaning again, readying the room for the new choir's arrival. With the able help of Ikea, Amazon, and the Maintenance Department Manager who, conveniently, happens to run Girl Guide troupes, we came up with excellent solutions for individual storage for all members of the choir, as well as secure long-term storage for music, and clean, reliable cupboards for cassocks and surplices. The Organ Scholars and I spent several days prettifying the room, putting up pictures on walls, labelling pigeon-holes and cassock hangers, organising the sewing kit, sharpening pencils, and finally, bedecking the room with colourful bunting for its first use.

The practical advantages of our new Choir Vestry are obvious: there is ample and secure space for storage of personal items; the surplices have a reasonable chance of remaining white; the newly-built music desks will be excellent for sectional rehearsals; there is a piano available for choir members to learn music before services; and my 16-year-old collection of annual choir photographs actually has somewhere to be displayed. Most importantly however, there is no need for the choir to remain silent in the Vestry. For me, this is the most valuable aspect of the room.

Members of a liturgical choir spend the majority of their time together performing ceremonial duties: processing in carefully-formed lines, standing and sitting collectively at appropriate times, leading formal worship, being silent during services, and concentrating intensely during rehearsals. However, in the privacy of the Choir Vestry, communal banter, social chatter, and hearty laughter are positively encouraged. Vestries are often mildly subversive places of order and disorder which provide a haven from the solemnity and order of liturgical services: the bottle of sherry secreted in a pigeon-hole, the irreverent cartoons on the notice-board, the Doctor Who action figure which magically appears in a different place every week. Indeed, in the lay clerks' Vestry at Ely Cathedral, there is even a darts board (appropriately resting on an adjustable music stand) which allows the adult members of the choir to vent their various frustrations.

These social activities are as important to building ensemble as are the hours spent working on sound, tuning, and processions. The Choir Vestry is the space where they can (literally) let their hair down, chat noisily without fear of rebuke, and interact informally in a way which is impossible when they are in chapel. In many respects, Choir Vestries are the most human domain in liturgical buildings. They are the secular sanctuaries where those involved in the often tiring and demanding business of liturgical music-making can become that strange and precious thing—a community. Not having one's post-service disrobing procedure interrupted by elderly Fellows in wheelchairs is merely an added bonus.

The Elusive "Tied Quaver"

A perennial question with which choir members interrupt rehearsals runs as follows: "Where does the final consonant go?" This legitimate enquiry can be particularly irritating when asked by someone who only achieved 60% accuracy in the preceding phrase. Now, I am a stickler for final consonants, some might argue to a fault. Nonetheless, if by the end of a rehearsal, a choir's consonants are perfectly together but the notes are still wrong, one wonders about their conductor's priorities.

In theory, of course, this question should not need to be asked by anyone from a well-trained choir. However, confusion inevitably arises with that very British[145] of choral quirks, the tied quaver, or eighth-note. How many times have you seen this:

O   God.

---

145. Re: http://jandrewowen.com/en/2015/03/19/tied-eighth-notes-in-choral-music/. I do not believe that Gabriel Fauré was doing the same thing as RVW, Howells, et al. Fauré's occasional tied eighth-notes simply indicate the duration of the note he wanted, i.e., a dotted-quarter-note for the final syllable of 'luceat', with the 't' occurring on the rest.

and agonised about where the 'd' should be placed? (This example is taken from Howells' *Like as the hart*.[146]) Perhaps those of us who are particularly OCD about final consonants can be forgiven for having forgotten that 40% of the previous phrase was inaccurate.

Historically, these pesky eighth notes began to appear inconsistently in the early works of Elgar (there are a number of instances in the 1897 *Te Deum and Benedicite Op. 34*, for example). Vaughan Williams was the first to use them habitually, though his application of them is also inconsistent (see below). The tied eighth-note is especially ubiquitous in the works of Howells, Finzi, and Leighton, and the like, and has for many years perturbed singers and conductors alike. Fortunately, many contemporary composers (James MacMillan, Jonathan Dove, Cecilia McDowall, et al.) seem to have abandoned them.

So, what is that tied eighth-note for? Is it correct to place the consonant directly on the note, or should it occur on the ensuing rest? What were the composers' intentions? And, assuming they had intentions for those consonants, what on earth did they mean by adding a tied eighth-note to a word ending in a vowel—as in this example from Vaughan Williams' *A Choral Flourish*?[147]

My personal practice is consciously inconsistent. I consider each instance individually, and base my decision on tempo, style, harmony, and context, varying my verdict from bar to bar. I do not teach my choirs a specific 'policy', which is why that aforementioned question occurs. In an informal survey of cathedral and Oxbridge colleagues, I was not surprised to find that they follow this route as well. Those who do attempt to abide by a policy inevitably stray from it on a regular basis.

It is widely agreed that tempo is the most important factor in deciding where to place the consonant. In general, at a faster speed, the consonant is

146. Howells, Herbert. *Like as the hart*. OUP. 1943.
147. Vaughan Williams, Ralph. *A Choral Flourish*. OUP. 1956.

placed directly on the tied note. So, in the quick middle section of the Magnificat from Leighton's *Second Service*,[148] placing the consonants on the tied note enhances rhythmic clarity, and keeps contrapuntal ensemble precise.

On the other hand, in a slower, more lyrical work, placing the consonant on the rest after the tied note creates subtle and less perceptible joins between phrases. For example, in Howells' *O pray for the peace of Jerusalem*,[149] the consonants in the opening and closing sections are most musically placed on the rests (or at least this is true at the tempo at which I take the piece!).

Frustratingly, composers themselves were inconsistent. In Vaughan Williams' setting of *Let all the world*,[150] the following two phrases occur within three bars of each other. Surely they are not meant to be sung differently?

148. Leighton. Kenneth. *Second Service (Evening Canticles)*. Novello and Co. 1972.
149. Howells, Herbert. *O pray for the peace of Jerusalem*. OUP. 1943.
150. Vaughan Williams, Ralph. No. 5 from *Five Mystical Songs*. Stainer and Bell. 1911.

Elgar's anthem "The Spirit of the Lord" (from *The Apostles*)[151] contains the following three examples of tied eighth-notes, each of which demands a different interpretation.

For 'poor', a tied eighth-note is provided for no final consonant (the 'r' is not pronounced when singing with a standard English accent).

Putting the 's' of 'captives' on the rest creates a more refined connection between the phrases.

The complexity of the syncopation and the *rallentando* in the accompaniment makes putting the 's' of 'righteousness' on the tied note by far the simplest and tidiest solution.

A particularly awkward example of the phenomenon occurs in Howells' *Magnificat in B minor*,[152] during the quicker middle section, which is conducted in half-notes.

151. Elgar, Edward. *The Apostles Op. 49*. Novello. 1903.
152. Howells, Herbert. *Evening Service in B minor*. Novello. 1955.

Howells'
original:

My
alternative:

Placing the 't' on the tied note itself makes the gap feel unnaturally long, and inevitably someone comes in early after the rest. On the other hand, it is mathematically very difficult to place the final 't' of 'seat' on an eighth-note rest when counting in half-notes. My (undoubtedly controversial) solution is actually to rewrite Howells (!) which fortunately works well harmonically in this case.

There is, of course, no right answer. Composers themselves were varied in their approach, and it is a relief that the practice seems to have fallen out of use. As to why it was introduced originally, one theory is that the tied notes were added to encourage less-accomplished singers to hold long notes with conviction right to the end. Since many of the works in which they first appeared were oratorios written for amateur choral societies, this conjecture seems plausible.

The former Director of Music at King's College, Cambridge, told me that he had actually asked Howells about the tied eighth-notes many years ago. Howells "didn't comment in detail", presumably "preferring decisions in this area to be made by conductors."[153] Consequently, it looks as if we are required to make an informed and musical judgement in every individual case rather than trying to construct a universal policy—but mark up your choir's scores before the rehearsal, in order to avoid being asked that old familiar but irritating question!

153. Stephen Cleobury, personal correspondence, 29 August 2016; quoted with permission.

July 2022

A Modest Proposal

"**D**ear Ms MacDonald, I hope you won't mind me writing to out of the blue like this. We spoke briefly at a recent [Selwyn College] Feast, at which I babbled my admiration for the glorious sound of the Chapel Choir. The occasion stayed with me, and has prompted a thought I'd like to lay before you."

Thus began an email the subject of which provides the tagline for this column. The thought laid before me in the subsequent paragraphs comprised an invitation for Selwyn College Choir to provide music for a new BritBox Agatha Christie adaptation, written, directed, and starred in by the author of this communication—none other than Hugh Laurie, undergraduate at Selwyn from 1978-81, and now an Honorary Fellow of the college. The novel in question, *Why didn't they ask Evans*, is set in a village in North Wales. The protagonist is (rather improbably) the organist at the local parish church, where his father is the vicar. There are various scenes which required a choir and an organist, and Hugh's connection with Selwyn pointed to us as the obvious choice to fill these roles.

The request seemed at first to be nearly as fanciful as Jonathan Swift's 1729 original "modest proposal"[154] (in which he suggested that impoverished Irish families might make money by selling their children to the

---

154. Swift, Jonathan: A modest proposal, Dublin 1729.

aristocracy for food). Nonetheless, after deciding the email was genuine, I contacted college authorities to ask permission to accept the offer. Once agreement-in-principle had been confirmed, there began lengthy negotiation of dates, contracts, logistics, timing, risk assessments, Covid protocols, and so on.

Finally, the day arrived. The production team, including Hugh Laurie, arrived in college in time for Saturday brunch in the dining hall, one of the busiest meals of the week. You can imagine the pointing and whispering from students and staff while eggs and hash browns were consumed. Choir and organist then gathered in chapel for a three-hour session, to record the audio for two hymns, Mendelssohn's Wedding March, Bach's Prelude in B minor (BWV 544), and a 1908 music-hall song "All the nice girls love a sailor".

The two hymns, "O! Iesu mawr, rho d'anian bur" (O Jesus, let thy Spirit bless) and "Ti dymunwn fyw" (I'll walk beside you), were both to be sung in Welsh—fortuitously, one of our alto choral scholars was a native-speaker, so acted as language coach. "Ti Dymunwn Fyw" is commonly sung by a boy treble, so I arranged it for Alfie, 12-year-old Ely Cathedral chorister, who was accompanied by organ and choir. "All the nice girls love a sailor" is a rather bawdy and unreconstructed number, which is referred to throughout the show by various characters. Our choral version of it, in my post-modern arrangement which combines madrigal, part-song, and barbershop,[155] closes the final episode of the series, and provides an intentionally light ending to the dark tale. (Any of you who know the song will be relieved to know that I only set verse 1.)

Michael, the organ scholar, had to follow very particular performance directions. In the relevant scene, the Bach is played in the church by a sinister character called Mr Angel, who is suspected of murdering several people—this was perhaps the only time Michael has been asked to play the organ "in the manner of a contract-killer". In episode 3, the Mendelssohn Wedding March is played by Gladys, an elderly spinster who deputises from time to time for the vicar's son. Michael was charged with playing it enthusiastically but badly, and he did a spectacular job of this,

---

155. Published by August Press, Tennessee, and available from J. W. Pepper

despite being an FRCO prize-winner. Hugh explained the requirements and the context of the scene, and then he and I went to listen in the chapel below. We were in hysterics as Michael played, and I'm rather surprised that isn't audible in the final edit!

The choir were delighted a few months later to be invited to be involved in the filming as well. The crew had taken over a village church in Surrey as the location for the scenes in which our music was featured. We were bussed down south over a couple of days to mime along to our own recordings of the hymns. We brought our cassocks and surplices (which the production team insisted on calling "costumes") and enjoyed the glamour of hair-and-makeup before our scenes. I'd taken advantage of eased Covid restrictions a week earlier and had my hair cut for the first time in months, which made me very unpopular with the historically-assiduous stylist. Rather than a relatively quick French-braid, they had to give me a 1930s "finger wave" which took ages, and required a dispro-portionate number of bobby-pins to hold it in place. Ely chorister Alfie (whose voice had changed by the time of the filming, so it was a good thing we were miming) receives pride of place at the beginning of epi-sode 2, with me peering over his right shoulder, and Michael enjoyed the double role of singing in the choir at the same time as heart-throb actor Will Poulter mimed his (Michael's) organ accompanying.

Finally, a year after the initial email was received, *Why didn't they ask Evans* was released on BritBox. It was fascinating to see how Hugh (a fine musician himself of course) integrated his imaginative music choices (including our contributions) into the programme. It's a terrific mini-series—watch it if you can!

Chapter 14

A Selection of Guest Columns

Over the years, a number of my colleagues have contributed columns which have discussed the choral set-up in their cathedrals/colleges/ churches. I have permission from the authors to publish a small representative selection of those interesting and informative columns here.

Curry, Qur'an and Choral Evensong

Alexander Berry, Bradford Cathedral

The daily commute from my home in the UNESCO world heritage site of Saltaire, West Yorkshire, takes me along Bradford's infamous Manningham Lane. The names of its colourful shops (Hashim's Hairdressers, al-Falaah Supermarkets, Al-Mu'min Bookshop) betray the strong Pakistani Muslim demographic of the inner city. Within the Bradford inner ring road, all but one of the wards have a Pakistani Muslim majority, and almost a third of all Bradfordians are now followers of Islam.

It is in this context that I find myself doing the job of Director of Music at Bradford Cathedral. The cathedral is the only Church of England church in Bradford city centre: a beautiful medieval parish church, extended in the 1950s and 1960s. There are several so-called 'parish church cathedrals' in the UK, which were consecrated as the populations of the industrial centres of Victorian Britain expanded exponentially. This is exactly what happened in Bradford: as the centre of the British wool and silk trade, the city's mills were one of the largest employers in the country, leading to fabulous wealth for the mill owners and abject poverty for the workers. With the labour shortages after World War II, Commonwealth citizens from Pakistan and Bangladesh (former East Pakistan) came to fill jobs in the now declining textile industry.

This is a very different story from the that of the famous old English Cathedrals, many of which were monasteries or great pilgrimage sites for centuries, and some of which sit on large financial endowments and have an annual turnover of over several million pounds. A good number of these cathedrals also have a choir school, usually a fee-paying prep school, from which cathedrals can draw their choristers. This means that a rigorous weekly programme of rehearsals can be drawn up to fit with the school timetable, full attendance being assured by generous scholarships.

Like the old cathedrals, at Bradford we have two separate treble lines of boys and girls, and sing at least five fully choral services every week. There is no choir school, and our choristers come from over twenty schools in the local area. One boy hails from the delightful market town of Ilkley (of the famous song, "On Ilkla Moor Baht 'at"—look it up)[156], and it takes him about an hour to get to the cathedral through rush hour traffic in time to rehearse before evensong.

Having no choir school means that recruitment takes up quite a lot of my time. It's very easy to get the children excited and on board, but persuading the parents is often more difficult. Sometimes the children's enthusiasm is quashed by the schoolteachers themselves—"Remember, you can't go t' cathedral if you go t' mosque". This latter point is actually untrue. Two of our recent recruits come from a Muslim family, whose parents are so pleased that their daughters are having a musical and spiritual education. I recently asked the girls' father if he would be happy to leave contact details, some of which contain confidential information. He had no qualms at all, the cathedral being a "house of God". We also have two boys of Pakistani origin whose father is one of the leaders of the local Asian Christian congregation, but has decided to make the cathedral his home church.

Living in a city with such a mix of ethnicities and religions creates many and various wonderful stories. In the 2011 census the Muslim community outnumbered the Jewish community by 129,041 to 299. The fine local synagogue of 1880 was barely able to function, with declining membership and emergency repairs that could not be supported by its small

---

156. Yorkshire folksong: https://en.wikipedia.org/wiki/On_Ilkla_Moor_Baht_%27at

congregation. The fund-raising effort to repair the synagogue was led by the now senior vice president of the Bradford Council for Mosques, Zulfi Karim, in conjunction with the chairman of the synagogue, Rudi Leavor, himself a refugee from Nazi Germany. Karim is also the founder of the World Curry Festival, which last year held its opening banquet in Bradford Cathedral, to encourage what Karim calls 'gastrodiplomacy', bringing people together through food. The interfaith diplomacy is so strong here that Leavor often leaves the synagogue keys with Karim when he is away from the city.

The importance of interfaith relations cannot be understated in a city like Bradford, not least in the aftermath of the Manchester Arena suicide bombing, which caused the death of 22 civilians (https://en.wikipedia.org/wiki/Manchester_Arena_bombing). On 23rd May 2017 a prayer vigil was held in Bradford Cathedral led by the Bishop of Bradford in conjunction with leaders from faith groups across the city. As the choir sang the very simple chant, "Kindle a flame to lighten the dark and take all fear away", Christians, Muslims and members of all faiths and none came to light candles in memory of the victims. For our young people, this holds such strong educational importance: these local acts of solidarity form the building blocks of an open and diverse British society.

Running a choir in the faded grandeur of a former industrial city may be far removed from the Barchester Towers idyll of life in an English Cathedral. However, in a country of declining church attendance and increased secularism, Bradford's patchwork of churches, mosques, temples, and gurdwaras makes it a great City of Faith. For me it is incredibly fulfilling that the cathedral and our choir play an important part on that stage.

Alexander Berry was appointed Director of Music at Bradford Cathedral, about 30 miles northeast of Manchester, in 2017, at the age of 27. He is the youngest Cathedral Organist in England. He was a chorister at Lichfield Cathedral, and after completing a degree as Organ Scholar at Queens' College, Cambridge, he held assistantship posts at Ely Cathedral and Magdalen College, Oxford, working respectively under Sarah MacDonald and Daniel Hyde.

The Diocese of Leeds' Singing Programme

Thomas Leech, Roman Catholic Diocese of Leeds

Chancing on the inner-city sanctuary of Leeds Cathedral during weekday vespers, its chant and polyphony eclipsing rush-hour commotion, you might imagine a historic choral institution, a select group of choristers educated in an exclusive school. For our team, the heart of our work isn't found here amid musical, architectural, and liturgical splendour; indeed even the cathedral choirs could be described as a by-product of our core mission as the Diocesan music department.

For a recent conference paper, I spent some happy hours looking at how English cathedral choirs defined themselves publicly via their websites. The choir that devoted 13 words to faith, and the remaining 462 to a list of past concert engagements, broadcasts, recordings, and *Gramophone* accolades was typical: a sentence or two about worship, a competitive reference to the age of the foundation, explanation of the education choristership provides, and lengthy evidence of professional brilliance. This is reinforced by many cathedral and collegiate choirs' social media presence, where the "music list" and quality of performance hold sway.

These self-portrayals seem to seek confidence from temporal factors and betray nervousness, ambivalence even, in the relationship between the church and its mission, the professional musicians, the children they work with, and the outside world. We often hear that choirs bring the ancient buildings to life; while they are clearly less expensive to maintain than a building they are nevertheless a costly enterprise. Is it sustainable or even desirable to spend upwards of £250,000 [$329,375] annually on a music programme that works with between 32 and 50 children and employs ten adults? I wonder if cathedral choirs—like the buildings themselves so often appear—are for many more of a middleclass heritage product than "living stones".

This brings us to our programme at the Diocese of Leeds, a model that retains those self-proclaimed assets of cathedral choirs (musical excellence, education, tradition) with both worship and evangelisation on a very substantial scale.

Our formal charitable objectives charge us to support the mission of the Catholic Church through "the advancement of the Catholic religion" and "the promotion of Catholic teaching in the Diocese and beyond." The Diocese's latest annual report summarizes our efforts thus: "Central to the programme of youth evangelisation is the Diocese's Music Department. The core programme of the musical and liturgical education is the Schools Singing Programme."

So our choirs have at their core the evangelisation and subsequent catechesis of the participants; most of this work takes place not in the rarefied atmosphere of our beautiful cathedral but in the noise, energy (and occasional chaos) of numerous schools. Musical achievement, educational benefits, and social outcomes are all real and very welcome, but necessarily secondary.

Our choral directors race across Yorkshire during the day, working with some 3,500 children weekly (over 100 groups across 53 schools), returning to their bases to run our elite choirs: six boys' choirs, six girls' choirs, five mixed children's choirs, two youth choirs, six university choirs, and an adult choir, all drawing their membership from our school sessions. We are staffed by six full-time and one part-time musicians, a development administrator, two organ scholars, one choral conducting scholar, and twelve choral scholars. Our choirs are hugely diverse both socially and culturally—much of our work takes place in some of the UK's most deprived areas. Funding comes from schools, parishes, the Diocese, and a number of key partnerships (including Leeds Trinity University and Leeds College of Music), and our horizons are broadened through international links, including Notre Dame University and the University of El Paso, whose students and staff have made a number of visits to observe, study, and participate in our programmes.

The choirs draw families into the church. We know that improved singing in the school environment enriches school worship, and it's wonderful to see children who have started work with us aged six in a noisy classroom now singing at some of the 350 sung liturgies at the cathedral, representing the Catholic voice on national BBC broadcasts and making acclaimed recordings of sacred music. We can safely say that these are children who would not have these opportunities if we weren't doing this work. Similarly, it takes special staff to have weeks that encompass singing games with five-year-olds, teenage youth choirs learning Tomkins for a performance with the Gabrieli Consort, solemn Mass in Latin, and preparing the *Knabenchor* part for Mahler 8!

If the clergy, the altar servers, and the choir all have grey hair, then we are running the church into the ground. A liturgical music programme worthy of investment must prioritise evangelisation and young people on an industrial scale—surely expenditure on exclusively adult professional choirs is a short-sighted waste of precious resource and wilful neglect of the future of both children and church. Let's be brave enough to question the existence and rationale of cathedral choirs, let's question what our motives as church musicians are, and in a society that seems so dangerously fractured let's make sure that the church can respond in a way that isn't exclusive or retrograde. We talk so much about children being the future—they are also the present and they deserve the very best we can bring them.

Let's give some of ours the last word here: "Choir improves my belief in God." "Everyone has different backgrounds and we all sing together in unison." "I'd like to stay in choir for a really long time!"

Thomas Leech is the Director of the Diocese of Leeds' Schools Singing Programme. He was Organ Scholar at Downing College, Cambridge, and has numerous broadcast and recording credits. He has received the Worshipful Company of Educators Masters' Award in recognition of his work for the Diocese.

April 2018

A New Team of Choristers

James Lancelot, Durham Cathedral

Nobody who heard Richard Seal[157] speaking at the 1991 Precentors' Conference in Durham about starting a team of girl choristers at Salisbury Cathedral could fail to be moved by his vision or commitment. While I was not without some misgivings, Richard's talk kindled a flame for me which was never quite extinguished.

Looking back a quarter of a century later, it is strange to recollect what a radical step this seemed to be. But times change, and social attitudes with them; and Salisbury's example increased the pressure on other cathedrals to follow suit. Not only that, but for me at least the lack of human rights for women and girls in many parts of the world has been such that, whatever the musical arguments, for English cathedral choirs to remain bastions of male privilege would be downright contrary to the Church's witness.

I was clear that in admitting girls we would ensure that they held equal status with the boys. Given that Durham Cathedral has its own choir school, the Chorister School, within its precincts and as part of its foundation, it made sense that the girls should be pupils there, boarding

---

157. Richard Seal (1935–2022); Organist and Master of the Choristers at Salisbury Cathedral from 1968-1997.

just as the boys do, and within the school's age range of 8 to 13. The fact that the choristers board enables us to recruit from throughout the UK; indeed, most of the current choristers live too far from Durham to be able to commute daily. Parity with the boys also meant equality of scholarship level, and (in the fullness of time) an equal number of services, singing together with the gentlemen of the choir. I never allowed the term "girls' choir" to be used; the girls are full choristers in exactly the same way as the boys, and their training is in the hands of the Master of the Choristers and Organist, assisted by the Sub-Organist, the Assistant Organist and the Organ Scholar, just as is the boys'.

We held auditions in 2008, and I immediately realised what talent we had been denying ourselves, as one promising candidate after another presented herself. Because some of the successful candidates already attended the school (or joined it immediately), we were able to do some preliminary work with ten of the girls, rehearsing twice a week, before the project officially got under way with the arrival in September 2009 of the other twelve choristers-elect. Training and rehearsals could now begin in earnest, in preparation for the girls' first service on All Saints' Day, 1 November, and the Advent and Christmas services which followed. Public reaction was widespread and almost unanimously positive, and the cathedral was full—and emotionally charged—for that first Evensong.

For the girls, as for me, those initial weeks and months were unforgettable, as a team of committed, enthusiastic and musical girls experienced for the first time the privilege and excitement of being part of this ancient foundation with its iconic building (having shared such a privilege myself as a child, I could empathise with their enthusiasm). We were hugely lucky in the quality of this team; they rapidly set themselves high standards which they have passed down to their successors, who have maintained them richly.

Training the initial team was a fascinating experience. The boy choristers and the gentlemen of the choir were role models, of course; but the girls had to learn for themselves, too. Early morning practices might involve a visit to the cathedral to practise projecting their voices (calling or singing) from one end of that vast space to another, discovering the need to inhabit the building vocally and learning how to fill it with sound. Visitors were not always sure what to make of this!

In terms of repertoire, I was clear that alongside more straightforward (but never banal) music it was necessary to tackle challenging music from the outset, even if it meant repetition of the same music in some services. Movements from a Palestrina Mass featured early on, and Christmas morning featured a Poulenc motet (only 100% accurate in the service itself, leading to some high fives under the music desk).

Gradually we worked towards the goal of equal frequency with the boys, achieving this just ten months later in September 2010. Each team of choristers sings seven services every fortnight, with weekend duties alternating so that every chorister has the chance to sing Matins and Eucharist on Sunday mornings.

What of the effect on the boy choristers? It was providential that just as the girls arrived the boys found themselves on live television and every sports page singing at a memorial service for the footballer Bobby Robson,[158] and then participating in a recording with Sting;[159] there was no danger of their being overshadowed. The advent of the girls has meant that the boys not only have more free time at weekends, but also more rehearsal time for the music they sing, and more time also for theory tuition and instrumental practice: a win-win situation.

For me, inaugurating this new top line and sharing with the girls their new experiences has been perhaps the highlight of my career. The standards they have achieved speak for themselves, and the spiritual, human and musical dimension they have added to the cathedral's worship and community is without price. It was a long wait since Salisbury led the way, but it was worth it.

Dr James Lancelot is Canon Organist Emeritus of Durham Cathedral, where he was Master of the Choristers and Organist from 1985 to 2017. He was responsible for the foundation of Durham Cathedral Consort of Singers in

---

158. Bobby Robson (1933-2009); English footballer (i.e., soccer player). He was coach of the England team when they won the 1966 World Cup.

159. Sting (b. 1951); English singer-songwriter; lead singer of the Police from 1977-1984.

1997; this enabled women to sing in the Cathedral as part of a choir which belongs to the foundation for the first time. He spearheaded implementation of the Chapter's decision to introduce a team of girl choristers into the cathedral choir in 2008. In retirement, he spent six months as Acting Director of Music at Worcester Cathedral, and continues his career as an organ recitalist.

May 2018

A Life at King's College Cambridge

Sir Stephen Cleobury
(this column is included by permission of his widow, Lady Cleobury)

Since Sarah MacDonald invited me to write this short piece about my work at King's, the college has announced that I shall retire on 30 September 2019. I am not going to dwell on that now, except to reflect that, as is the case for most of us, the burden of administration has increased during my professional life, and that this has the potential to make it more difficult to keep centred on the preparation of the daily repertoire. I remember the organist of one prominent cathedral telling me that he often found himself at meetings all day and came to choir practice in the late afternoon having had no time to think about the music. I am not going to miss the administrative work, even though I believe myself to be quite good at it, for it is the music which actually makes me want to get up in the morning. Indeed, you certainly become a morning person if you have to face a group of twenty or so young children shortly after 8 o'clock on a daily basis!

My first dean at King's, John Drury,[160] used to refer to these morning rehearsals as representing the 'engine room' of the choir, recognising that this is where the foundation of each successive year is built. Equally

---

160. The Very Revd Dr John Drury (b. 1936); Dean of King's from 1981-1991.

important are the full rehearsals in chapel before services, for in those collegiate choirs which remain exclusively undergraduate ensembles, about one third of the choral scholars are coming to what is to me familiar repertoire for the first time. Meeting this challenge is part of the stimulating nature of my job. Meeting it successfully requires careful planning of repertoire and rehearsal.

One of the great benefits of the ecumenical movement has been the opening up of new areas of repertoire, so that we can now sing music from the Catholic and Orthodox traditions as well as traditional Anglican church music. In fact, there is so much to choose from, it tempting to be too ambitious. Equally, there is no longer any excuse for performing second-rate music, even though, of course, there can be no definitive judgement in that regard.

I am fortunate at King's in having quite a free hand in terms of selecting music: there is no precentor seeking to dictate what I do (a practice deprecated as long ago as the 19th century by S. S. Wesley).[161] I have sought to discharge this privilege responsibly, being greatly guided by the insights into liturgical history and practice which I gained during my time as Master of Music at Westminster Cathedral in the aftermath of the Second Vatican Council [1979-1982]. While it may sometimes be possible to guess at a current recording project from a perusal of the music list, it will not be possible to determine what we are to do at our Advent Procession by noting the anthems being performed from October onwards.

Early in my time at King's I introduced a termly music list (such as we had at St John's where I was organ student) to replace the 'scheme' which appeared fortnightly. This idea has now been copied by almost all colleges. It takes time to prepare this, but it enables me to have more of an overview of the repertoire. When I have finished the first draft, I look at each week to see whether it has sufficient variety and whether there will be sufficient time to prepare the music thoroughly. This is the point where I need to put a brake on my more extravagant ideas. I have tended to keep a

---

161. Wesley's clashes with the Precentor at Winchester are discussed in Horton, Peter. *Samuel Sebastian Wesley: A Life.* OUP. 2004.

relatively small core of settings of the canticles, which might be sung two or even three times a year, so that I can present a wide range of anthems reflecting the different liturgical seasons and feasts, many of which, necessarily, appear only once in the year.

Important practical considerations concern the length of the different elements of a given service. If we are doing Psalm 78 with its 73 verses on the fifteenth day of the month, we will not need to be tackling Byrd's *Great Service* that day.

Obviously, special care needs to be given to Christmas. The Choir does not want to be presented with new music on Christmas morning after *The Festival of Nine Lessons and Carols*. We usually perform a Mozart mass on Christmas morning: I make sure this has been performed earlier in the term. We are about to have our fourteenth *Easter at King's* festival, and each year we perform one of the Bach Passions; I have found it both effective but also useful to programme the chorales as introits during Lent. One thing I learned very early on was that it is not a good idea to learn new or less familiar music on tour. (I had tried to be accommodating to our promoter in New Zealand who did not want the same programme as we were offering in Australia.)

Having planned the repertoire with these considerations in mind, it is then a matter of organising rehearsals effectively and carrying them out efficiently. In this, the experience I gained in London at Westminster Abbey and Westminster Cathedral has been invaluable. At the Abbey I had to be able to rehearse Evensong in 18 minutes (provision is more generous now, I think). You certainly learn not to waste time. The recipe for success is to be thoroughly prepared yourself, to prepare the performing material carefully (I am an avid marker of copies), and to encourage good habits of attention and quick response from the singers.

All this is easy to say: I hope that, as I approach retirement, I am beginning to learn how to do it.

Sir Stephen Cleobury (1948-2019) directed the Choir of King's College, Cambridge for 35 years. At King's, he developed the daily service repertoire, commissioned new music, had developed the choir's activities in broadcasting, recording, and touring. He conceived and introduced "Easter at King's"

from which the BBC regularly broadcasts, and the series of high profile per-
formances, "Concerts and Kings". He also helped to inaugurate King's own
record label. He was chief conductor of the BBC Singers and the Cambridge
University Musical Society, and remained active as an organist and conduc-
tor, concertising all over the world. In 2019, he was knighted for his contribu-
tions to choral music. He died on St Cecilia's Day 2019.

October 2020

How Shall We Sing the Lord's Song?

David Price, Portsmouth Cathedral

There's a good deal of comment just now on social media about cathedral music. Here's what I'm thinking, for those interested. "How shall we sing the Lord's song (Psalm 137:4) in a strange land?"

When the Choir Year came to a close in July 2020, as ever, there was a chance to reflect on all that had taken place in Portsmouth Cathedral, on tour and in concert, during the previous ten months. We celebrated the myriad opportunities to sing in our wonderous building; to sing to God; to sing to and with each other; and to aid those who attend services and concerts here in their journey of faith—or their quest for solace and calm.

We celebrated Christmas when we welcomed thousands through our doors. We celebrated our tour to Finland in January—a trip that feels a world away now. We experienced the now-distant world of choral singing in close ensemble to a packed house in snowy Lapland. Back home we celebrated Monday evensongs with the Choral Scholars and Lay Clerks, with the timeless simplicity of plainsong. We celebrated the small successes of new boy and girl choristers, and we celebrated our leavers who had offered years to the choir—for some of them, half a lifetime—as they move on into senor school and university. But what of recent months? Much of it was a kind of bereavement. Yes we managed online rehearsals, virtual evensongs, and choir socials. But this is only half of it. Not even half.

All choirs thrive when they sing together—that is the point of singing in a group. The sum is greater than the parts. It is even more so for cathedral choirs: the daily round of rehearsals and services define us. Portsmouth choristers normally have over fourteen hours of contact time *every week* with the cathedral and its music staff. Through this remarkable offering of time and talent, a vast well-spring of musical endeavour and a joyful exploration of faith is made possible. We watch boys and girls develop their music-making from tentative steps through to expert and professional leaders. We see Choral Scholars learn to hone their skills, and we benefit from the experience and insight of our Lay Clerks who in turn watch and learn from their peers.

All this ceased abruptly in March when much of the world stopped. The Song School was deserted and the choir stalls and pews were bereft of life. School ties forlornly left amidst dishevelled robes were a metaphor for the messy nature of our shutting down. The physical ties of school and cathedral stopped abruptly, and we were tasked with maintaining virtual and spiritual ties.

And what has happened in the meantime? Children and adults alike have risen to the challenges, online rehearsals undertaken and virtual evensongs attempted. But all of this frenetic activity has only been a holding pattern. The much-celebrated virtual life of choirs has had a place in our coping strategies but it is no more than that. We need daily interaction; our youngest boys and girls learn by osmosis from being surrounded by their more experienced elders; our adults blend with their colleagues in time and timbre as much by telepathy and honed camaraderie as by any direction from the conductor.

For the music staff, the monotony of all the necessary administration and its daily aggravation is made worthwhile by the creative interactions that frame our daily routine; the privilege of rehearsing an energetic group of children at 8 o'clock every morning culminating in more rehearsals after school with the sole aim of producing music at daily Evensong in the cathedral is the reason I, and so many of my colleagues, entered this profession.

All this hangs in the balance as we await advice and as much certainty as we can. But we will also need our share of confidence, some bravery and a bit of faith. For if we falter at this moment, our choral tradition will hang in the balance—and could indeed be lost, a generation of singers will be abandoned and our timorousness will be judged.

Much energy is going into lambasting a number of other cathedral Deans and Chapters across England just now as they variously navigate complicated moments in their own contexts. None of us who are outside their walls know enough to comment usefully as yet. We should marvel at the commitment of the Church of England to its choral tradition—for even in these stormy times, the C of E is one of the most generous patrons of music and musicians in England. Cathedrals are primarily about sacramental worship and the arts. Both point us to the divine. The Lockdown has shown us that both of these things matter deeply to people and we must urgently reclaim them before it is too late.

David Price is Organist and Master of the Choristers at Portsmouth Cathedral, where daily round of choral worship is led by various combinations of boy choristers, girl choristers, professional Lay Clerks, university-age Choral Scholars, and a choir of mixed adults. In addition to his duties at the Cathedral, David serves on the Council of the Royal School of Church Music.

August 2022

Let All Mortal Flesh Keep Silence

Tim Popple, Bristol Cathedral

In 2020 the world fell silent.

Silence has its place. Arguably it is the most important part of music, because it looks beyond itself, to the notes which follow. Think Bruckner's *Ave Maria* (Bruckner, Anton. Ave Maria. Vienna 1867), with the thrilling silence between each iteration of "Jesus". Or the excitement of the resounding echo in the silence between each "Alleluia" in Bairstow's *Let all mortal flesh* (Bairstow, Edward. Let all mortal flesh keep silence. Stainer & Bell. 1925). But each silence is a moment which points to the music around it. In 2020 the music stopped, and that silence continued, and continued, and continued. The mortal flesh was kept silent.

As choral singers, as organists, as musicians, it seemed like the music would never return and, if it did, would it ever be the same? Because we veiled our faces, and we stood with fear, and we lost not just the music, but everything that went with it. The camaraderie, the friendship. The family. We lost the fun.

The knowing glance when your desk-mate finally gets the note right they had failed resolutely to manage in rehearsal. The post-service debrief dressing down. The moaning about that one hymn coming up again. The endless debates over which Wood in E Flat setting of the evening canticles is better. (It's No.2. Obviously.) (Wood, Charles. Evening Service in E flat no. 2, Sterhold & Hopkins. 1934) The pub trip where the world is put to rights, the perfect Evensong devised, the latest gossip from friends at other churches, cathedrals, chapels devoured as hungrily as the pack of pork scratchings with your pint. All of this, the unspoken necessary catharsis to the changes and chances of this fleeting life: all of this was lost too.

And I missed it. I missed Handel and Howells of course, but I missed humour, too. I even missed hymns. Even that one hymn. So I thought, fine: I'll do it myself. I'll bring that familiar sense of belonging we have as choral musicians, and share it. And so I created *In quires and places where they meme*[162], usually just referred to as *Quire Memes*, because it is a very silly, long name. It's somewhere I can indulge my particular sense of humour with others who can consume it and say, "yes, that's the very specific music world I know and love and miss".[163]

I have no policy *per se* but, if I had to consider rules I subconsciously follow, they might be these:

a. It has to be niche. We're a community of people singing music written anytime between 500 years ago and last Tuesday morning; in buildings a thousand years old; with children who have never known anything other than life under a Conservative government. We're a really weird group, and I lean into that.

b. It has to be relevant. This is vague: relevant could be something written centuries ago, but which is well-known, and some of us have sung recently. Or it could be a response to whatever political chaos is happening right now.

c. It is, by and large, heartfelt. It's not intended to be mean-spirited, or nasty, or punching down. It's why I joke about John Rutter (we love you, John!) more than I do about things I actually don't like. Because behind the ribbing, is respect. Behind the laughter, is love.

---

162. The title is derived from a rubric in the Book of Common Prayer "In Quires, and places where they sing, here followeth the anthem".

163. You can find the Quire Memes accounts at facebook.com/quirememes and twitter .com/quirememes, and buy niche choral merchandise at quiresandplaces.myspreadshop .com (US/AUS site) and quiresandplaces.myspreadshop.co.uk/ (UK/EUR site).

There really is no greater strategy behind this. I'm just one choral musician, making humorous content for other people who love choral music. I diversified the account into merchandise, with very much the same lack of strategy, and simple mindset: I'd wear niche clothing about choral music; maybe others would too. It keeps me in beer. (Which, as a choral singer, is of course very important.)

From a handful of followers when I started in August 2020, the brand has grown to (at the time of writing) over 10k followers across Facebook and Twitter. Posts range from the silly (Ryan Reynolds as choral music books) to the poignant (New "O antiphon" announced: "O micron") to the delightful (Cathedral scholars singing my alternative words to Here is the Little Door))Howells, Herbert. Here is the Little Door. Stainer & Bell. 1920). And, occasionally, not even a meme at all (marking the passing of Simon Preston) (Simon Preston, organist (1938-2022).

The only other diversification was an inadvertent foray into political advice, when a (poorly-made) meme was seemingly (though never proven to be) taken literally by someone deep in the Welsh Government. They subsequently produced official advice indicating that tenors spread the coronavirus more widely than other voice parts (https://www.classicfm .com/music-news/coronavirus/welsh-government-deletes-tenors-fake -news-advice/). The Welsh Government has since made up for this error by trebling the funding for music education across Wales.

What's next? Well, this continues to be something I enjoy creating, and people enjoy consuming. And, while choirs are now singing again, and pubs are serving beer again, the appetite for specific jokes poking fun at the distinct lack of alto parts in Howells' music, or setting national news stories to psalm chants, continues undiminished. There is more to come.

In a world where we were cut off, isolated, and silenced, my hope was that the account, in some small way, brought people together, connected them, and gave a voice to a familiar community. A community that extends beyond the individual choirs with whom we were prevented from singing, to a larger group of people who find weirdly specifically niche memes as funny as I do. My continued hope is simply to enable people to both "laugh and sing" (inevitably, Psalm 65).

And we sing exultingly the hymn—yes, even that one hymn—Alleluia!
Anon.

The identity of the author of the Quire Memes account (that prolific composer and writer "Anon.") has been a poorly-kept secret in choral circles, but publication has forced him to emerge from the stalls. Tim Popple is an Alto Lay Clerk in Bristol Cathedral Choir (this may explain a great deal of the jokes he aims at altos). He has previously sung with The Fitzhardinge Consort, St Woolos Cathedral Choir, and Carlisle Cathedral Choir. His love affair with choral music began at the age of eight as a chorister at Durham Cathedral. When he's not working, making memes, designing niche clothes, singing Evensong, or socialising afterwards, he watches films with his two teenage children, explores the local food and drink scene with his wife, and pretends to be a dinosaur for his young stepson.

Parish Worship in a Northeast Coast Fishing Village

Andrew Reid, Harrison and Harrison Organ Builders Ltd

Sarah MacDonald asked if I would write about the English Choral Tradition in my corner of England. Presently that is Cullercoats, on the North-East Coast, traditionally a fishing village, which has embraced Newcastle commuters and tourism in recent years.

In the 1880s the Sixth Duke of Northumberland decided to build a church in memory of his father, appointing as architect John Loughborough Pearson (also architect of Truro Cathedral and St John's Cathedral, Brisbane). Pearson designed a miniature cathedral, stone-vaulted throughout, with a vast spire, sitting evocatively above the beach. The contemporaneous and tonally unaltered TC Lewis organ of two manuals and 26 stops is a TARDIS[164] of a musical instrument. Its bold, Schulze-like Great chorus and Cavaillé-Coll-inspired reeds are further enhanced by the warm acoustic.

---

164. A TARDIS (Time and Relative Dimension in Space) is the ship used by the fictional BBC character Doctor Who. It is known for being bigger on the inside than it is on the outside.

St George's has seen its musical peaks and troughs. As with most churches, musically speaking, you get out what you put in. It takes energy to run a choir—there are no shortcuts—and, outside those establishments with full-time musicians, that energy is often circumscribed by the Director of Music's day job. Perhaps this is indicative of a wider difficulty; many of the First World problems of the Anglican Church seem to relate to commitment, be it of singers and musicians, or of wider patterns of attending, worship, faith, giving and living.

We have a choir of 25 children and adults. Average attendance on a Sunday in term-time is around 14, with fewer in the holidays or on major feasts. When the choir numbers 18 or more it can make a pretty full sound.

When we lived in Peterborough I ran the music at All Saints' Church, where I inherited a Choir Club. Children came to play with friends after school on a Friday, with some sort of guided activity: craft, cookery, or such like. Then they moved effortlessly into an hour's singing. They didn't think of themselves as attending a rehearsal: they were going to Choir Club—we taught them singing by stealth! This idea has moved to Cullercoats with us.

Our musical time starts with breathing, humming, vocalising and singing exercises, encouraging those who can't yet read music or text fluently. We then learn the hymns, Responsorial Psalm, Gospel Acclamation, anthem and perhaps a descant, alongside music for future weeks. I always spend at least 20 minutes on the hymns. Choristers learn to follow the notes with their finger, sing them to 'na' or sequential numbers, keep pulse and breathe in phrases; they discover rhythms, pitch, and intervals.

The hymns are also where we learn theology. We work out why they are chosen, what the references mean and where they come from, what the images signify, and what the hymnwriter is saying. We leave plenty to mystery and the imagination, but the bits and pieces picked out over time form a framework of Biblical study. The adults rehearse fortnightly. We then put everything together in 20 minutes on a Sunday morning—that final rehearsal is invaluable. It's enough to get everyone on message but not to peak; it leaves space for the liturgy which follows.

Excluding time at university I have to date spent 17 years alike in professional and amateur church music. I love both. Working with professional musicians means a high standard of sight-reading, breadth of musicianship, availability of forces required, regularity of attendance and commitment. Working with amateurs emphasises aspects which exist in good professional choirs too but can at times be overlooked: corporate and individual effort, the ability to over-achieve or 'go beyond', building others up, joy, a sense of wonder, worship.

In a professional choir there are few musical weak links, especially among the adults. In an amateur choir those with the least experience learn from and are carried by those with more. When this works it feels wonderful, largely because of the challenges overcome in the process. That people with little or no musical, vocal or choral background can encounter a vision of glory while singing is a marvellous thing. That was me aged 8; at some stage it was all of us.

Building a choir in a small community is not unlike building a church. The common bond of geographical proximity is something to cherish. In a professional choir the sacrificial common bond may be the standard of the music-making. In an amateur choir this endeavour is enriched by delight in local communal participation and the drawing out of skills from those who thought theirs were limited. Their flourishing becomes a source of joy for the whole choir, and a wellspring of prophetic beauty and leadership for the Church.

As I grow older I value more and more the community of saints, flawed, imperfect, distracted and impoverished, which makes up the Church. The ability to worship together in community is an extraordinary gift and a foretaste of even greater joys. I cannot begin to understand how hard it must be for those who try to remain faithful alone in places of persecution.

We are promised that what we do now as a minority, against the odds, judged by many in society, will one day become the summation of our desire and the restitution of our natural state. Then the resources of a Westminster Abbey or a Cullercoats will be irrelevant. Wherever we are we can as yet but glimpse through a glass darkly the beauty of that worship.

Andrew Reid was Managing Director of Harrison & Harrison, Organ Builders until 2022, and he directs the music at St George's Church, Cullercoats, a post he combines with other freelance work. He was formerly Director of the RSCM and before that Director of Music at Peterborough Cathedral. He held Assistantship posts at both Westminster Cathedrals and Westminster Abbey.

Epilogue

November 2017

Psallam Spiritu et Mente[165]

I recently found myself in the unusual position of preaching a sermon. I was asked to reflect on the role of music in liturgy, and for my text, I chose the motto of the Royal School of Church Music: *Psallam spiritu et mente*; "I will sing with the spirit, and I will sing with the understanding also." (1 Corinthians 14: 15). For me, these words sum up the role of music in the context of liturgical worship. Like many of you, my vocation is that of a liturgical musician. As well as being a liturgical musician, I am a baptised, confirmed, and communicant Anglican. I express my faith through music—indeed, I'm not very good at expressing it in words.

Liturgical music offers something less concrete and less logical than a typical sermon. Deductive theological reasoning may attempt to convince my *mind* that "his banner over me is Love",[166] but Bairstow's beautiful

---

165. This column is presented here in its original extended form (that printed in TAO was an abbreviated version of a sermon I preached in Selwyn College Chapel in April 2016).

166. Song of Solomon 2: 4

setting of those words successfully convinces my *spirit* that it is so. The intangible results of the latter argument are actually more convincing for me than the conclusion of a logical verbal discourse, which, to be honest, doesn't normally end well for invisible omniscient beings who live in the sky. I am persuaded that music can point towards the divine, and can help us to look beyond ourselves and our petty disagreements. Music can raise the soul, move the heart, and direct us towards God. *Psallam spiritu.* I will sing with the spirit.

Notwithstanding this desire for mystical and musical transcendence, in pursuing my vocation, I have spent many years developing my professional skills, and I have several degrees and diplomas in a variety of disciplines, including piano, organ, composition, analysis, and conducting. I am very demanding of myself, of my singers, of my students, and of the composers I work with. I expect serious preparation, hours of practice, technical ability, perfect intonation, and a thorough grounding in Fuxian counterpoint. *Psallam mente.* I will sing with the understanding also.

Is it possible to reconcile these two apparently conflicting tendencies, the mystical yearning of the spirit and the analytical rigour of the mind? There is an age-old argument that those things which are technically perfect are emotionally dead—that things unconstrained by rules are likely to have greater vitality. In music, for example, the dry constraints of Baroque counterpoint may seem less expressive than the emotionalism of nineteenth century Romantic repertoire. The New Testament analogy would be to argue that glossolalia, or speaking in tongues, without regard for syntax and grammar, is closer to God than the Old Testament rigours of the Law.

Yet the spirit and the understanding—transcendence and technique, if you prefer—are not only completely reconcilable with each other, but are also mutually dependent. Hours of scales at the piano make possible emotional expressiveness in performance. Knowing how to prepare, strike, and resolve suspensions correctly facilitates the creation of spiritual ambience in choral composition. The development of well-supported, centred vocal technique enables singers to give meaning to the performance of text. Organists who neglect to practise left hand and pedal exercises regularly, will struggle to lead a congregation effectively in the worshipful singing of hymns. Neither the spirit nor the understanding is sufficient alone.

That there is music at all in the context of Christian worship supports this. We are one of the three so-called Book Religions, and we are reminded every Christmas Eve that "in the beginning was the Word".[167] There are many words in the Bible that deserve to be spoken and expounded upon verbally. But music adds another dimension, and can help congregations to hear rational discussion in new and enhanced ways. An appropriately selected and skilfully played organ voluntary won't contain any 'therefores' or 'consequentlys', but it can present a convincing argument nonetheless.

Edgar Bainton's classic and masterful setting of Revelation 21: 1-4[168] provides an excellent example of a choral work that appeals to spirit and understanding, while demonstrating both the rational and the emotional response of the composer to the text. Contrapuntally and technically, the anthem is tightly constrained, replete with canons at the octave, tenth, and fourth, double imitation, inversion, compound melodies, fluent functional diatonic harmony, and many other structural features. It is a testament to the rigorous training in music theory that Bainton received at the Royal College of Music under Henry Walford Davies and C. V. Stanford in the late nineteenth century. At precisely the golden section of the anthem (yes, I counted the bars), its best-known tune occurs.

This is undoubtedly one of the most emotionally charged moments in the liturgical repertoire. Ironically, it often brings tears to people's

---

167. the opening of the Gospel according to St John.
168. Bainton, Edgar (1880–1956). *And I saw a new heaven*. Novello and Co.

eyes—sometimes for the wrong reasons. The melody is completely exposed. It soars directly though the most vulnerable points of the tenor voice, known in the trade as the *primo* and *secondo passaggi*. These are places where the voice has natural transitions that can be difficult to negotiate, especially for young singers. Bainton's melody moves through these regions with a poignancy and lyricism that defies the technicalities of its compositional construction. To be precise, it's a compound melody harmonised over a contrary motion bass line incorporating an internal dominant pedal followed by a pedal on the sub-mediant and ending with a cadence in the relative minor. Yet even if you know what all of that jargon means, you'll hear far more than that when you listen to those bars. If you're listening prayerfully, you will also hear a promise of forgiveness and of consolation. The spirit and the understanding are fully entwined in this Edwardian gem.

Music's ability to evoke both an emotional and an intellectual response is also useful in demarcating the liturgical year. The events in the life of Christ (from the Annunciation through to the Ascension) and also of the Church year (from Advent to All Souls) are marked with specific music, and appropriate repertoire choices are often more powerful than lengthy sermons. The opening solo verse of *Once in Royal David's City*, immediately puts us in the mood for Advent and Christmas. The evocative counterpoint of Allegri's *Miserere*, with its famous top Cs (however inauthentic they may be), moves us into the frame of heart and of mind required on Ash Wednesday, with no need for theological explanation. The anticipatory organ B flat in the first bar of Patrick Hadley's anthem *My beloved spake* embodies Easter. The fanfare-like opening launching onto the dominant pedal under that first top F 'rise up' is revivifying every time. After the more contemplative middle-section, the confidence of the recapitulation of 'rise up', with its top A flats fearlessly outdoing the range of the phrase's first statement and its unexpectedly twisted harmonies is emotionally exhilarating indeed. To put it bluntly, the opening bars of that anthem are much more likely to dispel any lingering doubts in me, than if that text were merely read aloud and then preached upon.

Finally, there is an educational aspect to all of this, particularly in the context of a school, college, or university chapel. Choirs and congregations alike need to be exposed to a wide variety of the very best liturgical music, in order to feed their spirits and deepen their understanding. Vacuous and emotionally manipulative music is as damaging as dry, cerebral repertoire that lacks soul. In the Anglican choral tradition, the canon encompasses the counterpoint of Palestrina, Aleotti, Byrd, Tallis, Bach; the melodic genius of Mozart and Haydn; the technically sophisticated Romanticism of Brahms, Bruckner, Rheinberger. It also includes the great responses to the Oxford Movement composed by Elgar, Bairstow, Stanford, Harris, Bainton; the challenging 20th-century liturgical repertoire of Hadley, Howells, Britten, Leighton; and, more recently, the best of the mystical works of the so-called Holy Minimalists, John Tavener, Cecilia McDowall, Eric Whitacre, Jonathan Dove, James MacMillan, Paul Mealor, Morten Lauridsen. I select carefully from this great canon. The intricate counterpoint of the *B minor Mass* will lead some of us to transcendence; for others it will be the joyous triumphalism of Stanford's *Magnificat in C*, or the incense-filled cluster chords of Eric Whitacre's *Lux aurumque*. Fortunately, there are twelve gates into the City of the New Jerusalem[169]— perhaps one for each degree of the chromatic scale—so we don't all have to follow the same path to get there.

To sum up, the role of music in worship must be to move both heart and mind, to challenge both emotion and intellect, to be inspiring and also rigorous, to point to the divine and also to strive for excellence in human endeavour. And this is because we all *possess* both heart and mind, both emotion and intellect, we are capable of being inspired and also of being rigorous, and striving for excellence in human endeavour is itself the essence of the divine—we were created in God's image, after all. So, sing with the spirit, and sing with the understanding also, to the best of your ability, at all times. *Psallam Spiritu et mente!*

---

169. Revelation 21

APPENDIX

COMMERCIAL RECORDINGS – Sarah MacDonald

RECORDINGS SCHEDULED FOR 2022-23

recording date	role	title/description	label
09/22	conductor	Eternal Ecstasy II (Selwyn College Choir, Cambridge)	Regent Records
07/23	conductor	Choral music by Bryan Kelly (Selwyn College Choir, Cambridge)	Regent Records

RECORDINGS CURRENTLY IN PRODUCTION

release date	role	title/description	label
2024	conductor	Choral music by Joanna Gill (Selwyn Choir, Cambridge)	Regent Records
2023	solo pianist	Bach Goldberg Variations (Steinway model-D, Ely Cathedral)	Regent Records
2023	conductor	Multitude of Voyces vol. 1 complete (Selwyn Choir, Cambridge)	Regent Records

| 2023 | conductor | Choral music by Stuart Turnbull (Selwyn Choir, Cambridge) | Regent Records |
| 2023 | conductor | And to be the glory: upper voices canticles vol. 2 (Ely Girl Choristers) | Regent Records |

RECORDINGS AS CONDUCTOR

year	details	label
2022	Faces in the mist: Choral music by Richard Peat (Selwyn Choir/Ely Girl Choristers)	Regent Records
2020	Sacred Ayres: Choral music by Paul Ayres (Selwyn Choir, Cambridge)	Regent Records
2019	Garment of Holiness: Choral music by Iain Quinn (Selwyn Choir, Cambridge)	Regent Records
2019	Music for Christmas by Ben Parry (Selwyn Choir/Ely Girl Choristers)	Regent Records
2018	Utrumne est Ornatum: music by Mark Gotham (Selwyn Choir/Ely Girl Choristers)	Regent Records
2018	An Ely Christmas (Ely Cathedral Choir: Girls and Layclerks)	Regent Records
2017	Marvellous Light: music by Ben Ponniah (Selwyn Choir, Cambridge)	Regent Records
2016	All Angels cry aloud: Music by John Hosking (Selwyn Choir/Ely Girl Choristers)	Regent Records
2016	To be a light: Evening Canticles for upper voices vol. 1 (Ely Girl Choristers)	Regent Records
2016	Christmas from Selwyn (Selwyn Choir, Cambridge)	Regent Records
2015	Eternal Ecstasy: music of rapture and transcendence (Selwyn Choir, Cambridge)	Regent Records
2015	O Come, Emmanuel: Christmas music by Alan Bullard (Selwyn Choir, Cambridge)	Regent Records
2013	Choral music by Phillip Cooke (Selwyn Choir, Cambridge)	Regent Records
2012	Milles Regretz: music for lutes and voices (Selwyn Choir, Cambridge)	Regent Records
2012	Songs of Innocence: music by Gary Higginson (Selwyn Choir/Ely Girl Choristers)	Regent Records

2012	Pergolesi 'Stabat Mater' and other music for Lent (Ely Girl Choristers)	Regent Records
2012	Wondrous Cross: choral music by Alan Bullard (Selwyn Choir, Cambridge)	Regent Records
2010	God be in my head: choral music by Paul Edwards (Selwyn Choir, Cambridge)	Regent Records
2009	Come out, Lazar: choral music by Paul Spicer (Selwyn Choir, Cambridge)	Regent Records
2009	A lover's complaint – *Choir & Organ* cover CD (Selwyn Choir, Cambridge)	Choir & Organ
2008	A Candle to the Glorious Sun: John Milton/ Martin Peerson (Selwyn Choir, Cambridge)	Regent Records
2008	Sing reign of fair maid: Music for Christmas (Ely Girl Choristers)	Regent Records
2007	Master-Pieces from Selwyn College (Selwyn Choir, Cambridge)	Priory
2006	Christus vincit: Music by Colin Mawby (Selwyn Choir, Cambridge)	Kevin Mayhew
2006	Songs of Welcome (Newnham College Choir, Cambridge)	Priory
2005	The Moon of Wintertime: Music for Christmas (Selwyn Choir, Cambridge)	URM Audio
2004	One day in thy courts: Settings of the Psalms (Selwyn Choir, Cambridge)	Priory Records
2003	Complete New English Hymnal Vol. XIV (Selwyn College Choir)	Priory Records
2000	Herbert Howells: Evening Canticles (Selwyn Choir, Cambridge)	Herald AV
1998	Charlie's Prospect National Film Board (*incantatus*, Halifax, Nova Scotia)	NFB Canada
1995	Saints & Sinners (Robinson College Choir, Cambridge)	MLR Discs

RECORDINGS AS PRODUCER

year	details	label
2019	Choral Music by Vaughan Williams (Robinson College Choir, Cambridge)	Regent Records

2006	Lady on the Silver Thorne (Spiritus Chamber Choir; Aidan Oliver, conductor)	Toccata Classics
2004	Louis Vierne Songs (Rachel Santesso, soprano; Roger Vignolles; Andrew Reid)	Deux Elles
2002	Picking of Sticks: Early English dance (Orchestra of the Age of Enlightenment)	1AM Productions
1999	J. S. Bach: Orgelbüchlein (Anne Page, organ, with Cambridge Voices)	Merlin Audio
1994	Abroad as I was walking (Jesus College Choir, Cambridge)	MLR Discs

RECORDINGS AS ACCOMPANIST

year	details	label
2014	Vaughan Williams Five Mystical Songs (Little St Mary's Church Choir, Cambridge)	Regent Records
1998	Choral Evensong (Robinson Choir, Cambridge)	Robinson Discs
1990	His beauty doth all things excel (St John's Choir, Victoria, British Columbia)	SJD Audio
1990	A choral flourish (Exultate Chamber Singers, Toronto, Ontario)	Novadisc

PUBLISHED COMPOSITIONS – Sarah MacDonald

KEY

August – August Press, LLC, Tennessee, USA
Chichester – Chichester Music Press, Hampshire
Encore – Encore Publications, Kent
OUP – Oxford University Press
RSCM – Royal School of Church Music
Selah – Selah Publishing Co. Ltd., Pittsburgh, USA
SJMP – St James Music Press, USA
MoV – Multitude of Voyces, UK

ORGAN SOLO

2023	Commission for two further voluntaries	OUP
2022	Fugue on 'Gonfalon Royal'	OUP
2022	Choral Variations on 'Kingsfold'	OUP

| 2021 | Trio on 'Attende Domine' | Stainer and Bell |
| 2020 | Prelude on 'Solothurn' | OUP |

LITURGICAL WORKS

2023	Missa Brevis (SATB and organ); for St Timothy's Church, Winston-Salem, NC	Selah
2023	Evening Canticles Westcott Service (upper voices)	Encore
2022	Evening Canticles Third Service (lower voices)	Encore
2021	Advent Responsories (SA + lower voices)	RSCM
2021	Preces and Responses (mixed voices)	Encore
2021	Hymn 'Hope' (words by ++Justin Welby)	Encore
2020	Preces and Responses (upper voices)	Encore
2020	Hymn 'Nelson' (Sing, my soul, his wondrous love)	Selah
2019	Evening Canticles in A flat (mixed voices and organ)	RSCM
2018	Advent Responsories (mixed voices)	Encore
2017	Evening Canticles Second Service (upper voices and organ)	SJMP
2017	O Come, O come, Emmanuel (mixed voices)	Encore
2012	Evening Canticles in A flat (upper voices and organ)	SJMP
2010	Evening Canticles Thomas Morley Fauxbourdons (upper voices)	RSCM
2010	Evening Canticles Tonus Peregrinus Fauxbourdons (upper voices)	RSCM
2009	Preces and Responses (upper voices)	Encore

ANTHEMS & CAROLS

2023	To see a world in a grain of sand (SATB and brass); commission for The Sixteen	Encore
2023	Four carol arrangements for choir, brass, organ; commission for The Sixteen	Encore
2023	Ave verum corpus (canon for unison voices)	SJMP
2023	Drop, drop, slow tears (arrangement for two-part voices and organ)	SJMP

2023	This joyful Eastertide (arrangement for two-part voices and organ)	RSCM
2023	Schmücke dich (arrangement for two-part voices and organ)	RSCM
2022	Love has come (mixed voices and organ)	Encore
2022	Love has come (mixed voices and organ)	Encore
2021	Now the green blade riseth (arrangement for upper voices)	Chichester
2021	The Wondrous Cross (upper voices)	Chichester
2021	The Infant King (SA + lower voices)	RSCM
2021	The Angel Gabriel (arrangement for mixed voices)	Selah
2021	Riu, riu chiu (arrangement for mixed voices)	Selah
2021	Hymn for the Feast of St Joseph (lower voices)	MoV
2021	Bethlehem's Star (arrangement for mixed voices and organ)	MoV
2020	Tomorrow shall be my dancing day (arrangement for lower voices)	Chichester
2020	A new Psalme (upper voices and organ)	Encore
2020	Keep me as the apple of an eye (upper voices and organ)	Encore
2020	After this, we will return (lower voices)	Encore
2020	Five introits (mixed voices)	Selah
2020	O Beata Trinitas (upper voices and organ)	MoV
2019	To minister (women's voices)	August
2019	Take delight in the Lord (mixed voices)	August
2019	All manner of thing (upper voices and organ)	SJMP
2019	The wounds of Christ (SA and lower voices)	RSCM
2019	Arise , Shine (mixed voices)	Encore
2019	Crux fidelis (mixed voices)	MoV
2018	The Huron Carol (arrangement for mixed voices)	RSCM
2017	Gaudete, Christus est natus (arrangement for mixed voices)	Encore
2014	Andrew's Song (upper voices and organ)	Encore
2013	This joyful Eastertide (arrangement for lower voices)	Encore

2010	Cherry Tree Carol (arrangement for upper voices and organ)	Encore
2010	The Holly and the Ivy (arrangement for upper voices and organ)	Encore
2009	Miserere mei, Deus (upper voices)	Encore

Secular

2023	All the nice girls love a sailor (arrangement for mixed voices); commissioned for and conducted on Hugh Laurie's "Why didn't they ask Evans" BritBox miniseries	August
2019	Flow gently, sweet Afton (arrangement for mixed voices)	August

INDEX

ABOUT THE AUTHOR

SARAH MACDONALD is a Canadian-born UK-based organist, conductor, pianist, and composer, where she is Fellow and Director of Music at Selwyn College, Cambridge, and Director of Ely Cathedral's Girl Choristers. She has been at Selwyn since 1999, and was the first woman to hold such a post in an Oxbridge Chapel. Sarah studied at Toronto's Royal Conservatory of Music Glenn Gould Professional School, and at Cambridge University, and her teachers were Leon Fleisher, Marek Jablonski, John Tuttle, and David Sanger. She has toured extensively as a conductor and organist, and is in demand internationally as a director of choral and organ courses. She has made over 35 commercial recordings, and her liturgical works (over 50 published titles) are performed regularly throughout the world. She holds the Fellowship of the Royal College of Organists (RCO), and is a winner of the coveted Limpus prize. She is an examiner for the RCO and for Cambridge University's Faculty of Music. Sarah received the honorary ARSCM in recognition of her contribution to choral music. She is a Patron of the Society of Women Organists, President of the School Organists' Association, and an Honorary Patron of the Herbert Howells Society. In 2022 she was appointed Organist to the University of Cambridge. She is the first woman to hold this historic ceremonial role. In her spare time, Sarah is a keen amateur photographer.

Milton Keynes UK
Ingram Content Group UK Ltd.
UKHW010023160823
426897UK00003B/44